THE GREAT FAMINE
IN SKIBBEREEN

The Great Famine
in Skibbereen

PETER FOYNES

Irish Famine Commemoration Skibbereen Ltd

Published by Irish Famine Commemoration Skibbereen Ltd.,
Sutherland Centre,
North Street,
Skibbereen,
Co. Cork,
Ireland.

© Irish Famine Commemoration Skibbereen Ltd., 2004.

ISBN No. 0-9547269-0-1

First published in 2004.

Print origination by Inspire Design and Print, Skibbereen, Co. Cork, Ireland.
Printed in Ireland by Inspire Design and Print, Skibbereen, Co. Cork, Ireland.

All rights reserved. No part of this publication may be copied, reproduced or transmitted in any form or by any means, without written permission of the publishers.

CONTENTS

Preface		vii
Acknowledgements		ix
Chapter 1	Before the Famine	1
Chapter 2	The Onset of the Blight	19
Chapter 3	The Winter of 1846-1847	45
Chapter 4	Temporary Relief and the Final Solution	63
Chapter 5	Conclusion	81
Appendix		93
List of Benefactors		95
Index		97

PREFACE

The Great Famine was one of the defining periods of modern Irish history and we live with its effects to this day. The town of Skibbereen has become an icon of this period, associated the world over with the events of the mid-1840s.

This book is a description of events in Skibbereen and its hinterland during the worst years of the Famine, from late 1845 to the winter of 1846/47. The emphasis is on a narrative of events through the period, allowing the reader to understand the interplay of cause and effect, understandable misjudgement and wanton negligence which led to the horrible scenes which contemporaries described. The question of culpability in such an immense human catastrophe is a complicated one which the readers can decide for themselves.

While human error, and worse, is a part of the story of Skibbereen, so also are the finer aspects of human nature. Many of the townspeople of Skibbereen responded bravely and unselfishly to the distress of their neighbours. Many government relief officials recognised the futility of their task, yet continued to labour tirelessly on behalf of strangers. For some, their efforts cost them their lives.

If the story told in these pages keeps the memory of these men and women alive, a good will have been done.

Peter Foynes,
March 2004.

ACKNOWLEDGEMENTS

The Skibbereen Famine Commemoration Committee would like to acknowledge the work of the author, Peter Foynes, who, through his involvement in the development of the Famine Exhibition at the Skibbereen Heritage Centre, brought much valuable material to light. The members of the Committee resolved that this accumulated research material should be made available to the public and should be published in book form.

A special word of thanks is due to:

Gerald O'Brien – for his diligent and painstaking work in compiling the index; and
Jerry O'Sullivan – for co-ordinating the various strands of the project.

Special thanks are due also to the enthusiastic and energetic members of the Famine Commemoration Committee:

Noel O'Driscoll	Chairman
Marie Cregan	Secretary
Denny O'Sullivan and Dave Barry	Joint Treasurers
Charles McCarthy	PRO
Gerald O'Brien	Vice Chairman
Seamus Ryan	
Jerry O'Sullivan	
Sean Connolly	
Cathal O'Donovan	
Billy O'Brien	
Sean Scully	Committee Members

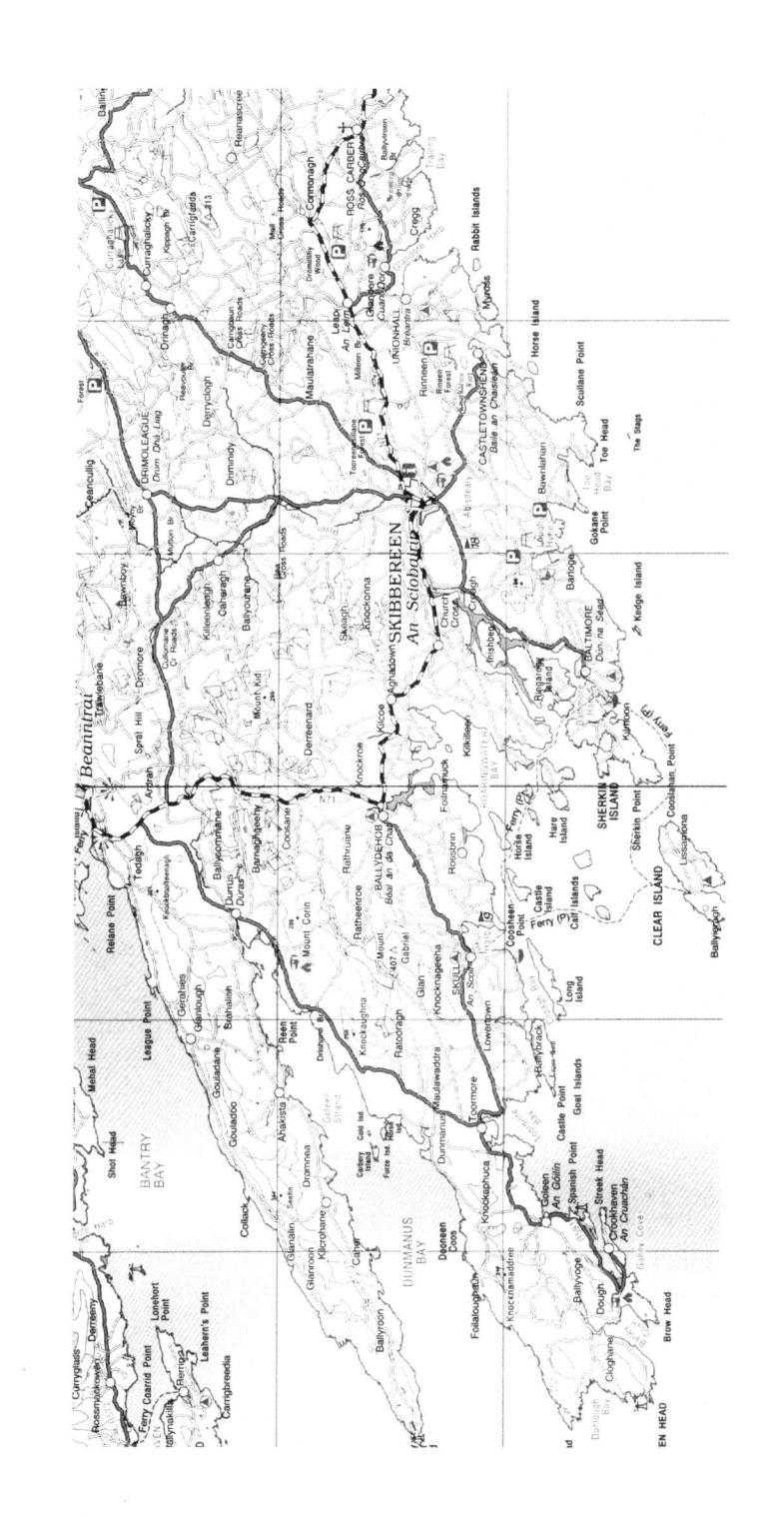

Figure 1. Map of West Cork (Ordnance Survey Ireland Permit No. 7825)

Chapter 1
BEFORE THE FAMINE

Skibbereen was a thriving commercial town in the first half of the 19th century. Horatio Townsend, in his survey of the County of Cork of 1810, wrote:

> Skibbereen, without patronage or encouragement, has, from the mere circumstances of its situation, become populous, thriving, and wealthy. ... Here are bolting mills, porter and beer breweries, and but lately possessed an extensive distillery of whiskey. It has a crowded market on Saturdays and four yearly fairs ... The circumstances, to which this town owes its rapid advancement are a great and increasing population in the neighbouring districts and the want of any rival to share with it in supplying their wants.

Samuel Lewis's account in his Topographical Dictionary of 1837 confirms the impression of prosperity, though he notes some decline since the beginning of the century.

> This place formerly had a very considerable trade, arising from the manufacture of woollen cloth, linen, checks and handkerchiefs, which has altogether declined. ... In the town are capacious storehouses for corn, and a considerable quantity of flour is also exported from the mills ... a porter brewery, upon an extensive scale, was established in 1809; it is the property of Daniel McCarthy Esq., ... The supply of provisions is very abundant, particularly fish and poultry; pigs and sheep are also sold in great numbers.

William Thackeray, in his account of his visit in 1842 described the town as an "active and flourishing town".

While there were other urban centres in West Cork, such as Ballydehob and Schull, it was Skibbereen that dominated. The town's prominence in the locality was confirmed by the presence of two banks, a Custom House and a courthouse, as well as Methodist, Anglican and Catholic places of worship. The recently opened (1843) Workhouse was also situated in Skibbereen, and the town was the administrative centre of the Poor Law Union. The Poor Law Union extended over an area of 236,000 acres and consisted of the area west of a line that began east of Leap, north to beyond Drimoleague and then to the coastline west of Durrus. (The Union was so large it was thought necessary to divide it in 1849 and create the Schull Union). Skibbereen's role at the centre of the Union, combined with its commercial predominance in the locality, ensured that the town became the centre of the relief effort that was undertaken from 1846 onwards.

At the apex of pre-Famine Skibbereen society were the large landowners. The most prominent of these (with a contemporary estimate of their incomes) were:

> Lord Carbery – £15,000;
> R.H.H. Beecher, Esq. – £4,000;
> Mr. Henry Newman – £ 4,000;
> The O'Donovans – £2,500;
> Rev. M. Beecher – £1,000;
> Messrs. Townsend and Wright – £1,500;
> Mr. Townsend, White Hall – £2,000;
> Mr. French – £1,000;
> Mr. S. Lavis – £1,000;
> Sir William Wrixon-Beecher – £10,000;
> Rev. Stephen Townsend – £8,000;
> Lord Audeley – £8,000.

The combined annual income of these estates was £50,000.

The list illustrates the concentration of land-owning. It disguises the fact that the Skibbereen Union was a poor area. The rateable valuation of its land and buildings was less than £1 per head of population, the second lowest in the country. This low capital value of the area was compounded by the comparative absence of resident landlords. One contemporary asserted that two out of three landlords were non-resident. Of those listed above, Lord Audley, Stephen Townsend and Sir William Wrixon-Beecher, whose total combined income was more than half of the total of those listed, were absentees. While a resident landlord was not always a benevolent one, in general resident landlords offered more possibility of employment, were more involved in improving their estates and were more committed to their community than the absentee landlord. Absent landlords also meant that a proportion of the rental income was being exported from the area, rather than invested locally.

In the middle bracket of pre-Famine Skibbereen society, below the head landlords, were the strong farmers, land agents, middlemen, professional men, clergymen and merchants that went to make up the body of the respectable classes of society. Of the 9,432 land holdings in the Union in 1845, 30.87 per cent were between ten and 20 acres, 25.66 per cent between 20 and 50 acres and 5.6 per cent above 50 acres. In all, some 60 per cent of the holdings were above ten acres. The 1841 census shows that 216 families were involved in the professions, 626 were involved in trade or manufacturing and some 480 persons were involved in the provision of lodging.

As in any community, this middle band of respectable people, many of whom became active in the relief programme, was a varied group. They included: McCarthy Downing, the Skibbereen solicitor; Daniel McCarthy, brewer and vice-chairman of the Board of Guardians, also from Skibbereen; James McCarthy, a farmer and middleman from Goleen; John Collins, a gentleman farmer of c.100 acres from Oldcourt; Henry Newman, a farmer and land agent; Thomas J. Hungerford, a land agent from Rosebank, near Skibbereen; Thomas Marmion, merchant and agent for the Rev. Townsend; R.B. Townsend, Rector of Abbeystrewery; Constabulary Sub-Inspector George Minchin – to name but a few. These relatively comfortable persons formed but a small proportion of the society. This much is apparent from the 1841 Ordnance Survey map, where the number of houses significant enough to be included on the map can be counted; and that in an area of almost 100,000 acres.

Below the respectable middle bracket was the vast majority of the community. Pre-Famine Skibbereen was a densely populated area, something both Thackeray and Townsend noted. The Skibbereen Poor Law Union had a population of 104,508, the eighth largest in the country, with a density of over 400 people to the square mile, in contrast to the County average of 200-300 per square mile. Thackeray describes:

> The people ... flocking into the place in their hundreds ... There was only one wretched village along the road, but no lack of population.

Not only was the area densely populated, but that population was growing. The 1831 census gives a population of 38,338 for the Barony of Carbery West (East Division). Within ten years, that number had risen to 43,531 (some 7,963 families), a 13.5 per cent increase in ten years. The vast majority of that population lived in poverty.

In an agricultural society such as pre-Famine Skibbereen, almost three-quarters of the population of the Barony were chiefly employed in agriculture. The fundamental determinant of economic status was access to land. By this criterion, the majority of the population was poor. In 1846, 42 per cent of the population of the Skibbereen Union were landless, while another 16 per cent of the population (3,082 holdings) occupied holdings with a rateable valuation at or below £4 (which translates roughly into five acres). Given that contemporaries believed that at least ten acres was required to make a "comfortable" living, the precariousness of the existence of almost 60 per cent of the population is apparent.

The poorest were the agricultural labourers. Two sorts of agricultural labourers were to be found in pre-Famine Skibbereen: the cottier tenant; and the conacre man. Rev. Thomas Tuckey, of Dromdaleague (now Drimoleague), described the position of the cottier tenant to the Poor Law Inquiry of 1836 thus:

> The agreement between the landlord and cottier tenant is generally of this kind; the farmer agrees to employ such a man as a regular labourer. He then sets him a house, engaging to give him every year a certain portion of ground, from half to an acre, on which to put his manure for a potato garden; he generally allows him to keep a couple of sheep on the farm at 2s. a quarter each for their grazing; sets him a portion of bog for turf, and tillage for flax. For all these the tenant has to pay by his labour and, of course, receives the difference only after the amount of these several charges ...

Rev. Tuckey went on to remark:

> If the cottier be not a labourer to his landlord, of course he must find money to pay his rent, and any other charge to which he may be subject.

In the summer of 1847, Fr. Mathew gave a detailed description of the pre-Famine economy in West Cork to the Commission on Colonisation:

> *Will you have the goodness in the first instance to direct your attention to the state of those poorer classes before the failure of the potato crop, and subsequently to the condition of the same class after that calamity?*

Before the Famine

– It was my conviction that the labouring poor in the west of the County of Cork were the most destitute of any in Ireland.

Was that the condition of things even before the failure of the potato crop?
– Yes.

In what way did that destitution manifest itself so far as was represented by the wages of labour?
– In the west of the County of Cork there was very little local employment. The people had wretched cabins, they were poorly clad, badly fed, and in a great degree uneducated.

Was there a demand for the labour of the able-bodied poor in that district?
– No local demand. Those persons generally supplied labour to the inland parts of Ireland – Tipperary, Limerick, Kilkenny. They emigrated at the commencement of the corn harvest, and remained until after the potato-digging and then returned home.

Are the Committee to understand that there was a certain internal migration of those classes in Ireland in that same way that exists from Ireland more generally for the harvest work in England?
– Precisely the same ...

Can you state the extent of employment which a mere potato garden affords to the Irish cottier peasant?
– A potato garden employs the cottier peasant more than half the year in preparing the ground for the potatoes. The females of his family are also employed in the same manner, the male in digging and preparing the ground, the female in sticking the potatoes, then again in trenching those potatoes, and shovelling those potatoes, and afterwards for a couple of months they are employed in cutting turf and saving it to boil those potatoes. Almost the whole time of these poor people is taken up in the cultivation and dressing those potatoes.

Supposing the case of a cottier peasant holding a plot of land sufficient to provide him with potatoes, at what time of the year does he generally begin the preparation of the land for planting those potatoes?
– The cottier tenant should begin in March to prepare the ground for the potatoes, digging the ground, or, if he can borrow a horse to plough it, and in collecting manure and putting on the manure. Then the wife is employed in planting those potatoes, and afterwards in picking them and pitting them. There is a small portion of April and May employed in digging the furrows; and there is shovelling the furrows and weeding the potatoes. The labour would not be over till about the middle of June or the end of June in general.

The Great Famine in Skibbereen

For what number of hours of the day would the man be generally employed upon his potato ground in the day?
– A poor man in his own garden is master of his own time, and would go out an hour or two or three hours in the morning, have dinner at twelve o'clock, and then work again till six in the evening. From that time the labour connected with planting the potatoes is closed.

What interval of time occurs before the subsequent labour of digging the potatoes begins?
– They are generally perhaps three or four months before digging the potatoes.

About what time of the year does the digging of the potatoes conclude?
– The latter part of November.

Is there any employment for the cottier between the planting of the potatoes and the digging them up?
– Yes, weeding in July and in August. Perhaps there is a second shovelling if the potatoes are luxuriant.

Does that subsequent work of weeding and shovelling afford any considerable amount of employment for the cottage labourer?
– Certainly not.

Then, from the month of November up to the potato planting the following year, has the cottager tenant any effective demand for his labour?
– No. He is generally employed in preparing for the next year's crop. If he has not the cattle to assist him in making manure, he must employ his time during the year in raising sand and other matters to prepare for the next crop.

Practically speaking, is there any effective or continued permanent demand for his labour on his own land in that interval of time?
— No, there is not more than I have mentioned. Cutting turf and drawing it home occupies a great deal of time.

That is in the summer.
— That is in the summer.

But there is no analogous occupation between the month of November when the potato digging ceases up to the time in the spring when the potato planting begins?
– Very little.

Will you now describe the condition of the conacre cultivator of potatoes; has he any more effective demand for his labour than that which you have described in the case of the cottier?

Before the Famine

– He has not so much. He does not get the land for the conacre into his hands till late in May generally.

In many instances is not the cultivation of the conacre carried on by allowing the tenant to dig a green field, or by planting potatoes in land which the farmer, the lessor of the conacre tenant, has already manured?
– In the County of Cork there is very little of the kind of cultivation referred to; that is, by digging up green sod and planting potatoes; there is a great deal of it in the County of Tipperary. The generality of the land is light in the County of Cork, and it is generally tilled by burning; the ground is raised up, and the sods are burnt, and the potatoes planted in the ashes

Then, in the case of the conacre man, his condition is worse in relation to the demand for his labour than the condition of the cottier tenant who is working his own land?
– It is so far worse that he is not so much employed on his own land; but the conacre man contents himself with planting the potatoes in that way, and then shovelling and digging them and leaving them, and then such of them as remain in Ireland go off to Tipperary, Limerick, Kilkenny, Waterford, Carlow, or to other inland counties to get employment there in saving hay and cutting the harvest and digging potatoes, and they come home in the latter part of October or early in November to dig their own crop.

Does such a conacre tenant give any work to the lessor of the conacre?
– Those persons are not much to be depended upon; when a farmer or a gentleman wants labour those persons are employed upon their own little farms.

How does he pay his rent for the conacre?
– Those that emigrate to cut the harvest and dig the potatoes bring home as much with them as will pay for the conacre; others, who do not, pay their rent by the sale of part of the potatoes, or they sell a pig fattened, or part of the potatoes.

But they do not give work in lieu of rent?
–Not to the poor farmer, for he has servant boys whom he gets cheap and feeds poorly.

For the conacre man, the issue was to find cash to rent a garden; with that he had the possibility of growing enough to keep himself and his family. Without it, utter destitution loomed.

Rents for conacre could be high; according to the evidence of John Collins, a gentleman farmer of Oldcourt, near Skibbereen, given to the Commissioners appointed to enquire into the occupation of land in Ireland, in 1844 (generally known as the Devon Commission):

The Great Famine in Skibbereen

He [the labourer] gets a very bad acre of land from the farmer and he pays a very high rent for it. There is £4.5s charged by the farmers for some ground. Another description of ground he is charged £3 or £2 for.

The absence of continuous employment ensured that the position of the agricultural labourer was always going to be a precarious one. National evidence suggests a working year of 140.5 days paid employment for such people, which, on a daily rate of 8d, gives an annual income of £4.13s.8d. The evidence from the Skibbereen area is consistent with this. In the parishes of Roscarbery and Kilkerranmore, not more than 100 labourers out of 1,100 had constant work. In the parish of Creagh, in which the greater part of the town of Skibbereen lay, only 45 out of 341 labourers were permanently employed.

The Poor Inquiry of 1836 gives an account of the periods of unemployment of labourers in the area, using information provided mainly by local clergymen and magistrates. The only disparity is between those witnesses who suggest that it is the winter months between November and March when labourers are unemployed and those who suggest that it is those months and the period from June to harvest when the labourers have no work. James McCarthy, a comfortable farmer and middleman from Goleen, was asked by the Devon Commission whether the labourers got sufficient work to enable them to live comfortably and he replied: "No; there are very few instances of persons in that condition". Fr. Mathew made the same point in his evidence to the Colonisation Commission:

> *How many months of the year are those cottier tenants and conacre persons out of employment altogether?*
> – If the cottier farmer does not migrate to work on other farms, I suppose he is pretty nearly half a year partly idle.
>
> *Without any employment either on his own property or on others?*
> – Very little employment.
>
> *Do you think that this want of employment is felt as a grievous evil by the labouring classes?*
> – I think it is.

A second impediment to the labourer's wellbeing was the unreliability of the potato crop. Fourteen partial or complete failures of the

Before the Famine

potato crop have been recorded in the 26 years between 1816 and 1842. The effect of this on people who had invested the larger part of their cash income in the growing of potatoes can easily be imagined. The unreliability of the crop also meant that farmers who let the land insisted on the rent being paid in advance, not being willing to wait for the potato harvest. For people with a very limited cash income, this was an obvious constriction on the amount of land they could rent. The position of labourers in general was deteriorating in the years leading up to the Famine. Rev. Alcock, of Durrus, told the 1836 Poor Inquiry:

> I have no doubt it [the condition of the poor] is considerably deteriorated, owing, I conceive, to the small remunerative price for every article of agricultural produce. Still, unquestionably, the population has increased.

Another witness told the Inquiry:

> No decrease in the population but a decrease in employment, and in the expenditure of money; the low prices of the past year have disheartened the farmers and paralysed their exertions, and, of course, they do not employ, nor can they afford to employ, as many hands as they formerly did in making improvements &c. in their farms.

These accounts, and others, suggest that poor agricultural prices were restricting the opportunities for hire of any kind.

Housing conditions confirm the impression of widespread poverty in the 1840s. They also illustrate the marked divisions of wealth within pre-Famine Skibbereen society. Of the 7,963 families enumerated for Carbery West (East Division) in the 1841 census, 122 were housed in dwellings of the first class while 4,204, some 56 per cent of the total number of families, were housed in dwellings of the fourth class (one-room mud cabins). In the town of Skibbereen itself, where 964 families resided in 1841, 316 of those families were in dwellings of the fourth class, while just 40 were in dwellings of the first class. However, there were variations. Baltimore, with 34 dwellings, had none of the fourth class and 20 of the first and second class. Castletownsend had 167 dwellings, of which 123 were of the first and second class and only one of the fourth class.

Thackeray described the cabins that he saw in Bantry:

> The wretchedness of some of them is quite curious; I tried to make a sketch of a row which lean against an old wall, and are built upon a rock that

tumbles about in the oddest and most fantastic shapes ... These are, it appears, the beggars' houses ... such places were never seen! As for drawing them, it was vain to try; one might as well make a sketch of a bundle of rags. An ordinary pigsty in England is really more comfortable. Most of them were not six feet long nor five feet high, built of stones huddled together, a hole being left for the people to creep in at, a ruined thatch to keep out some little portion of the rain.

The conditions within these cabins are well-documented and offer a sad chorus. Fr. David Dore, Parish Priest of Caharagh described conditions in 1836 as follows:

> These cabins are of mud, mortar and stone and furnished with nothing but what the wretched inhabitants may have of their own. They are not supplied with bedsteads, and as to comfortable bedding, it is a thing almost unknown in a labourer's cabin.

A Skibbereen witness described them as:

> Miserable beyond description. I have seen farmers without a table or a stool. They are frequently without bedsteads and plenty of straw is not universal.

Rev. Richard Townsend told the Poor Inquiry that: "the greater number, of course, are very wretched". Accounts of their diet and clothing confirm this. Fr. James Mulcahy, Parish Priest of Myross and Castlehaven, told the 1836 Poor Law Inquiry that: "the potato is the only food, with sometimes a little milk or fish; the clothing in generally wretched".

Rev. Townsend reported:

> Potatoes their ordinary diet, sometimes with fish, sometimes with salt fish, and in dear seasons without either and alone; their clothing depends on having constant employment or not, and also on their propensity to drunkenness or sobriety.

Even in good years, when there was an adequate potato crop, there was an interval between the consumption of the old crop and the arrival of the new crop. At the best of times the preferred variety of potato, the lumper, did not keep beyond August. Other food had to be found until the new crop in October. If the potato crop was poor, then those hungry months could be considerably extended. Various

Before the Famine

devices were resorted to, such as sale of the pig, food from more fortunate neighbours, fish, pawning of clothes. Another was early picking of the crop. Thackeray, on his journey from Skibbereen to Bantry, noted:

> The wretchedness of them is quite painful to look at: many of the potato-gardens were half dug up, and it is only the first week in August, near three months before the potato is ripe and at full growth.

Seasonal scarcity was a fact of life for many labourers and, as the modern historian James S. Donnelly has remarked: "Surely, many half-starved".

We are fortunate that the Devon Commission of 1844 heard the evidence of a labourer, Michael Sullivan, from the parish of Abbeystrowery. It is illuminating to quote him at some length:

What are you?
– A labouring man.

What quantity of ground do you hold?
– I hold no ground. I am a poor man. I have nothing but my labour.

Under whom do you hold your ground?
– Under a farmer called Daniel Regan; just a house and an acre of ground.

What do you pay for it?
– I pay £3; £2 for the acre of ground and £1 for the house.

Have you the acre of ground always in the same place?
– Different acres from time to time. The acre I have this year I cannot have it next year; he will have it himself. I must manure another acre, and without friends I could not live; without having some respectable friends who assist me, I could not appear as I am.

What rate of wages do you get?
– I get 6d a day every day he calls me; but I am not bound for to get employment constant.

Have you constant employment?
– No; but whenever he wishes to call me he gives me 6d a day and my diet; and then at other times I go down into the country and earn £1 or 30s, according to the wages there.

Where do you generally go?

The Great Famine in Skibbereen

– To the lower part of this County. I may work in the County of Tipperary or Limerick.

Is that at harvest time?
– Yes; I went out in harvest time and work in digging potatoes.

What family have you?
– I have five children.

Are there seven of you to be supported?
– Yes.

What age is the eldest child?
– One of them is 12 years the 6th of May last; the other nine and so on.

Are any of the children employed by farmers?
– Not one.

How do you manage upon 6d a day to support the family?
– My landlord has a road making for the use of the farm, and has employed the tenants there, and I cannot deny but I have employment at the present hour.

What is your general food for the family? ?
– Nothing at all but dry potatoes.

Have you fish?
– Not one, except they may bring a pen'orth home in a month; but it is not once in a month, or once in three months. If my poor wife sells her eggs, or makes up a skein of thread, in the market, she may take home with her a pen'orth or two pen'orth of something to nourish the children for that night; but in general, I do not use 5s of kitchen from one end of the year to the other, except what I may get at Christmas.

Have you generally milk with your potatoes?
– Not a drop. I have no means of getting it. I would think myself middling happy if I could give the five children that: and if they were near a national school, I could give them schooling. A better labouring man than what I am cannot afford his children any schooling, and even some of the people called farmers in the same place.

Are there any free schools?
– Not convenient to that place.

Are you anxious that your children be taught to read and write?

– Yes; and so I am striving, but without the assistance of my good friends I could not do it.

What does your wife make by the week from her eggs?
– I cannot give you the account of that. She may make 2s.6d or 3s now. She may be the means of making up that. That is not regulated as it ought. The farmer has a corn field convenient, and we must keep the fowls from the corn field.

Have you not a little garden attached to the house?
– Yes, for 400 cabbages or so.

Have you a pig?
– Yes.

Have you a pig-house?
– No.

Where is he kept?
– He must be kept in some part of the house, in a corner.

Have you any room for a pig-sty outside?
– No. I might make room for the pig, if I was sure of the house for a second year, but I do not mean to go to the trouble: and many the same as me do not so, not being sure of the house for a second year.

What bedsteads have you or bedding?
– I have a chaff bed and bedclothes that would do my own business but I am in want of a second one. I cannot afford to have it. I cannot complain myself but I could complain for others. There are others of the poor working class, as I am myself, who have no beds, nor more than a gentleman or even a wealthy farmer would think too good for his pig, and they may lie in the clothes they wear for the day.

While there is copious evidence to indicate that the labourers in pre-Famine Skibbereen endured a wretched existence, establishing the degree and extent of poverty among those who held land is a more complicated exercise. Acreage held may not be a sufficient indicator, as ten acres of good land may be more productive than 15 acres of poor or indifferent land. One indicator available is one that contemporaries used; the £4 valuation. Persons whose holdings were valued at or below £4 were not obliged to pay the rates; the burden fell entirely on the landlord. Assuming that a rateable valuation translates into an acreage of five acres (an arguable but defensible position) we can conclude that persons holding five acres or less were considered to be poor.

Contemporaries believed that the condition of small farmers in the early 1840s was as bad, if not worse, than that of the labourers.

Daniel McCarthy, the brewer from Skibbereen, told the Devon Commission that the condition of the "small tenantry" was "considerably disimproving". Henry Newman, the farmer and land agent from Bettsborough, near Skibbereen, was of the view that:

> The only difference between the small farmer and labourer is that the farmer is a little better housed; the condition of both is extremely bad.

Others took a slightly different view. James McCarthy believed that: "the labourers, having no responsibility attached to them, are better off than the small tenantry". Thomas Townsend, from Smithville, asserted that:

> ... the holding of the small farmer is not sufficient to maintain his family and pay his rent. I do conceive that the labourer is better off than the small farmer, having no taxes of any kind to pay.

Irrespective of whether one believes that the small farmer was better or worse off than the labourer, it is apparent that both groups were living at, or close to, subsistence level before the arrival of the potato blight, and these two groups accounted for at least 58 per cent of the population of the Skibbereen Union.

Structural factors in the agricultural economy contributed to the disaster that was to come. The agricultural economy was labour-intensive. In Tipperary in 1812, according to one account, a farmer hired 42 men to dig an acre for potatoes, 12 girls and eight boys to plant it, 12 men to shovel it, 12 women to weed it and 38 men to dig out the potatoes. During haymaking, four or five men followed the scytheman. The "lazy bed" technique, which was used for growing potatoes, was, contrary to its name, a "laborious system of culture".

The pressure of high rents meant that there was limited opportunity to build up reserves for lean times.

> "The rent is too high" – Charles McCarthy, Upper Lissall;
> "I am obliged to pay the rent and the times are hard" – John Hayes, Roscarbery;

"I have a very good landlord: he is a considerate man, but wishes to get the most he can" – John Collins, Oldcourt.

Such remarks can be multiplied.

Of course, it would be surprising if tenants said anything other than that their rents were too high, but there is objective evidence to support their position. Given a fixed amount of land and a growing population needing that land, then the laws of supply and demand dictate that the price of land, and the rent, will increase. The safety valves of emigration, higher productivity or non-farm income did not exist for the weakest. The option of bringing waste land into production seems to have been exhausted by the 1840s. Some smaller tenants took land at a rent they knew they could never afford. John Collins of Oldcourt told the Devon Commission:

> I think the want of land is so great they do not care upon what conditions they hold, so that they are left in possession ... all they want is land; they say we will have a few years out of this land. They will make an offer for land which they are conscious they cannot pay.

Widespread dependence on the potato was another feature of pre-Famine Skibbereen society. Density of population, ease of cultivation, high nutritional content and limited access to land combined to make the potato an obvious choice of crop. In Skibbereen, this tendency was reinforced by ease of access to sand and seaweed, which were used as fertilisers. Thackeray, describing his approach to Skibbereen, wrote:

> ... on the road great numbers of country carts; an army of them met us coming from Skibbereen, and laden with grey sand for manure.

Fr. Mathew believed that the "facility of obtaining sea manure, sea sand and seaweed" allowed the very widespread cultivation of potatoes.

The devastating effect of unprecedented failure of the crop in three years out of four between 1845 and 1849 should not blind one to the fact that cultivation of the crop can be seen as a sensible way of meeting the food requirements of the population of the time. The potato is a highly efficient food source. In Britain, during the First World War, nutritionists calculated that an acre of wheat could feed

The Great Famine in Skibbereen

2.08 persons, while an acre of potatoes could feed 4.18 persons. Combined with buttermilk, potatoes provided all the proteins, calories and minerals needed. The quality of this diet, when available, is borne out by the fact that studies of Irishmen in the British services before the Famine show them to have been taller than their English counterparts, suggesting a nutritious diet as a child.

Dependence on the potato in pre-Famine Irish society was extraordinary. An adult male consumed between ten and 14 pounds of potatoes daily for most of the year and the rest of his family in proportion. If we assume a household of two adults and four children (probably an underestimate), then daily household consumption of potatoes must have been in the region of 30 pounds a day. A contemporary noted that:

> The Englishman would find considerable difficulty in stowing away in his stomach this enormous quantity of vegetable food, and how an Irishman is able to manage it is quite beyond my ability to explain.

The importance of the potato extended beyond its role in human diet. The potato was a major source of animal food; the labourer's pig and hens were fed on potatoes. Nationally, it is estimated that half of the potato crop was fed to animals. The potato was also, in effect, a form of currency, as the farmer paid his labourer in land on which potatoes could be grown or received conacre rent for such land. It was also a means of acquiring cash. Potatoes were sold at market by those with sufficient surplus to do so. The potato was at the centre of the complicated web that was the pre-Famine agricultural system. The failure of the potato crop had effects far beyond those for whom it was simply the main foodstuff.

What was true nationally was even more marked in Skibbereen. In March 1846, the Skibbereen Poor Law Guardians estimated that 18 out of 20 of their population depended solely or mainly on potatoes for food. Even allowing for the possibility of exaggeration, this is an astonishing figure. Nonetheless, contemporary accounts support it. Rev. John Wright, of Creagh, told the Devon Commission that:

> Many of the poor people who have a small quantity of ground have potatoes entirely. I have seen some ground they have had 40 years under potatoes, without any other tillage ...

A writer in the Cork Examiner in September 1846 noted that Skibbereen had long been remarkable:

> ... for the vast quantities of potatoes which it produced annually; in fact, the extent of the population was so great and at the same time so poor that the extent of ground sown was incapable of producing any other crop sufficient to support them.

J.H. Marmion, a local landlord, noted that the markets of Cork and Waterford were "principally supplied" from Skibbereen and that he himself had exported 2,000 tons in one season. Fr. Mathew told the Commission on Colonisation in June 1847 that the Cork market was very dependent on potatoes brought by boat to Cork from Skibbereen, Schull and "all round that country".

Skibbereen, on the eve of the Famine, was a poor, densely populated, largely agricultural community, weak in capital (and credit resources). The potato was central to the economy. In addition, a significant portion of the population was wholly or mainly dependent on the potato for sustenance.

In hindsight, it is easy to believe that this society was a "disaster waiting to happen". But it should not be forgotten that the system worked. The island of Ireland was able to produce enough food to support a population of eight million (and growing) and be a significant exporter of food. One need only mention the Cork Butter Market, which, in the 1840s, was the largest such market in the world. Death from starvation was practically unknown, even though the potato crop failed regularly. The evidence from height statistics has already been mentioned. Agrarian outrages in the Skibbereen area were practically unknown. At the dinner for the annual Skibbereen Agricultural Show, held in late October 1845, the diseased potato was a matter of concern, but it was but one topic of discussion among many, which included the improving price of butter and the improvements in agriculture generally in the area. The existence of an Agricultural Show at Skibbereen testifies to a general air of improvement in the region.

In pre-Famine Skibbereen, as in pre-Famine Ireland in general, much of the population lived in conditions that we now find unacceptable, but there was an equilibrium in that society. Captain Pole, an officer of the Relief Commission, wrote in a letter of April 1846:

The Great Famine in Skibbereen

There is a tide of fixed distress in this country, which never ebbs; a stranger cannot well discern its level, but an inhabitant understands every wrinkle on its surface.

Chapter 2
THE ONSET OF THE BLIGHT

On 2 September 1845, the arrival in Ireland of a new disease, which affected the potato crop, was first reported. The disease, known variously as the blight, distemper, the rot, the murrain or the blackness, originated in the United States and spread across continental Europe and Britain that autumn. Accounts from the United States described the affected potatoes as being:

> ... subject to dry rot, attacking some in the hill, and some in the heap, and fatal to the whole wherever it makes its appearance, causing them to rot and emit a very offensive stench.

In late October, Alexander O'Driscoll, a Skibbereen landlord and middleman, rode for some days around Crookhaven, where he found that the disease was spreading rapidly: "The poor people are in tears and nothing less than a famine is expected". Speaking at the annual dinner of the Skibbereen Agricultural Show, Mr. Somerville of Drishane asserted that the use of proper pits for storage would arrest the putrefaction, a view that was subsequently propounded by Rev. Dr. Traill, Rector of Schull. The dispensary doctor for Skibbereen, Dr. O'Donovan, believed that pits were useless. Henry Marmion of Coolish insisted that it was everyone's duty to buy corn to avert a famine.

In early December 1845, a "large and influential meeting of the inhabitants of Skibbereen and the gentry and the landed proprietors of the vicinity" was held at the Courthouse in Skibbereen. There was agreement that one-third of the potato crop had been lost. McCarthy Downing suggested a fund be collected to make:

> ... some provision against the famine which seemed to threaten them and, which, if it came at all, would come in the spring and summer seasons (hear,

hear) ... I fear that if we apply to the Government they will answer our demands with another Commission (hear and laughter).

Rev. Webb from Schull believed that they should apply to the Government in the first instance. A motion was proposed demanding the commencement of public works. Rev. Dr. Traill argued that relief works would not be enough and that it was necessary to take measures to preserve the crop and again explained his pitting system. Henry Townsend proposed that they apply to the Government for assistance in deepening the Ilen and building military barracks in the town. This "would be productive of greatest good to the town which was likely to become a town of the greatest importance".

In the event, the Government had already set up a Relief Commission in November 1845 and its correspondence gives a picture of the developing situation in Skibbereen and its environs during the winter of 1845-46.

In January 1846, Thomas Baldwin, of Skibbereen, told the Commission:

> There is no danger of want in this district if the provisions are left in the country; but I fear that the prices will be high towards the end of the season. The people who are likely to suffer most are the small farmers in the mountain districts and the labouring classes generally.

From further west, John Merrick, of Schull, echoed Mr. Baldwin's view:

> ... I do not apprehend famine, but fear that the low acre tenants and labourers will suffer severely from the dearness and scarcity of provisions, if some public employment is not afforded them in the ensuing summer, and would humbly suggest the building of piers in this harbour and other places along the coast ...

R.S. Fleming, from Ballydehob, told a similar story:

> ... I think there is a sufficiency of potatoes in the country for the consumption of the population, however as to the small holdings, the tenants will not have a sufficient supply and unless they are able to obtain employment they will suffer severely.

The Onset of the Blight

In February, however, James O'Sullivan, clerk to the Poor Law Guardians of Skibbereen, reported that:

> ... the disease is on the increase and that the sound portion [of the potato crop] is being purchased and exported from this district.

The first significant public response from the Government, other than the setting up of the Relief Commission, did not come until the end of February 1846 in the form of instructions for the establishment of Local Relief Committees. Though lengthy, the document is worth quoting in full. In tone, and in content, it gives an authoritative statement of the relief policy of the Government, the assumptions underlying that policy and the means to be employed to implement it.

INSTRUCTION TO COMMITTEES OF RELIEF DISTRICTS
(Extracted from the Minutes of the Proceedings of the Commissioners appointed in reference to the apprehended scarcity).

The Commission had under their consideration the necessity of establishing Local Committees, properly organised in the several districts where destitution is likely to prevail, through whose superintendence the approach and progress of distress in such Localities may be watched, and the means of relief administered according to the instructions of the Government.
IT IS RESOLVED
I: That Lieutenants of Counties be requested to form Committees for conveniently sized relief districts, in those cases where it shall be established, on good and sufficient grounds, that very considerable loss of the potato crop has been sustained and that extreme distress is near at hand. That these Committees be comprised of the following classes:
Lieutenant or Deputy Lieutenant of the County;
Magistrates of Petty Sessions;
Officer of Board of Works;
Clergymen of all persuasions;
Chairman of Poor Law Union of the Locality;
Poor Law Guardians of Electoral District or Districts;
Coast Guard Officer, where available;
Resident Magistrate;
And such other active and intelligent gentlemen as the Lieutenant may select.
II: That each Committee should hold regular periodical meetings at a place or places to be fixed by them, where all Committee business should be transacted; and that regular minutes should be kept of their proceedings in a book to

be supplied to them from this Commission and that three members should be a quorum.

III: That such Committee should make themselves acquainted with the provisions of the Act 1, Vic., cap.2 and the amendments to this Act now in progress, through Parliament, which are intended to afford a summary method of affording relief by means of Public Works; observing that it is desirable, in order to facilitate the operations of that statute within the district, that all Memorials from Special Sessions held under this Act should be accompanied by proper plans, sections and estimates of the works proposed to be constructed.

IV: That a most important duty of the Committee will be to promote, by every means in their power, the most profitable and most natural sources of employment in their district, by stimulating private enterprise, by urging the improvement and drainage of farms and estates, and by promulgating a knowledge of the facilities afforded by the Legislature for these objects, many of which are now under the consideration of parliament, to meet the present emergency.

To supply the Committee with the necessary information, copies of the following documents will be forwarded to them:

Address to the Landed Proprietors, from the Royal Agricultural Society.
Act 1, Vic., cap.2 for facilitating Public Works.
Estate Drainage Act.
Amendments of Drainage Act.
Amendment of Board of Works Act, enabling proprietors to borrow money for improvements.
Grand Jury Presentment Act.
Fishery Piers Act.

V: That it is evident, and also in strict accordance with the views and instructions of the Government, that the landholders and other ratepayers are the parties both legally and morally answerable for affording due relief to the destitute poor, and the same parties are, from their local influence and their knowledge of the situation and wants of the people in their neighbourhood, best able to furnish such relief without waste or misdirection of means employed.

That the means to be adopted by the Officers of Government are to be considered merely as auxiliary to those which it is the duty of the persons possessed of property in each district to adopt.

That the Local Committee should, therefore, put themselves in communication with such persons, and should solicit subscriptions from them proportioned to their means, and to the extent of distress in the locality to which they belong.

That where, notwithstanding such subscriptions, some assistance is likely to be required from the Government, a list of the sums subscribed, together with a list of the landlords who do not contribute, should be confidently brought under the notice of the Lord Lieutenant, who after due consideration of the

case, will determine the sum to be contributed from the funds at his disposal in aid of the local subscription.
But those landlords are not to be considered in the list of persons refusing to contribute, who, by farm drainage, by other works of a more general nature on their estates, or by residence and employment, enable their tenants to meet the present emergency without an appeal to the public assistance.
In cases where there may arise a scarcity of food within a district or the price of food may have been artificially raised, the Government will be prepared to transmit to the Local Committee at cost price, including the expense of carriage, a quantity of food corresponding to the amount of the subscriptions paid in for that purpose and to place that food in the hands of the Local Committee for distribution on their own responsibility, at cost price, or as wages of labour to destitute persons employed on local work or, when absolute destitution is united with inability to labour, in gratuitous donations.
VI: That some very few and particular instances may occur in which the necessary relief cannot be afforded by funds derived from the proprietors, or voluntary associations, of the district. In such instances, stations will be established in the distressed localities for the distribution of relief, subject to the rules hereafter detailed. The distribution of such relief will be conducted by the Commissary General, through the agency of the Commissariat, of the Coast Guard, or of the Constabulary, with the co-operation of the Local Committee of the District, whose duty will be particularly directed to the selection of proper objects for relief, the preservation of the stores and the accounts of their appropriation, which will be duly entered on their records.
VII: That, in cases, wherein any assistance is afforded by Government, either in aid or local subscriptions or otherwise, the following rules are to be invariably observed in the administration of relief:
1st a task of work shall be required from every person capable of giving it, who applies for relief;
2nd the payments for the work performed shall be made in food, and shall in every case be limited to such a quantity of food as will be sufficient to support the workman and the helpless persons of his family;
3rd if, in any case, it be impracticable to pay in food, the payments in money shall be limited to what is absolutely necessary for the above purpose;
4th gratuitous relief will be afforded only to those persons who are entirely incapable of giving a day's work, and who have no able-bodied relative on whom they are dependent, and in these cases only in which their reception in the Workhouse of the Union to which they belong, is, from want of room, impracticable; and, lastly,
5th the works in which destitute persons are employed shall be in prosecution of some public improvements, approved of by this Commission, with or adjacent to the distressed locality, and shall be such as will be capable of being brought at once to a close when the circumstance of the people are improved.
VIII: That the Committee should obtain Townland lists, with minute reports of the circumstances of each family for which relief may be made; that at their meetings, certificates or tickets should be given to such only as are ascer-

The Great Famine in Skibbereen

tained to be without means of providing food for their families; that such certificates or tickets be the authority to the Superintendent of the Public Works for receiving the persons to whom they are granted; and that a Register of all certificates or tickets granted to be supplied for that purpose by this Commission.

IX: That the Committee should be prepared with plans or suggestions of small useful works of public improvement, for the employment of the destitute poor, in all cases where relief is given to the able-bodied; on which plans the County Surveyor will report to this Commission.

X: That the Secretary, or person officiating as such, of the Committee, should take charge of the books, correspondence and other documents; and in those instances in which it may be necessary to keep an account of the appropriation of public stores, the Commission will take means to procure from the Constabulary Force a person capable of discharging that duty, for which a proper book will be supplied him.

J.P. KENNEDY, *Secretary, Castle Dublin, 28 February, 1846.*

The first point to be noted about this document is, in a sense, its actual existence. In addressing the problem of distress arising from the blight, the Government had the option of using the existing mechanism for relief of distress, the Poor Law, which had been introduced to the country in 1838. This option was considered by the Government but was discarded for a number of reasons. One was the belief that the function of the Poor Law was to address endemic destitution but the function of relief activity was to address the current food shortage, and, as Sir Randolph Routh, Chairman of the Relief Commissioners, put it:

> ... it is very necessary to maintain this distinction, for the former may be said ... constantly to exist, whereas our duty is immediately directed to the scarcity arising from the diminished crop.

Cost was another consideration. It was believed that the burden on the rates to meet the extraordinary current circumstances would be too great. As the Home Secretary, Sir John Graham, put it in a letter to the Lord Lieutenant, it "would not be in the pecuniary interests of the ratepayers". A third objection to using the Poor Law for relief was that it would introduce an undesirable precedent, that of outdoor relief, i.e. the giving of assistance to people without requiring them to enter the Workhouse.

The Onset of the Blight

In the body of the Instruction, Cap V explicitly states the fundamental principle of the Government's relief effort:

> ... the landholders and other ratepayers are the parties both legally and morally answerable for affording due relief to the destitute poor ... the means to be adopted by the Officers of Government are to be considered merely as auxiliary to those which are the duty of the persons possessed of property in each district to adopt.

The assumptions and attitudes underlying this emphatic belief in the primacy of local effort and the minimisation of Government intervention are many and mutually reinforcing. Other aspects of the relief effort changed, but this principle remained a guiding light.

Simple economy was one: the Treasury did not wish to incur any expenditure that could possibly be avoided. There was, further, an opinion in Government circles in London that the Irish landlords were feckless and had neglected their property and their tenants over the years. The British Government had no intention of obliging the British taxpayer to meet expenses that were properly those of the Irish landlords. On a broader level, ideas about the role of Government in the 1840s were far less interventionist than they are now. This was particularly true in the case of the economy, where the prevailing view was that the best way to manage the provision of goods and services was through the unimpeded action of the markets.

There was, in addition, the moral element. For people to receive something for nothing was immoral; it was de-moralising. The authorities in Whitehall already had sufficient doubts about the moral fibre and industriousness of the Irish labourer and small farmer not to wish to encourage these lax tendencies by giving anything away for nothing.

The relief programme of 1845-46 was a tri-faceted, multi-layered relief effort, quite sophisticated in many ways. The first element was the provision of employment. Ideally, the local landlords would provide employment, at no expense to the Exchequer, on their own property, (Cap IV). This was never likely to be a significant factor in Skibbereen, due to the low number of resident landlords. Failing that, works at the public expense would be undertaken, ideally small ones (Cap IX), "capable of being brought at once to a close when the circumstances of the people are improved" (Cap VII, para 5). Public expense in this context meant, generally, the Exchequer contributing 50 per cent of the cost and the local ratepayers the remainder. With the money earned from this work, it was felt that the poor should be able to buy their own food.

The second element of the relief project was the management of the food market. Again, there was a staggered system. Ideally, from the Government's point of view, all that would be necessary would be for the Government to import a certain amount of corn and store it; the mere fact of it being potentially available for release on the market would be sufficient to keep prices down. Authority had been secretly given in December 1845 to import corn worth £100,000 from the United States, the first consignment of which was delivered to Cork on 1 February 1846.

If the mere presence of an unknown quantity of corn in Government storehouses was not enough to depress prices, then this corn was to made available to local Relief Committees, at cost price, for resale (Cap V, para 6). This mechanism of purchase and resale locally was to be funded by local subscription. The Government, in the person of the Lord Lieutenant, could choose to supplement these subscriptions if, and only if, he was satisfied that the contribution of the local men of property was sufficient.

The third, and last, resort was the direct provision of food to those in need (Cap VII). Here, also, we see a staggered system. Public assistance was only to be granted in return for work. Payment was to be in the form of food, sufficient only to meet the requirements of the labourer and his dependants. Money was to be given only if food payment was not an option. The rationale here seems to have been that payment in food would be seen to be a humiliation and would thus discourage all but the "truly deserving" from accepting it. If a person was incapable of work then that person must depend on his or her able-bodied relatives. If such did not exist then it was the Workhouse, unless it was full. It was only when all these options had been exhausted that the question of "gratuitous relief", i.e. direct provision of free food, arose.

The importation and distribution of food by the Government was intended as a means of manipulating the price of food in the local market "by throwing an opportune supply into several localities, to restrain, within due limits, the market prices". The Government did not see any need to distribute food directly to the needy population.

The Onset of the Blight

In this, they were reflecting a commonplace view. The Quakers, for example, did not believe that food should be distributed freely. While the Instruction allowed for this to happen, it was hedged about with such restrictions that it is fair to say that the Government neither wanted nor expected it. Such manipulation as there was going to be of the supply side of the supply-demand equation was to be very limited.

The mechanism by which all this was to be implemented was the Local Relief Committee, typical membership of which was given (Cap I). Their function was to collect funds, identify and list the deserving poor, acquire and distribute food if required and, in general, liase with the Relief Commission in Dublin and other appropriate bodies.

The Government was not alone in its estimate of the situation. On 23 March the Cork Examiner published a letter from Mr. W. Herbert Saunders, of Grenville Place, Cork, who wrote:

> The Government having taken provident measures to secure a sufficient supply of cheap food in Ireland and to disseminate it after a judicious plan amongst the people, I am of the opinion that public meetings convened for any other purpose than to carry out those measures are superogratory ...

It was not until 24 March 1846 that the appropriate divisions for the County of Cork were decided; the ninth district was to be the Barony of West Carbery, of which Skibbereen was the centre. This intentionally-delayed reaction of the Government, intended to minimise dependence on the Government, was to become a characteristic of the following years.

The urgency of the situation in Skibbereen can be gauged from the speed with which the community reacted to central Government actions. On 24 March a preliminary meeting was held in the town. Resolutions were passed asking that the Government supply Indian corn to the town "in order to lower the present high price of provisions, and also to relieve the indigent poor of the locality" and asking for public and private support for public works which again included "widening the bed of the Ilen so as to enable barges to come up to the town at all times" or the "paving and draining of the town of Skibbereen". Four days later, the secretary of the Committee established at that meeting, Thomas Hungerford, wrote to the Commission in Dublin, applying for the appropriate forms and other documentation.

On Thursday, 2 April, another, larger, meeting was held at the Courthouse in Skibbereen, specifically to appoint a Relief Committee. At the meeting Daniel McCarthy of Lough Ine Cottage told the meeting that:

> Whatever wish or difference of opinion might have existed some time ago since there was now but one opinion as regarded the frightful state of destitution amongst the people.

Richard Beecher, of Hollybrook observed that:

> ... there was great destitution amongst the humbler classes. There were many poor persons who would be most willing to work, and who could not get labour; and there were also persons who from age or other causes were unable to work. He wished to know how they meant to act in those cases? ... regretted to say that farmers were holding back their provisions, speculating on the distress of the people ... The farmers were holding them back and selling them to persons who carried them off to other places.

Mr. McCarthy Downing told the meeting that he had been told by the Mayor of Cork that it was the supply of potatoes from Glandore that was keeping the price in the Cork market reasonable. Rev. H. Townsend observed that the reason for sending potatoes out of the country was that: "... they were rapidly decaying, and that it would be better to sell them at once than have them rot on their hands".

The next matter discussed was what was to be done. There was general agreement with Daniel McCarthy, who told the meeting that:

> It was not his wish that gratuitous relief be widely distributed but that the Committee should have a fund to lay up provisions and give to the people a good and sound article of food at a moderate price.

Employment through public works would give wages to purchase the food.

Which public works and how they were to be funded remained a matter of discussion. McCarthy Downing believed that they should delay opening a subscription list until "they had heard from the rich landed proprietors", in particular the absentee landlords. Henry Newman argued that "something should be done immediately, for great want prevailed". Others pointed out that collections had already begun in neighbouring districts, such as Schull and Kilmoo. Mr. Robinson, a land-owner, said that on his estate his men were employed by him on useful works and not a single man wanted relief, which was why he was making the modest contribution of £5. He drew attention to the Government stipulation that landlords who offered work privately should be regarded as having contributed to the relief effort. McCarthy Downing thought this a bad principle:

> ... for there were many destitute persons who had no landlords to look up to, though the praise of the meeting was certainly due to Mr. Robinson (hear, hear).

Rev. Mr. Wright, agent of Sir W.R. Beecher, told the meeting that Sir William had advised him that he would be willing to support the dredging of the Ilen "but he did not authorise him to state what sum he would give (laughter)". A letter was also received by the meeting from Charles Anderson, an engineer from the Lower Road, Cork City. He advised that the dredging of the River Ilen would be expensive and impracticable. Instead, he recommended deepening the harbour at Oldcourt and constructing a rail link between Oldcourt and Townsend's bridge, Skibbereen.

It was agreed that a subscription list be opened immediately and that the Committee would meet every Thursday hence at the Work House. Relief Committees were set up in the same month for Roscarbery and for Myross. In Myross, the secretary, Edward Powell told the Relief Commission that the Committee was necessary to:

> meet the urgent and increasing distress in this vicinity ... a large and very poor and populous district ... the landlords in this vicinity will be forthwith applied to for pecuniary aid.

At the Roscarbery meeting, a Committee was elected and a subscription list established.

The situation continued to deteriorate. Jeremiah O'Callaghan, a frequent correspondent to the Cork Examiner from Skibbereen, wrote:
> There is not time to be lost, famine has set in with all its horrors and will inevitably carry off many who could now be advantageously employed on public works.

On 24 April 1846, the Constabulary reported that:

> ... a number of persons, consisting of about 100 individuals of the very lowest order, marched through this town [Skibbereen] this morning, preceded by a man who exhibited a spade with a loaf of bread on the top, signifying want of labour and want of food ... The want of employment is severely felt in this locality ... the National School (a very large building) is finished and the majority of labourers have no work.

The demonstrators then presented a petition to the Petty Sessions and withdrew only when assured that corn was expected and that employment would be provided.

J.J. O'Sullivan, clerk to the Poor Law Guardians reported, on 28 April, that:

> I know of a labourer having purchased a weight of 23lb for eight pence, his day's hire, and of the weight he did not get even one that he could eat; potatoes reached nine pence yesterday ... potatoes that are known to be rotten to the heart – that under ordinary circumstances would not be considered food for pigs, five pence per weight was freely paid yesterday morning ...

The relief mechanism began to establish itself in the same month. By 7 April 1846, the Relief Committee had collected over £200 and was able to report to the Commission:

> ... that as the chief land-owners have not yet paid anything much more is expected and that as the price of provisions here is very high the Dublin Relief Commission is requested to order for this locality Indian corn flour to the amount the contributors already paid, together with a proportionate quantity from the Government to be distributed by the local Committee in such manner as may appear best to them for relieving the distress in this locality.

On 21 April, the Skibbereen Relief Committee submitted bank statements proving the local contributions, adding:

> ... The urgency of distress and the high price of potatoes forces the Committee to forward the subscription list in its present imperfect state but they have no doubt of getting in a much larger amount which is required and which will be speedily collected as the landed proprietors have not sent in their subscriptions ...

At the end of April the Skibbereen Committee began to intervene in the market. J.J. O'Sullivan reported that: "the Relief Committee opened a sale of oatmeal ... this sale keeps down the market ...". On 8 May Mr. O'Sullivan was reporting:

> The Relief Committee of this town continues to sell oatmeal of a very superior description at 2½d per quart and Indian meal at 2d per quart – potatoes have in consequence fallen 3d per weight – where potatoes could not be had last week the market is crowded with them now and the famine panic has entirely disappeared. The timely donation of £120 from Government will enable the Committee to extend greatly their usefulness. On Saturday last there were £18 received in the Committee's depot for meal sold in quantities varying from one pint to four quarts.

On 21 May, the Skibbereen Relief Committee was selling Indian meal at a loss of £2.10 to £3 per ton. The price of potatoes had fallen to between 6d and 8d in the Skibbereen market and "very little demand for them owing to the exertions of the Committee". On 15 May the Government opened its Cork grain depot for sales of grain to Relief Committees. That week it was arranged to deliver ten tons of meal flour for resale to the Skibbereen district – five tons to Castletownshend and five to Mill Cove. The Myross Committee acquired three tons of meal from commercial sources in Cork later in the month.

There was activity on the public works front also. On 13 May, public works to the value of £889 6s. 9d were sanctioned for West Carbery of which £500 was for the town of Skibbereen: "several gentlemen also bore testimony to the great destitution and want of labour prevalent in Skibbereen". Later in the month, the local magistrates agreed, at the request of Rev. Wright, Rector of the parish of Creagh, to call a further such meeting. There is, however, no evidence that these works were commenced.

It appeared that the relief system was working. Advertisements for meal for sale to Relief Committees were a commonplace in the Cork Examiner. The urgency apparent in April is absent. On 3 June 1846, the Examiner reported that "the potato and corn crops give a most cheering promise of an abundant harvest". Additional supplies of meal were supplied to the Coast Guard Stations in Castletownshend, Glandore, Baltimore, and Crookhaven. The Myross Committee acquired additional meal from Cork in June and July.

Fr. Mathew wrote to Trevelyan in June to congratulate him on the success of the relief operation:

> It will gratify you to be assured that the wise and generous measure adopted by the Government has been attended with complete success. A frightful famine has been warded off, and the inhuman speculations of corn, flour, potato &c. dealers has been confounded.

The Government also believed that its work had been a success. It ceased purchases of grain in June. In July it was decided to bring operations to a "decided, though gradual, close". On 21 July the Board of Works was instructed to bring to an early close any works not required for the relief of urgent distress. The Relief Commission itself was disbanded on 15 August.

However, the underlying problem of the unemployed labourers and the high price of potatoes persisted in Skibbereen.

On 31 July, Sub-Inspector Minchin of the Constabulary reported that:

> ... a large collection of labourers, about 200 in number, with spades and shovels, went through this town this morning. They called when the relief meal is given out and threatened to take it. On being remonstrated with, they desisted and went round the town and vicinity demanding money and food. From the threats used by them that they would kill the cattle, etc. This movement is considered to be the forerunner of serious depredations; under the circumstances it will be essentially necessary to adopt prompt measures to guard against an outbreak. It would be most desirable to have a military party here. The most heartrending distress exists here, from the want of employment and food, the inhabitants are in the greatest possible fear for the safety of their lives and property.

Constabulary reports from Abbeystrowery confirm the difficulties of the labourers. Here the proportion of land given to conacre had collapsed from 5.4 per cent in 1845 to 1.35 per cent in 1846, a 400 per cent decrease. In the event, the acreage of potatoes sown in the new season mattered little.

The Cork Examiner reported on 15 June:

> We regret to say that in every case where the plant has approached maturity ... the disease of last year has manifested itself.

Sir Reginald Routh confirmed this to Charles Trevelyan, Head of the Treasury in Whitehall, on 14 July: "I am sorry to say it seems to be that the general opinion is that the disease is reappearing". Subsequent reports confirmed the presence and the widespread extent of the disease.

The Government decided to change its approach to deal with the coming season. The new scheme was embodied in new legislation passed in August, formally known as "An Act to Facilitate the Employment of the Labouring Poor for a limited period in distressed districts in Ireland", but generally known as the Labour Rate Act. The implications of the Act were outlined in a Treasury Minute of 31 August, supplemented by revised Instructions to Relief Committees issued on 24 September.

The new scheme differed from the old in that, this time, Governmental effort was to be concentrated not on the supply of food but on the provision of employment through public works. The supply of food was, as much as possible, to be left to the private sector. In areas where the commercial infrastructure was not sufficiently developed, i.e. the western seaboard, food depots were to be established by the Government for the sale of food. These "depots will not be opened while food can be obtained by the people from private dealers at reasonable price". This policy was in keeping with:

> the pledge that has been given, not to interfere in any case where there is a reasonable expectation that the market will be supplied by mercantile enterprise.

The degree of local control was also to be reduced. Public works could only be instigated at the behest of the Lord Lieutenant and were to be managed by the Board of Works. This time it would be the Board officers, not the local Committee, who were to decide who was eligible for relief. On the other hand, the cost of the works was to be met entirely by the local ratepayers via a loan from the Government. This was unlike the previous system, where the Government met 50 per cent of the cost of public works. Other conditions were added, which were to have important consequences.

> In order to prevent labourers from being induced to leave their proper employment and to congregate on the Relief Works, in the hope of getting regularly paid money wages in return for a smaller quantum of work than they

have been accustomed to give, the following Rules ought, in their Lordships' opinion, to be strictly observed; ...
The wages given to persons employed on any Relief Works should, in every case, be at least 2d a day less than the average rate of wages in the district. And the persons employed on Relief Works should, to the utmost possible extent, be paid in proportion to the work actually done by them.

It would only be a slight simplification to say that it is the two rules quoted above that lay behind the disaster that was to follow in the next three months.

The dominant official figure in the implementation of the new policy was Charles Trevelyan. To understand the official approach, it is necessary to know something of Trevelyan.

Charles Trevelyan was an extraordinary man. He was one of the most influential civil servants in English history. Head of the Treasury by the age of 32, his reforms created the modern English civil service, and, by extension, that of much of the world. He was *the* civil servant, par excellence. He advised and guided his political masters, but it has never been suggested that the policies he pursued were contrary to the wishes of those masters. Trevelyan's personal commitment to the relief project cannot be doubted, as he himself would have been the first to point out. He worked all hours, took scarcely any leave, and even moved into lodgings close to the office to save time. Nothing escaped his attention. Technical details of hand-mills, soup boilers, soup recipes, cattle's heads and tails, all figure in his correspondence. He also made a personal donation of £25 to the British Relief Association, which was more than many of the Skibbereen landlords did.

He had very clear views on life and society. For Trevelyan, dependence on others was a moral disease. Self-improvement came through self-reliance: material improvement came through moral regeneration. He brought these beliefs and his evangelical zeal to his work in the public sphere. He believed himself to be battling on the side of enlightened moral progress. Trevelyan seemed to have a particular distaste for spending public money. He regarded Edward Chadwick, the great public health reformer whose work saved the lives of thousands of the London poor, as a reckless spendthrift who "had never shown any feeling about the public money except to get as much as he could of it". This, in Trevelyan's eyes, made him unfit for public office.

The Onset of the Blight

Trevelyan has often been characterised as the villain of the Irish Famine; the hard-hearted bureaucrat more concerned with penny-pinching and adhering to economic doctrine than with assisting the starving, caricatured by Anthony Trollope, in the fictional character of Sir Gregory Hardlines in his novel, *The Three Clerks*. But this picture is too simple. Trevelyan was never merely a mouthpiece or a dispassionate backroom adviser. His exceptional drive, ability and influence ensured that. But nor was he an ogre, single-handedly driving an inhumane policy with the purpose of perpetrating genocide on the small farmers of West Cork. Trevelyan was a man of his class and of his time. The moral, ethical and economic assumptions he held, in common with many others, were unexceptional in the English context in which they were formed. Whether they could be applied to a society like Famine Ireland was another question.

The new relief policy reflected a number of government concerns. The grain merchants were opposed to Government intervention in the trade and they had exerted pressure, successfully, to have it stopped. The Chancellor of the Exchequer told the Commons: "... many merchants had declared that they would not import food at all if it was the intention of the Government to do so". Hence the "pledge" referred to in the Treasury Minute. The Government itself had always been uncomfortable about that part of its relief operation. As early as April 1846, Commissary-General Hewetson of the Relief Commission had written to Charles Trevelyan, indicating that: "I have always sought to excuse rather than commend the interference of Government on the present occasion". He went on to argue that the best method of relief was to create employment and allow people to buy food. Trevelyan was in complete agreement. Excessive intervention by the Government in the markets was not a good thing. Trevelyan ordered *Thoughts on Scarcity* (1795), by the Irishman, Edmund Burke, to be sent to all senior relief officials. Burke begins his essay:

> Of all things, an indiscreet tampering with the trade of provisions is the most dangerous, and it is always the worst in the time when men are most disposed to it – that is, in the time of scarcity.

In July 1846, Routh argued to Trevelyan that despite the re-appearance of the blight they ought not to:

The Great Famine in Skibbereen

... suspend our arrangements for discontinuing the supply. Whatever may be done hereafter, these things must be stopped now, or you run the risk of paralysing all private enterprise and having this country on you for an indefinite number of years.

Concern over abuse of the system by local interests lay behind the decision to remove from the local Committees the right to offer employment to the needy.

The debate about the best means of affording relief that took place in official circles in the summer and autumn of 1846 has striking parallels with modern debate on how best to provide famine relief. The path chosen, of money for work, is an option that is strongly favoured by some modern authorities. As Amaryta Sen and Jean Dreze have pointed out:

> ... the strategy of employment provision with cash wages provides an excellent – indeed perhaps, unique – opportunity to take advantage of the administrative economies of using the market mechanism in the movement and distribution of food ...

However, Sen and Dreze do point out that work for money is necessary at an early stage in the crisis "when affected people are looking hard for alternative sources of income but do not yet suffer from severe nutritional deprivation". This was not the case in the autumn of 1846 in Skibbereen.

On 1 August, Constabulary Sub-inspector Minchin from Skibbereen reported:

> I beg to impress upon you the great failure of the potato crop, want of employment and consequent destitution that exists to an alarming extent in this part of the country amongst the working classes. A stranger would be at a loss to imagine where these wretched beings find means, small as they are.

On 17 August, a meeting was held in Skibbereen to address the question of the second failure of the potato crop. It was reported by Fr. Fitzpatrick, the administrator of the parish, that the "hungry hordes of labourers travelled the streets and the country with poverty depicted on their faces" and that "614 people had now entered the Workhouse". Dr. O'Donovan reported that cholera was now present, caused by eating rotten potatoes.

The Onset of the Blight

Again, Skibbereen reacted quickly to the Government's proposals. On 10 September another meeting was held in Skibbereen to apply for the establishment of public works under the new Act, the first such application to be made. Some ratepayers were uncertain in their support, fearful of the long-term cost. R.H.H. Beecher was prepared to support as many roads as possible but "strongly object[ed] to proceeding rashly which would only end in confiscation". Mr. Beecher's anxieties can, perhaps, be forgiven, as he had nearly bankrupted himself from a long legal dispute with the Earl of Bandon.

In the event, works to the value of £33,255.11s.0d were proposed. These included making a new road to Island Bridge, a new road from Drimoleague to Drimmoniddy, a new road from the Coast Guard Station to Sherkin Island, a new road on Sherkin Island, a new road from Baltimore to the sea, a new road from Baltimore to Church Strand bridge and a causeway and bridge across Myross Channel, to name seven.

The reporter present from the Cork Constitution recognised, though did not altogether approve, that fact that the scale of these works was motivated by the need to alleviate distress. "The sessions seemed to be carried away by the panic occasioned by the loss of the potato crop".

Whatever about the intentions and mechanics of the new policy of money for work, it was soon apparent that it had failed completely in its stated purpose of relieving distress.

Within less than a month of the first public works in Skibbereen being sanctioned, a worker on the relief works, Jeremiah Hegarty, had died. Within a month of Mr. Hegarty's death, another man, Denis McKennedy, had died. By December, famine had taken a grip. Understanding why Denis McKennedy and Jeremiah Hegarty died, and why the public works programme failed, lies at the heart of understanding what happened in the following three years.

At one level, it is very simple. Obliging undernourished, poorly clad men, and often women and children, to do physical labour from 6.00 a.m. to 6.00 p.m., six days a week during the winter months, does not improve their health. In the words of Sen and Dreze:

> ... the employment approach has the contrary feature of increasing calorie requirements precisely at a time when there is a strong case for reducing activity levels.

Frequent references throughout the winter of 1846-47 to labourers refusing to take work shows that the labourers understood this principle, even if the Government did not.

Winters in the early nineteenth century were colder than they are now. The winter of 1846-47 was a bad one. Accounts speak of a "biting easterly wind" traversing West Cork. The situation was made worse by the use of what was called task work. This was a system derived from clause 3 of the Treasury Minute quoted above:

> And the persons employed on Relief Works should, to the utmost possible extent, be paid in proportion to the work actually done by them.

Labourers were given a task, a value was put on the task, and they were paid when the task was completed. It was intended to allow diligent workers to earn above the average and give them time to work on their own plots when the task was completed. In practice, it meant that the starving, weakened labourers were incapable of earning sufficient money with which to maintain their families. The official version of task work was laid out in a Treasury Minute of December 1846:

> My Lords understand it to be ... as that to be performed in a day by each individual, in such as can be performed by an ordinary labourer with ordinary exertion in that time.

My Lords did not seem to appreciate that ordinary labourers with the capacity for ordinary exertion did not exist in the winter of 1846-47.

At another level, it appears that the mechanisms of communication and bureaucracy were not capable of delivering the policy objectives of central Government. Sen and Dreze suggest that this is often the case:

> ... if public works programmes suddenly have to be improvised from nowhere by bureaucrats unused to such a system.

To some extent this is what happened. The head of the Board of Works, Lt. Col. Jones, wrote to Charles Trevelyan in December 1846:

Our account branch is an enormous machine, and if you could pick out half a dozen clerks who are well acquainted with book-keeping, they would be of very great use to us; the difficulty is to find well-trained hands.

The applications for public works for East Carbery, which were begun in Ballydehob on 15 September, did not receive final approval until 28 December, although works started before the final paperwork was done. A witness at Jeremiah Hegarty's inquest reported that he had been working nine days without pay. Denis McKennedy died with three weeks' wages owing to him, because the money had gone to Clonakilty in error. In November 1846, 500 men were dismissed from the relief works in Myross with three weeks wages due to them, "in consequence of the money running out". The same happened on the Lisheenassingana road in December. This is not to say that the Board of Works was incompetent: the works scheme was an impressive achievement. Nor should the humanity and concern of many of the Board of Works officers be forgotten. Many of them were among the first to see the futility of what they were asked to do. That being said, delay meant death; and delays inevitably occurred.

There were other, more fundamental, reasons behind the failure of the public works programme.

One was that the Government misread the lessons of the preceding year's shortage. In August 1846, the Government, and the Relief Officers in general, were happy that the 1845-46 relief operation had worked. Newspapers, local committees and others agreed with them.

In the minds of the most senior people, an anxiety remained about intervening in the market by increasing the supply of food through importation. Successful relief from the food shortage had been achieved by a very limited intervention in the supply side of the food market. The net cost to the Exchequer of the grain imports had been in the region of £50,000. Why not do it better next time, then, by avoiding the supply side and by putting all the efforts into ensuring that the demand side of the food equation was managed properly? This was to be done by giving the people sufficient money with which to buy food. Such a scheme would be in keeping with current economic thinking and keep the merchant lobby happy.

The problem with this line of reasoning was that it misread the events of the previous year. The real additional supply of food in the 1845-46 period came, not from the imports of Sir Robert Peel, but from the labourers and small farmers. One-third of the potato crop was eaten by pigs or other farmyard animals every year. In a year of partial potato failure it was possible to avert catastrophe by diverting this food to human consumption, which is what happened. The number of pigs sold on the Cork Market increased five-fold in 1846, though they were largely half-fed. This could not be done in a year of complete failure. The new relief system was built, not on a proven record of achievement, as was thought, but on a misapprehension of what had happened in the previous year.

The failure to understand the mechanics of the Irish agricultural economy is apparent. A second, more fundamental, mistake was made by the framers of the work-for-money policy, which was the setting of the level of wages on the relief works.

As early as April 1846, Commissary-General Coffin pointed out to Trevelyan the particular problem that affected the labourer in times of potato shortage. Coffin noted that the labourer had little access to money:

> … his labour avails him only for the direct production of the food on which he depends for subsistence, the failure of that food leaves him incapable of profiting by the resources of the market.

Coffin also pointed out that there was plenty of food in Ireland, but that lack of purchasing power at home meant it was exported. The creation of public works would give people purchasing power and ensure sufficient supply of food.

Given that analysis, it only remained to decide at what level the wages should be set. This was straightforward. The wages on relief works could never be allowed to go above the general local average, because to do so would either force up the price of labour or, more likely, draw labourers away from working on the farms and onto the public works. To deprive a labour-intensive agricultural system of its labour in this way would completely destroy any hope the economy had of restoring food production. In practice this meant that wages could not be allowed to go significantly above 8d per day.

It is a plausible, logical, position that completely failed. Why it failed was outlined in a lengthy memorial sent to the Prime Minister, Lord John Russell by the Bantry Local Relief Committee and published in the Cork Examiner of 16 September 1847. Its length

The Onset of the Blight

precludes quoting from it in the detail that it deserves, but it is discussed here in some depth, both to outline its argument and to illustrate the point, that was to become increasingly apparent in the following months, that people on the ground recognised the extent to which, and why, the Government's relief policy was failing, while the Government did not.

Addressing the Prime Minister, they wrote:

> ... the Committee feel, my Lord, that ... it will be indispensable to call your attention to details and topics, of a nature heretofore perhaps considered too lowly to have engaged attention.

Recognising that the Treasury's setting of the relief wage was designed to keep the agricultural economy functioning, the Committee continues:

> This .. would be most wise and prudent provided that the ordinary and usual wages paid for those operations [normal agricultural work] were such as to enable the labourers engaged upon them adequately to support themselves and their families.
> But this is not the case – and why? Because ... the ordinary or average wages of 8d a day are applicable ... to a labouring community, living not only on a cheap, but on a self-raised food – a food procurable by labour – but they are altogether inapplicable to the condition of this same community when transferred to a food dearer ... in price, and only to be procured by money.

To paraphrase; the wages that appeared to be sufficient to allow people to grow and live on potatoes would not be sufficient to allow them to buy and live on corn.

A few simple calculations will illustrate this. Let us assume a household of two adults and four children. The adults consume ten lbs of potatoes each per day and the children five lbs each, a daily consumption of 40 lbs per household. As corn is half as nutritious as potatoes, it requires 80 lbs per household to maintain the same level of nutrition by eating corn. This works out at 87 cwt per annum. The Committee estimated a price of 12s per cwt of Indian corn. (This was a low estimate; prices were up to 17s per cwt by December.) This means the household now needs a daily wage of 34d per day.

The difficulty now is to explain how it was possible for a family to be able to live on 8d a day in pre-Famine times, yet this 8d was insufficient by a factor of four in the autumn of 1846.

The Great Famine in Skibbereen

One aspect that was not understood was the differing nutritional qualities of meal and potatoes. Yet even this does not explain the discrepancy.

> The Committee, therefore, respectfully would proceed to show to your Lordship that it is the score ground or conacre system which had produced generally the low rate of wages, now sought to be continued by the Treasury Minute; and that now that the produce of that system has failed, it is submitted that the rate of wages originated by it should cease also, at least for the present.

The paper then goes on to show that the labourers provided their subsistence not by money wages, but by a combination of money wages, their own labour and the potato. Money allowed them to rent land; their labour, and that of their family, allowed them to grow food. The fertility and high nutritional content of the potato that they grew provided subsistence. On the Bantry Committee's figures, a typical £10 investment in this system would produce the market equivalent of £15 worth of potatoes, enough for three adults. To buy this amount of food for cash would require working 485 days per year at 8d per day.

As the Committee pointed out, and as Commissary-General Coffin had realised, the labourer was a producer, not a purchaser, of his food. The low wages paid by farmers before the Famine were sustainable only by the hidden subsidy of the potato. Coming from a commercial "goods in exchange for money" understanding of how economies functioned, this was not appreciated by the Treasury. The new relief policy was, in the words of the Committee: "founded upon untenable principles, and cannot safely be persevered in".

If one looks at the situation in this context, then the question of who imported or exported how much corn, or any other food, becomes a secondary factor. The authorities saw no reason to attempt to manage supply by extensive purchase and imports in the autumn of 1846. They believed their analysis and management of demand was sound. Theoretically, it was. It was in the practical application of policy that errors arose. They failed to invest sufficient money to attract the supply of food, either by diverting corn from exports or other uses or attracting imports. If, however, the wages had been set any higher, the Government believed that it would completely undermine the agricultural economy.

The Government were unable to square this circle because they appeared not to understand the pivotal role of the humble potato, described by the Bantry Committee as:

> ... often referred to in gone by times with derision and contempt, yet ... the removal of which is likely to lead to much misery and confusion.

The potato was not only the primary food source of one-third to one-half of the population, it was also central to the whole agricultural wage system and the agricultural economy in general. Once the potato was lost, then, as Thomas Marmion said in Skibbereen in December 1846: "the fabric of society is dissolved".

Chapter 3
THE WINTER OF 1846-1847

The events of the winter of 1846-47 were inevitable, but the degree, and speed, of collapse is still remarkable. On Monday 13 October 1846, Denis McKennedy, of Coolnaclehy, died of starvation, despite being on the public works. On 16 October, the Cork Examiner reported the inquest held on the death of Jeremiah Hegarty who was found dead near Skibbereen. The report of Mr. Hegarty's death illustrates how conditions were.

> Mary Driscoll, sworn – Is daughter to deceased; saw her father last alive on Saturday 10th inst.; he took a little breakfast with her then; he eat all he got, but not enough; it was stirabout, made of barley meal; she had that morning for breakfast, for nine in the family, three pints of barley meal, but the child on her breast did not use any of it; her father's brother was one of the nine, because he was working on the road with her father; her father was seven days working on the road and one day waiting at it; the three pints were not sufficient food for them; they had no dinner that day, nor any other food for breakfast or dinner on Friday but a quarter of a weight of small potatoes; on Thursday they had about three pints of barleymeal; she had about a barrel of barley on the ground, but the landlord put a cross on it and would not allow her to use it; the landlord is Mr. O'Grady of the County Limerick; on Friday she eat some potatoes out of her own field in which there were a few still; she would dig a ridge of them – would be tired digging them before she could dig for one; when she saw her father on Sunday morning he was dead; as he didn't go home on Saturday night, she, her mother and others, went to look for him; deceased had no sickness, but on Friday complained that he was hungry; when she went home on Saturday night she had a little barley, her father would have got a share of it if he returned home; she eat none of it, because she was sorry for her father; neither did her mother; he didn't get enough to eat on any one day of the week; on Friday he eat none of the potatoes, to leave them to the children, because they used to be crying of hunger ... her father was eight days working without payment ... the cross was put on it by Curly Buckley and John Collins about three weeks ago or a fortnight, she thinks; she took about two firkins of barley out of it because she had nothing else; with the barley she had they had no milk, no bread, no anything; in order to

The Great Famine in Skibbereen

have as much plenty as she could, she used not even sieve or clean it; they would not like to use it all till Mr. McCarthy would be paid for the seed that he gave them on credit, though she was not asked for the price of it ... neither had they fire enough to warm them; her father did complain of cold; she has in pawn 12 lbs of thread, her husband's great coat and a quilt; her father pledged all he had two years ago; she pawned all she had to pay for the manure of the garden; her father's bed was a little straw scattered on the ground and some packing for his covering; the rain is down through her house; they had no turf cut for themselves, because they had no food for the people that would be required to cut it; her father never drank.

Michael Driscoll, sworn and examined – Stated that he is married to the daughter of the diseased ... deponent got but one day's work though six days looking for it, so many were the applicants for work and he did not like to be urgent; deponent himself could before do twice as much work as now; the coffin for the diseased was ordered by the Relief Committee; all the people about him were as badly off as him but they are at work now; the labourers about him have no other visible means of support but from the public works.

Daniel Donovan Esq., M.D. sworn – Stated that he had examined that day the body of deceased which the Police had brought into town yesterday ... His opinion as to the cause of death is, want of sufficient nourishment was the remote, and exposure to cold, the direct cause of his death.

John Kelleher sworn deposeth – He is a Steward on the Lick Road ... deceased attended regularly at work during the eight days he was employed ... on Saturday last about 2 o'clock he sat by the ditch, apparently very weak; he had shoes and stockings that were more harm than good to him so bad were they as well as his clothes; for the eight days he earned 4s.10d, two days being wet. ...

John Harrington sworn, deposed – Deponent is now working the ninth day on the same road and is not yet paid; but for the charity of others deponent himself would starve since he went to work.

This account anticipates many of the characteristics of later accounts of distress.

The size of the household: nine persons in all. An account from Skibbereen in mid-December paints a similar picture: "In the adjoining house I found nine persons stretched on the ground ...".

The depletion of economic reserves: by October 1846, Mr. Hegarty's daughter, Mary Driscoll, had pawned 12lb of thread, her husband had parted with his coat and his bedding and the late Mr. Hegarty had pawned all he had two years before. We can surmise, from the fact that they held grain, that the Hegarty family was not among the poorest. Similar stories were told by John McCarthy, of Litter, at the inquest for his father, Michael McCarthy, held on 26 November, and at the inquest of Michael Donovan, who died in Skibbereen sometime around 10 December, to name but two. In the three winter months of 1846-47, 40,000 pawn tickets were issued in the Skibbereen area.

The dependence on the potato: without it, apart from anything else, they were unable to acquire fuel to heat themselves. The family was not preparing their food properly, to minimise any waste. The verdict, death from exposure, not from starvation. Death from specifically "want of food" was only one of the many causes of death.

The difficulties with the works programme: Jeremiah Hegarty was working a six-day week for an average daily wage of seven pence farthing. John Harrington had been working for nine days without pay. John McCarthy's father had worked a fortnight without pay. Denis Bohane, of Kiladerry, who died in late November, had been working for 17 days without pay.

The poor weather and the tattered rags worn by the workers: this is a persistent feature of the accounts given at the inquests and by commentators.

The varied reactions of the better-off: these feature in the case of Jeremiah Hegarty and also appear in other accounts. Curly Buckley and John Collins "put a cross" on the Hegartys' barley, that is, they marked the barley for paying the rent, irrespective of the needs of the family. John McCarthy told the inquest jury that his father "held a farm, but the potatoes having failed, the landlord, Tom Dunston, seized our horse and corn, and we had to leave". In December, in the town of Skibbereen, a landlord of a cabin, on finding his tenants unable to pay the rent:

> ... removed the door from its hinges, he removed the window from its frame, he dragged off the wretched rags that covered the nakedness of a woman who lay in fever and left a family labouring under this dreadful disease.

An unnamed landlord was reported by Fr. Fitzpatrick as ejecting 75 paupers from his lands – half to the public works, half to the Workhouse, and "then he stated that he did not consider himself called upon to contribute, because he had no paupers upon his estate". O'Donovan Rossa recalled that his aunt, who was "pretty well off in the world", refused his mother any assistance after the death of his father and their eviction in April 1847. Against that, it must be noted that Mr. McCarthy gave the Hegartys seed on credit but had not asked for the price of it. Madame Townsend paid Denis Bohane's brother-in-law 10d per day regularly. Later in the crisis, she was active in distributing soup and continued to do so until at least April 1847.

The picture apparent in the inquest report is one which was to be seen again and again in the succeeding months. It is one of cumulative and accelerating distress. The first shortage had significantly diminished whatever reserves there may have been, including clothing. By October 1846, people were facing immediate and severe shortage. Without the potato, the capacity to endure physical labour, which was the main avenue of avoiding starvation, rapidly diminished. This becomes a spiralling decline. Without work, no food; the less food one acquired, the less the capacity for work. Assistance from neighbours remained a possibility, but that could not last long.

Not only were the faults on the Government management of food demand becoming apparent, but so also were those on the supply side.

Some realised very quickly that there would be difficulties with the Government's supply policy. Lt. Col. Jones, Head of the Board of Works, wrote to Trevelyan on 1 September:

> I am very much afraid that the Government will not find *free trade*, [emphasis in original] with all the employment we can give, a succedaneum for the loss of the potato ... It is really distressing to read the applications for assistance from Skibbereen and that district, where there is an abundance of fish close to their shore, lying upon the beach, and no salt to cure them.

On 5 September, Fr. Fitzpatrick wrote to Routh querying what exactly was meant by the term "reasonable prices" used in the Treasury Minute of 31 August. He also warned Routh that:

> [any price] ... exceeding the price at which the Relief Commissioners have been selling Indian meal during the last season, namely, one penny per pound, will inevitably be a famine price. ... if it is true, as reported, that the price of Indian corn meal is likely to run to £14 per ton ... a widespread famine must inevitably follow.

A Government depot was established in Skibbereen on 31 August, at a storehouse in North Street belonging to Mr. Baldwin. Government policy was that depots such as these were not to be opened for the

The Winter of 1846-1847

sale of meal until 28 December. On 14 September, the Relief Committee at Skibbereen advised Reginald Routh that:

> ... private speculation in the town had discontinued three weeks ago and that on *Saturday evening, the 12th inst., not a single pound of Indian meal or baker's bread was to be found in town* [emphasis in original].

They therefore applied for meal to be sold from the Government depot to have a supply to meet future demand:

> We shall only add, that the frightful state of this town and country, arising from the want of the necessaries of life, demands the most serious and immediate attention of the Government.

Routh accepted that occasional sales would be required, given the very great distress in the area, but instructed Mr. Hughes, the official in charge of the depot, to emphasise that:

> ... the efforts of the Government, unassisted by trade, are wholly unequal to meet this great exigency; that our supplies are derived from foreign countries and time must be allowed for their arrival in Ireland; that the towns in your neighbourhood must unite and import for themselves from Cork or Liverpool; that now is the time for the sale of home produce ... I cannot sufficiently explain to you the necessity of economy, for our means of replenishing your depot are very limited, and must continue so until the first arrivals from America.

Routh's anxieties were justified. On 14 October he wrote to the Marquis of Sligo stating the Government's position. The Marquis had written asking that the Government's grain depot at Westport, like that at Skibbereen, be opened.

Routh's reply is confused. He points out, correctly, that the quantity in the Westport depot, 150 tons, would make no substantial difference to the situation and that the high prices were caused by the current food shortage. "High price is the only criterion by which consumption can be economised". But by his analysis, high prices should attract imports or sales of local produce. That this was not happening was due, in his opinion, to the unsophisticated commercial infrastructure in the country: "the absence of respectable corn dealers". In fact, what was happening was that holders of grain were either consuming it themselves to replace the lost potato, hoarding in the expectation of higher prices later in the season or exporting to avail of the high prices abroad.

The Government then had two options. One was to intervene partially in the market. That would be absurd, as Trevelyan pointed out. The Government would be competing to buy food in the market against the private traders, the very people upon whom they had built their supply policy. This would simply push up the price of food for both. The second possibility was for the Government to take over entirely the supply of food to the country. Routh mentions this option in his letter to Sligo, but in terms that indicate that such a course was not within the bounds of his comprehension.

This situation had arisen, Routh points out, because:

> Neither the trade nor the Government could adopt any steps for the supply of food ... until the failure of the crop was known in September. [The only solution lay in awaiting foreign imports, but these] on the most favourable view ... cannot be accomplished with any effect in less than three to four months.

Commissary-General Hewetson made the same point to Trevelyan some months later: "December, January and February, when got over, will put us in a position, I hope, to do some real good". The end of February was too late for the labouring population of Skibbereen and its environs. The failure of Government policy had inevitable consequences.

On 30 September, 1,000 people marched into Skibbereen with spades and shovels, demanding food. Again, Mr. Hughes capitulated and allowed them to buy food from the Government store. On 7 October, troops were brought to Skibbereen. The correspondent of the Cork Examiner noted:

> The starving labourers of this locality witnessed their arrival with calm indifference ... Instead of bread they received a troop of mounted horsemen.

On 23 October, an alarm spread through the town that another army of starving labourers would invade and take any bread available. This never happened. The correspondent noted: "I am convinced that those who live a distance from the town would be unable, through exhaustion, to travel".

The Winter of 1846-1847

By the end of November, the Skibbereen Workhouse had 890 inmates, as opposed to 277 for the same period in the previous year. The month of December was one of unmitigated distress. Captain Huband, the Inspecting Officer for the Board of Works for County Cork, reported on 5 December: "The deaths have been numerous, but inquests held upon but a few". On 13 December, he reported: "... the people ... are dying fast. If snow should fall I fear the consequence will be a clean sweep of the greater part of the population westward of Skibbereen". A day later: "... the deaths are increasing". On 11 December, Inspector Pinchin reported that there were:

> ... several deaths in this district, though not sufficiently sudden to justify my reporting them as ... from starvation yet there can be no doubt but want of sufficient food is the cause.

On 16 December, Dr. O'Donovan:

> .... had no hesitation in saying that before the close of spring, half the population of this portion of Carbery would have been swept off the earth by starvation.

Detailed examples of the situation in December are plentiful. A series of accounts were published by the Cork Examiner in December 1846; in the following extract, the author accompanies Dr. O'Donovan on a visit to Bridgetown.

> The next house we visited was inhabited by a woman named Nelly Mahony, who was confined to her bed from a swelling in the legs, and whose only child lay alongside her in fever. A single garment, which it would be mockery to call a shirt, constituted the only raiment he had to protect him from the severity of the weather.
> Another habitation that I entered was tenanted by a poor man named Swiney, whose limbs were swollen to an extraordinary extent from a dropsical complaint, and who had not one ounce of nourishment in the house to supply his necessities. There he lay, extended on a sop of dirty straw, without covering, or defence of any kind against the biting frost that pierced his miserable cabin ... The next house that I went into was held by a man named Neal, who had worked on the public roads, but was compelled from sickness and exhaustion to resign that employment. Neal lay on the ground, labouring under a dropsical complaint and unable to supply himself with a morsel of food or drink. A few days since Dr. O'Donovan passed by the house and ... inquired of the inmates if Pat were dead and a voice from the interior replied

The Great Famine in Skibbereen

"I want some relief, Sir". He entered the house and saw the boy stretched dead, the father lying alongside him, suffering from dropsy, and unable to rise, and other members of the family similarly circumstanced. ... whatever little food they were at first supplied with ... was fiercely contended for by two meagre dogs that made this hovel their habitation ...

... In Bridge Street I visited upwards of 35 houses, accompanied by the respected and most indefatigable medical gentleman ... in every instance did I find no less than two members of each family extended on the bed of sickness, labouring under either severe fevers or confirmed dropsical complaints. In one or two instances I saw nine in family disabled by disease without a single individual to procure them nourishment of any description ... anxiously awaiting death to terminate their earthly sufferings.

... what I have detailed typifies the condition of the labouring population in every portion and outskirt of this densely populated town ...

The second extract is from an open letter to the Duke of Wellington by Mr. Nicholas Cummins, a Cork magistrate, published in the Times on Christmas Eve, 1846.

My Lord Duke,

Without apology or preface, I presume so far to trespass on your Grace as to state to you, and by the use of your illustrious name to present to the British Public the following statement of what I have myself seen within the last three days ... I ... went, on the 15th inst., to Skibbereen, and to give the instance of one townland which I visited, as an example of the state of the entire coast district, I shall state simply what I saw there.

It is situated on the eastern side of Castlehaven harbour and is named South Reen in the parish of Myross. Being aware that I should have to witness scenes of frightful hunger, I provided myself with as much bread as five men could carry, and on reaching the spot I was surprised to find the hamlet apparently deserted. I entered some of the hovels to ascertain the cause, and the scenes that presented themselves were such as no tongue or pen can convey the slightest idea of. In the first, six famished and ghostly skeletons, to all appearance dead, were huddled in a corner on some filthy straw, their sole covering what seemed a ragged horsecloth, their wretched legs hanging about, naked above the knees. I approached with horror and found by a low moaning they were alive – they were in fever, four children and a woman and what had once been a man. It is impossible to go through the detail. Suffice it to say that in a few minutes I was surrounded by at least 200 of such phantoms, such frightful spectres as no words can describe. By far the greater number were delirious, either from famine of fever. Their demoniac yells are still ringing in my ears and their horrible images are fixed upon my brain.

In 1847, McCarthy Downing recalled to Mgr. O'Rourke of Maynooth the first case of death from starvation:

The Winter of 1846-1847

> [It] occurred at South Reen, five miles from the town of Skibbereen. The case having been reported to me, as a member of the Relief Committee, I procured the attendance of Dr. Dore and proceeded to the house where the body lay; the scene which presented itself will never be forgotten by me. The body was resting on a basket which had been turned up on an old chair, the legs on the ground. All was wretchedness around. The wife, emaciated, was unable to move and four children, more like spectres than living beings, were lying near the fireplace, in which apparently there had not been fire for some time. The doctor opened the stomach, and repugnant as it was to my feelings, at his solicitation, viewed its contents, which consisted of a few pieces of raw cabbage undigested.

Unfortunately, Downing did not give a date for the event.

The rising tide of distress did not go unresisted. Sales of firearms increased. Captain Huband reported over the month that:

> ... the Carberies very unsettled, frequent plunderings of sheep and cattle and demand for money by mobs ... Task work has not been carried on satisfactorily in the Carberies ... the three Carberies are upside down ... there are such numbers out of work that outrage is certain to take place ... sheep-stealing has got to a head in some places.

On 10 December, Constabulary Sub-Inspector Pinchin reported that:

> ... about 30 or 40 unemployed labourers drove off the men at work on this line of road between Glandore and Ross this day, and said that they would not allow them to return except they were employed themselves. ... and this morning about 80 unemployed men passed through the village of Glandore, with spades and shovels, seemingly in much distress, looking for work, but committed no violence.

The Relief Committee and inquest juries were vehement in their criticism of Government policy in general and the relief works in particular. In their view, the works were too small, too irregularly paid and too mean-spirited in their execution to be of any use in relieving distress.

The inquest on Denis McKennedy famously brought in a verdict finding the Board culpable in his death: "this want of sustenance was occasioned by his not having been paid his wages on the Public Works". A similar formulation was used at the verdict on Denis Bohane. On 18 December, the Relief Committee debated whether they should resign en masse, and encouraged other Relief

53

Committees to do likewise. Thomas Somerville, Chairman, stated that:

> They were only made the tools of the Board of Works; they were only the medium of carrying out a vicious and bad system ... completely repugnant to their feelings as men of humanity.

Captain Huband had a correspondingly low opinion of the Relief Committees in Carbery. On 13 December he reported that: "the conduct of the Relief Committee of Skibbereen is of the worst possible kind, and violent in the extreme".

The efforts of the Skibbereen community were not confined entirely to heaping abuse upon the Board of Works and its agents. On 31 October, a Charity Soup House was proposed, to be located at Thomas Marmion's store on Ilen Street. This was in operation by 9 November. Rev. Caulfield, Rector of Creagh, was also dispensing soup from his house and was feeding "50 or 60 people" by the end of November. By the middle of December, the Soup Committee had acquired "an apparatus for ... the distribution of 160 to 170 gallons daily", although they were not always certain of sufficient funds to maximise use of the apparatus. According to the Committee, the quality of the soup was excellent and cost less than one penny for three pints. The correspondent of the Cork Examiner was less sure. Acknowledging that soup was the only gratuitous food in the town, he remarked: "and this food, it is conjectured by many, induces further bowel complaints, though it satisfies immediate want".

Another scheme in progress in Skibbereen in December was assisted emigration to England. There are references to emigration from the area taking place and this is confirmed by the rise in those departing the port of Baltimore. 901 people left the port in 1845 and 2,122 departed in 1846, but these, in the main, were the better off, with means to afford the passage.

Assisted emigration was instigated by Dr. O'Donovan and supported, in particular by the Skibbereen merchant, Mr. Swanton, who provided a vessel, and by other private supports. It was targeted at the poor, who were given passage and money. Only those who could provide evidence of being able to find employment in England, either by having friends or relatives there or by having been there previously themselves, were accepted. By mid-December, some 145 had been

The Winter of 1846-1847

sent, with a waiting list of over 700, which was increasing daily. Reports from those who had emigrated were favourable. The husband of Dr. O'Donovan's servant had written from Cardiff telling how he was earning three shillings a day and that work was plentiful. By early January, pressure of work forced Dr. O'Donovan to cease work on the scheme but he proposed to the Relief Committee that a special Committee be set up. Thomas Marmion, who seems to have been something of a firebrand, supported the suggestion on the grounds "that we spread fever and contagion amongst them (cries of oh, oh)". The proposal was agreed. The scheme continued until at least February 1847, and was the only one of its kind in the country.

In late November, the Relief Committee sent a delegation, comprising Rev. Caulfield and Rev. Townsend, to England to seek contributions to relieve distress. In particular, they sought permission to hold a nationwide church collection. They were unsuccessful in this, and in their fundraising generally, due, in their view, to misunderstandings among the English population about the situation in Ireland, but they did manage to meet senior Government ministers and officials, including Sir George Grey (the Home Secretary), and Sir Charles Trevelyan.

At their meeting with Trevelyan on 2 December, the clerics told him that normal agricultural activity had ceased. Because of the restrictions placed on the Relief Committee, worthwhile people had shifted their activity away from the official Committee, which was now merely listing names for public works. They also mentioned the soup kitchen and that deaths in the Workhouse were at a very high rate.

Trevelyan responded that it was his conviction:

> ... that the observance of the general rule of selling at a fair market price is indispensable because without it, dearth would become famine, and the creation of a class of dealers through which the new corn food may be distributed to the people would be impossible; but I did not understand that the Committee were precluded from giving ordinary relief in special cases.

The Reverends replied that:

> The case of all labourers employed on the Relief Works was special because the wages they obtained were insufficient to keep them alive at present prices.

The Great Famine in Skibbereen

Despite Trevelyan's routine response to the clergymen, after that meeting Skibbereen was on the agenda in Whitehall. The following day he wrote to Routh describing the meeting. The next day he wrote to Jones of the Board of Works: "I enclose another police notice of two more inquests at Skibbereen ... How do you account for these repeated deaths at Skibbereen ...?".

On 5 December Trevelyan suggested to Routh that "the whole or a portion of the Ceylon subscription be given to Skibbereen, where, judging from the number of deaths, the destitution must be frightful". Routh agreed and advised that he had ordered the depot in Skibbereen to be opened two days a week. On 12 December Routh reported that the depot was now open three days a week, with discretion to extend this if necessary. This was at a time when the fixed date for opening the depots was still 28 December. On 18 December, Routh was contacted by the Chief Secretary for Ireland, Henry Labouchere, "who is very anxious about the reports from Skibbereen". That day, Routh sent a senior official, Assistant Commissary-General Inglis, from Limerick to Skibbereen "to organise a plan for the relief of distress and to remain there until it is organised". A Board of Works Inspecting Officer, Major Parker, was appointed formally, for the East Division of West Carbery; informally, for Skibbereen. On 8 December, Trevelyan communicated to Routh his wish "to be furnished at the earliest practicable period with a detailed report of the measures which have been taken".

The Skibbereen Relief Committee itself had inquired of the Chief Secretary, on 14 December, if they could use the official relief fund for providing soup. Inglis arrived in Skibbereen on Saturday 19 December, and spent the following day meeting members of the Relief Committee and others, from whom he learnt that an active Soup Committee existed.

On Monday 21 December, a meeting was held at the house of Fr. Fitzpatrick. It was agreed that Inglis would lodge £85 to the account of the Soup Committee and that a second soup kitchen would be established in North Street, at a house owned by William Beecher and formerly used as a schoolhouse. This premises was also to house:

> ... an apparatus for preparing suitable food and drink for the sick poor in the district, as the poorhouse and the fever hospital contain a much greater number then they were intended to accommodate.

The Winter of 1846-1847

This was the first Government assistance specifically directed to a soup kitchen. It was a major change in policy. Inglis described it as "quite a new sort of Commissariat duty".

Trevelyan recognised this. Soup boilers were supplanting his sophisticated scheme of publicly funded demand being met by privately managed supply. On 5 January 1847, he wrote to Routh:

> I lament to have to express my opinion that this rude experiment of the public kitchen is the only thing which stands between multitudes of our fellow countrymen and death, and we are very anxious that it should be carried to the utmost possible extent in the districts in which it is required.

By the end of December, the Government was recommending to all Committees to provide soup. They even suggested a recipe. By 7 January, 1,500 people were being fed in Skibbereen, even though the second boiler had not arrived from Cork. By the end of the month, soup kitchens had become the cornerstone of relief policy, and they eventually arrested the tide of starvation, disease and death.

It is ironic that at the time the Government was beginning to recognise the failure of the money for work programme and move to a strategy of direct delivery of food, the situation in Skibbereen came to national and international attention. Nicholas Cummins' letter to the Times was instrumental in the formation of the British Relief Association, which paid a major part in delivering aid to Ireland; Trevelyan himself donated £25, one per cent of his salary. There were other ways in which information was carried abroad and relief funds received, in particular through individuals who sent copies of newspaper reports to friends or business acquaintances in Britain.

In December the Society of Friends sent three Cork Quakers to investigate reports of the situation in Skibbereen. As of 30 December 1846, subscriptions to Skibbereen relief had come from Cork City, Armagh, Cavan, London, Meath, Kildare, Sheffield, Molton Mowbray, Dublin and Allridge. Henry Grattan, the son of the famous Irish parliamentarian Henry Grattan, was among the contributors. According to Routh, too much money was finding its way to Skibbereen and "some of the poor ... have become sick from the sudden change to abundance".

In December and January of 1846-47, however, the tide of starvation, disease and death was rising. Inglis reported that "fever and

bowel complaints have reached such a pitch that the people begin to fear going near each other".
But the picture is a complicated one. Inglis goes on to note:

> This mortality is confined to a certain class of persons, who are always to be found in and about all towns in Ireland, such as labouring people and beggars. The country people generally never looked more healthy.

Colonel Fitzmaurice, another officer of the Board, had reported on the previous day that "the rural districts and those bordering upon the seashore is where destitution presses most severely". Nicholas Cummins found it unremarkable that he had no difficulty in acquiring "as much bread as five men could carry" in Skibbereen. Visitors in February found the same. Colonel Fitzmaurice also noted the availability of food: "there is still a large portion, both in the Commissariat stores as well as Mr. Swanton's extensive mills".

The report of Major Parker, a more sympathetic figure than his overworked colleague, Captain Huband, gives "a strange account of the state of things". It is dated 21 December, the same day that Inglis convened the Soup Committee meeting.

> The distress of this place is truly deplorable and heart-rending; its mortality is very great and likely to continue so ... the greatest number of deaths is in the Union Workhouse. ... It has been recommended by the priests from the altar, that it is better to save for the living instead of being at the expense of coffins for the dead; and, I understand, bodies are taken in coffins to the burial ground, taken out, and the coffins kept for conveying more for burial. A woman with a dead child in her arms was begging in the streets yesterday ... To narrate the many sad stories I have heard, would occupy sheets of paper ... nothing can exceed the miserable state of this place.
> It is a remarkable fact, that, although the flour and biscuit depot has been opened ten days, only £2.5s has been received for sales, the price being £17, while the retail price in the shops is about £18 ... no two persons of this place agree in explaining this circumstance ...
> I do not hear of any outrages; on the contrary, I hear of acts of the greatest patience and forbearance and I am sure the people suffering under so dreadful a calamity deserve any indulgence which can be reasonably be afforded ... On Saturday, notwithstanding all the distress, there was a market plentifully supplied with meat, bread and fish, in short everything. Those who have been entirely dependent on potatoes are, of course, the greatest sufferers; but as the resources of a rather better class are gradually diminishing, the demand for relief will not decrease, save by death. The poor are almost without clothing, having pawned everything.

The Winter of 1846-1847

To Colonel Jones, the availability of food in the midst of famine was no mystery:

> There is great distress and destitution in the town; no want of food, but the price demanded is so much beyond the means to purchase that the people starve in the midst of plenty.

While the image of people starving in the midst of plenty is a compelling one, it is deceptive. Assistant Commissary-General Bishop had reported to Routh on 5 December that the supplies of Indian meal in Cork were nearly exhausted. The Skibbereen market may have looked well-stocked, but its resources were never enough to address the scale of the shortage. 200 tons of biscuit and Indian meal were available in the Government depot on 15 December. The Union had a population of over 100,000. According to Mr. Swanton, who was a grain merchant, the 200 tons would be sufficient for no more than eight days. There was no guarantee that any more supplies would be coming. Judging by previous experience, things were going to get worse before they got better.

The food that was available was expensive, £17 per ton (compared to £10-£12 per ton the previous summer). The Committee agreed with Mr. Hughes that each deserving family was to receive no more than a quarter or half stone, the cost to be met by the Relief Committee.

While the Relief Committee was reselling food, the Government encouraged the extension of the soup scheme. On 8 January, Trevelyan authorised:

> Liberal donations to be made on the part of the Government in aid of the funds raised by local subscription, or ... in aid of sums contributed from other quarters.

That week, Assistant Commissary-General Bishop, who had replaced Inglis, toured West Cork encouraging the establishment of soup kitchens. By mid-January, kitchens were in operation in Baltimore, Glandore, Aghadown, Kilcoe, Carrighue and Castletown. In Skibbereen, he found "a degree of abject want and wretchedness which I have never before witnessed in any part of the world" and noted that the surrounding rural areas were worse. By 15 January,

Routh was directed to "double, or, if necessary, treble, the amount raised by local subscription".
The distribution of soup did help those who received it. An account dated 19 January noted:

> I have just returned from the south, the unhappy vicinity of Skibbereen. Soup is keeping thousands alive. It was a blessed plan. In a village near my residence they gave out daily 700 quarts at 1/2d per quart, at a loss under 10s per day. It is an amazing relief to the creatures on the road. They take a pint in the morning going to work, and the second pint on their return ... in the whole of West Carbery there is a most deplorable prostration, they have no seed of any kind.

However, throwing money at the local soup kitchens was never going to be the solution. It did not address the fundamental problem of the absolute shortage of food in the region, and in the country. In addition, relief schemes using direct distribution of food require an efficient logistical and administrative infrastructure to ensure that food is delivered, in a timely fashion, to those in need. This was not easily done in Famine Skibbereen.

Bishop reported on 16 January that:

> The difficulty of obtaining "boilers" for the "soup" is great, and causes at this moment an unfortunate delay – frequently of many weeks. This is very serious. If a few "iron boilers", varying in size from 60 to 120 gallons could be sent direct from Liverpool to Cork ... it would afford great assistance. There is a "foundry" in Cork where some few may perhaps be procured. I will make inquiries there.

On 9 February, the Relief Committee at Drimoleague and Drinagh asked for two boilers. As late as 7 March, the Agahadown Relief Committee had not received the two boilers that they had asked for even though their "need of them is daily increasing".

There was the further problem of human resources. In practice, the bulk of the relief effort came from the clergy, the town professional and mercantile classes and from some resident land-owners. There were not enough of such people.

In the Skibbereen Union only 5.6 per cent of holdings were over 50 acres, roughly some 330 households. Adding these to the 222 persons classified as being among the professional classes, gives a total of some 600 hundred individuals. By January 1847, the population of

The Winter of 1846-1847

the Skibbereen Union was still in the region of 100,000, at least one-third of whom were in severe distress. In March 1847, Rev. F.F. French was told by the local police officer that not 50 of the 3,000 families in the parish of Schull could survive without relief assistance. This disproportion between those in need of relief and those available to provide relief was even more serious because of the type of relief being provided – direct provision of food. As contemporaries recognised, food should be brought as close to the needy as possible, to avoid unhealthy congregations of sick people and to minimise the travel required from those weakened by starvation or disease. This was not possible in Skibbereen. The Union, at 236,592 acres, was the 13th largest in the country and included mountainous regions and islands. While the population was dense, much of it was dispersed into inaccessible areas. F.F. French wrote in March 1847:

> There was the most deplorable want of available agency and a consequent want of suitable measures to bring the food and the medicines within the reach of the people.

The shortage of human resources was matched by the absence of financial resources. In December 1846 and early 1847, financing the soup kitchens depended, in the first instance, on local subscription. The failure of many local land-owners to contribute to the relief effort was a regular complaint at Relief Committee meetings. Government donations, however generous, were always in some proportion to the local subscription. The high cost of food, and Trevelyan's insistence that it be sold at market price, further reduced the effectiveness of local subscription. There was, further, a more deep-seated problem.

Despite the appearance of a thriving town, Skibbereen was not a wealthy area. It never had the resources to meet the scale of need encountered in the winter of 1846-47. As Fr. Mathew had pointed out, the labourers had to leave the area to make a living. According to Swanton the merchant, in December 1846, 200 tons of food was sufficient for eight days. At £17 per ton (meal eventually peaked at about £19), this meant that £12,000-£13,000 would be needed per month. Swanton knew his business. When the Government did manage to get the direct distribution of food organised, in the late spring and early summer of 1847, at peak, some 49,000 persons were given food. At 2d per ration this works out to a monthly cost of £12,454. Both figures work out to approximately three times the entire monthly rent roll of all 12 of the largest landlords in the area. A fundamental plank of the Government's relief policy, "that the landholders and other ratepayers are the parties both legally and morally answerable for affording due relief to the destitute poor", was unsustainable.

As if that were not enough, what was for many the final hope of relief, the Workhouse, closed in early January. In December the Guardians had asked to be allowed to give relief outside the Workhouse. This was refused. By January the finances of the Workhouse were in tatters and it was in debt to creditors for supplies. There was serious overcrowding. One thousand, one hundred and sixty-nine people were housed in a building designed for 800, of whom 332 had fever or dysentery. Thirty-four people had died in the week ending 2 January, of whom ten had been admitted the previous "board day". Two hundred and sixty-six people had died between 10 October and 4 January, compared to ten for the same period in the preceding year. Seven members of staff were suffering from fever. The nurse and the apothecary were intending to leave. The Board stated that:

> In this awful emergency, with a house full to suffocation, surrounded by an atmosphere of pestilence, with a deficient exchequer ... with a population exhausted by want and starvation ... this Board has been obliged to adopt the painful alternative of closing the doors of the Workhouse against any further admissions.

Chapter 4
TEMPORARY RELIEF AND THE FINAL SOLUTION

Trevelyan wrote to the head of the Board of Works, Lt. Col. Jones, in January 1846, as follows:

> The tide of distress has for some time past been steadily rising and appears now to have completely overflowed the barriers we endeavoured to oppose it ... The question I have to ask you is whether the time has not arrived for having recourse ... to what we have been attempting to arrive at by many indirect means, namely, the outdoor relief of every destitute person.

The Temporary Relief Act of 1847, known also as the Soup Kitchen Act, was rushed through parliament in late January and became law on 26 February. Even before the legislation was enacted, the Temporary Relief Commission was established to implement the new system. Sir Reginald Routh was not appointed to the new Commission.

The Act envisaged the distribution of free food to three categories of people; the "destitute, helpless or impotent", "destitute, able-bodied persons not holding land" and "able-bodied persons who held small portions of land". Food could be sold to able-bodied employed persons whose wages were insufficient to maintain their families. Rations were set at 1.5 lb bread, or 1 lb biscuit, or 1 lb flour or meal, or two pints soup thickened with a portion of meal and a quarter ration of bread, biscuit or meal per adult, with half that for children under ten. Trevelyan had actually suggested to Routh in December that he and Lady Routh see if one pound of Indian corn would satisfy them for a day. Routh's reaction is not recorded.

The scheme was to be implemented by a new administration. Each Poor Law Union was to have a Finance Committee, appointed by the Lord Lieutenant, comprising between two and four "resident gentlemen" of the district. They were to supervise the local Relief Committees. Each electoral district within the Union, 20 in the case of the Skibbereen Union, was to have a Relief Committee. The composition of the local Committees was also ordained by the Lord Lieutenant, comprising the local Poor Law Guardians, the three principal local clergy, the resident justices of the peace and the three highest local ratepayers. Inspecting Officers were appointed for each Union, and their function was to liase with the local Committees and report weekly to the Commission in Dublin. The system was to be financed by a combination of local rates and charitable subscriptions as well as central Government loans repayable from the local rates and direct grants from Government.

Two traits characterised the new system. One was a concern, bordering on obsession, with preventing abuse. This seems to have been based, not on grounds of protecting the public purse, as all loans from the public purse were to be repaid, but an abhorrence of the possibility of the undeserving receiving anything for nothing. The first report of the Commissioners pointed out:

> Your Lordships are aware that the relief that we are now administering is not only of a temporary character, but necessarily of a nature contrary to all sound principles of policy.

Trevelyan was of the same mind: "To give to those not in want must do unmixed harm".

The second trait was that this system was explicitly characterised as one where the relief was to come from local sources. Inspecting Officers were instructed:

> You will cause to be constantly kept in view this essential difference in principle, that it is the Government is now coming forward to assist the local means and authorities, and not they assisting the Government.

The events of December 1846 and January 1847 had confirmed Trevelyan's belief that the Irish property owners were not meeting their responsibilities. In the 38 volumes of his private correspondence, Trevelyan only once criticised the aristocracy and that was in January 1847, condemning some Irish landlords for selfishness and others for "criminal apathy". The principle that "the landholders and other ratepayers are the parties both legally and morally answerable for affording due relief to the destitute poor" had been obscured in the public works phase. It was to become central in the succeeding years.

In tandem with the new relief scheme, the Government began to wind down the public works. On 16 February, the Treasury instructed that works "be discontinued as soon as the means of subsistence have been provided for the destitute in each neighbourhood ..." and in any case, within six weeks. By 10 March, numbers on the works were still increasing by 20,000 per week. The Treasury then took a more severe line. They instructed that from 20 March numbers be reduced by 20 per cent:

> Lords ... trust that the resources provided by this new system of relief [temporary relief] will, at an early period, be available for the greater part of those now employed.

Of course, this did not happen. In yet another instance of the administrative machinery proving incapable of responding quickly enough to the crisis, there were delays being in establishing the new system. The first report of the Temporary Relief Commission, on 10 April, admitted as much. Staffing was one problem. It was intended that officers from the Board of Works would transfer to the Commission as Inspecting Officers. This was not always possible; Skibbereen was a case in point. The local magistrate John Limerick reported that:

> We have had a deplorable loss in the death of Major Parker, who was most efficient and humane and I heard the gentleman who came to supply his place was so horrified at what he witnessed that he left the country.

Major Parker is buried at Creagh. The Relief Commission noted that in consequence of this:

> The business [of relief was] ... retarded, and that severe disease was rapidly increasing among a thoroughly dispirited population, we have sent two inspectors to that Union, among them a staff surgeon; considering that although his business would not be professional, medical knowledge and experience, would, in the Government Agent, be incidentally of great service.

Skibbereen was the only Union to have two Inspecting Officers, Joseph Samuel Prendergast, M.D. and John J. Marshall, and the only Union to have a doctor appointed.

In their anxiety to minimise abuse, the Commission created a mountain of paperwork, forms, cashbooks, receipt books, etc., 14 tons in all, which was not ready until 22 March. They further insisted that all the correct forms had to be completed before they would issue any funds:

> ... attempts have ... been made to obtain advances on the production of some very imperfect and summary forms and estimates; but we feel bound to require that the documents be completed in such a manner as to afford a full justification of the expense to be incurred.

The new Act did not come into effect in most parts of the Skibbereen Union until early May. The effects of the delay were, as ever, predictable. Public works remained the major source of relief and, as had been the case since October 1846, did nothing to stem the tide of distress. Food remained scarce and prices high. The catalogue of misery continued into 1847, with the difference that the scale had magnified.

On 6 January 1847, Jeremiah O'Callaghan reported on the continuing deaths on the works. A new term was coined: "road sickness". On 26 January Major Parker reported that the bad weather was reducing wages to 4d or 6d a day with meal at 2s. 8d to 2s. 10d a stone.

> I venture to write to ask ... [if] ... some special relief may be afforded by allowing more than half-pay? If something is not done, I am sure next week matters will be worse here than ever ...

On 13 February he reported:

> The mortality has been very great indeed lately, and there is a great deal of fever, dysentery dropsy &c. ... about 14,000 persons employed, the demands for employment are not satisfied.

On 27 February 1847 he wrote:

> From Skibbereen to Schull ... the people are literally famine-stricken ... westward from Skibbereen there is scarcely a trace of tillage of any sort. ... The men have lost their strength; how can it be otherwise? A little half-boiled meal and water is their whole support ... There is no hope for the people here; you

cannot rid them of the idea that they must starve. No poor man has either heart or strength to sow his field, even if you give him seed; so certain are they that death will take them before they could see it above ground.

A correspondent of the Society of Friends from Skibbereen reported on 6 February 1847:

> This place is one mass of famine, disease and death; the poor creatures hitherto trying to exist on one meal per day are now sinking under fever and bowel complaints – unable to come for their soup and this is not fit for them; rice is what their whole cry is for; but we cannot manage this well, nor can we get the food carried to the houses from dread of infection ... were it not for my strong reliance on Almighty God, I could not bear up against these scenes.

On 22 February, Elihu Burrett, the American philanthropist, visited Skibbereen:

> On our way [to Castlehaven] we passed several companies of men, women and children at work, all enfeebled, emaciated by destitution. Women, with their red, swollen feet, partially swathed in old rags, some in men's clothes, with their arms or skirts torn off, were sitting by the roadside, breaking stone. Men, once athletic labourers, were trying to eke out a few miserable days to their existence by toiling upon these works ...

In early March Colonel Jones told Trevelyan:

> ... I was told this morning ... that there is not a piece of seaweed to be picked up on the coast west of Skibbereen – all taken away for food by the people living adjacent to the coast.

It was also in the first three months of 1847 that outsiders began to report on the crisis and to link the name Skibbereen irrevocably with the Great Famine. Elihu Burrett, we have mentioned. The same month, James Mahoney visited Skibbereen and produced his famous images for the Illustrated London News. In the same month two Oxford students, Lord Dufferin, an Irish peer and great grandson of Richard Brinsley Sheridan, and the Honorable George Boyle visited. They brought with them £50 collected in the University, and accompanied the Reverend Townsend on a tour of the town.

> At length, Mr. Townsend singled out one [cottage]. We stood on the threshhold and looked in; the darkness of the interior was such, that we were scarcely

able to distinguish objects; the walls were bare, the floor of mud, and not a vestige of furniture. The poor have pawned nearly every article of furniture which they possess, in order to obtain food; the number of tickets at the brokers is almost incredible; many have thus parted with the means of future subsistence, as in the case of some fishermen, who have pawned their boats and nets, and so deprived themselves of the power of deriving benefit from the fish, which abound along the coast. We entered another at no great distance: over a few peat embers a woman was crouching, drawing her only solace from their scanty warmth; she was suffering from diarrhoea: there seemed scarcely a single article of furniture or crockery in any part of the hut. The woman answered the enquiries of Mr. Townsend in a weak and desponding voice; and from what we could gather, there appeared to be several other human beings in different corners of the hovel, but in the darkness we were totally unable to distinguish them.

This case is cited, not as an instance of extreme destitution, but as a proof of the miserable condition to which some, who were once in flourishing circumstances, have been reduced; for the woman, we were told, was the wife of a respectable tradesman, who but two months before was carrying on a thriving business; and the same reverse of fortune had been experienced by others likewise. Mr. Townsend assured us that in each of the surrounding huts we should witness the same or similar scenes, aggravated, perhaps, by the prevailing epidemic.

In February 1847, Sir Robert Peel remarked to the Dublin M.P., Sir John Gregory (of whom more later):

> The feeding of the people was the first duty of the Government, and they could by Government agency alone be fed in many parts of Ireland.

There is good evidence that the death rate in February, March, April and May 1847 increased dramatically, this despite the fact that substantial quantities of food had been arriving in Cork since February. One set of figures for the western part of the Union (which may be underestimated) suggests that 1041 people died in the four months of 1847. In the succeeding four months, February to May, 5,714 died. This was 13.2 per cent of the 1841 population. The pattern was mirrored in the Skibbereen Workhouse; 158 died in January, 370 died in March; 222 in April.

Jeremiah O'Callaghan's report of a visit he made to the villages of Reenbeg and South Reen in Myross in late April shows the effects of the preceding months on one community. A "wretched woman" holding a little girl "who appeared to be in the last stages of famine-consumption" told him:

"My husband and four children died of hunger; my eldest girl, 14 years old, died in the Skibbereen Workhouse, and I brought her corpse on my back and buried her in Myross churchyard." ... I asked her to give me some idea of the number of deaths that took place in the neighbourhood in the last three months. She said she did not well know, but she recollected Michael Walsh, her own husband, and four children; James Molony, his wife and six children; Jerry Wholane and four in family; James Whooley and four in family, and many others whom she could not then name. "There" said she, pointing to an old house, "is the place where the Molonys all died". I entered and there saw the floor strewn with the tattered garments of the late inhabitants. A few torn old hats and other fragments of furniture were all the remained to show that it was once the habitation of wretched mortals ... I quitted this slaughter-house with feelings I cannot well describe, and immediately I was at the door I was met by a gaunt female, who exhibited the living remains of her son ... The village of South Reen, or more properly speaking, the village of the dead, presented, if possible, to our view, signs of greater misery. It consists of about 19 houses, nine of which sent the entire inhabitants to another, and I trust, a better world.

Despite the delays in implementing the Relief Act, the soup kitchen system did succeed in arresting the tide of decline. Deaths declined in June and continued to do so into September when direct relief ceased and figures end. The number of persons receiving relief went from 49,229 daily in June 1847 (the third highest in the country) to 13,032 in September 1847. The Relief Commissioners' third report, on 17 June, specifically mentioned Skibbereen as an instance of the success of the scheme:

Although much wretchedness is still to be found ... there is now a provision made for every part of the Union, the population is gradually amending from their emaciated state, and the people are beginning to turn their attention to future occupation and improvements, that may tend to their permanent employment and subsistence.

The new scheme was not without its difficulties. On the advice of the Board of Health, it was decided that only cooked food should be distributed. As with many aspects of Government relief policy, this decision was informed by a variety of motives, some laudable, some less so. Food prepared by the Committee was more likely to be properly cooked than uncooked food given out. Cooked food also removed the need for the recipients to find fuel. The authorities further believed that distribution of cooked food meant that the reselling of food was impossible. It has also been suggested that the Government believed

The Great Famine in Skibbereen

use of cooked food would act as a disincentive, as there was a popular belief that receiving cooked food was humiliating. From the point of view of the Relief Commission, cooked food was "the most nutritious, the best test of destitution, and the most economical".

The spring and summer presented another problem. Famine fever was the generic term used to describe what is now understood to have been a combination of typhus fever and relapsing fever. The main source of public medical assistance was the Workhouse. Sickness there had been running at a high level since at least November, with an average of 315 cases per week between November 1846 and May 1847. It should be noted that this institution was designed for 800 inmates. The weekly number for the corresponding period in the previous twelve months was 71. By February, accounts from Skibbereen refer regularly to fever. Elihu Burrett left Skibbereen in part because of his anxiety regarding the fever. On Inspector Marshall's figures, 44 per cent of those who died on the west of the Union between September 1846 and September 1847 died of fever; 34 per cent of starvation and 22 per cent of dysentery.

Rev. French's account, written in early April 1847, of his visits to cabins in the Schull district are full of references to the fever. O'Donovan Rossa caught the fever in the late summer of 1847 and was not expected to survive. Major Parker was among the victims, as was Rev. Dr. Traill. In early March, Trevelyan was sufficiently concerned about reports of sanitary conditions generally, and of bodies being left unburied, to authorise relief funds to be used for burials, authorisation that had been denied the previous December. Rev. French reported that the magistrates were organising gangs of men to bury the dead. Temporary fever hospitals were opened across the Union during the summer of 1847: Leap; Skibbereen; Agahadown; Kilmoe; Tullagh; West and East Schull; and Caheragh. In their fourth Report, on 19 July, the Relief Commissioners noted the opening of these hospitals around the country:

> Wherever opened, they are reported to have been highly beneficial, but we regret to learn that the necessity for them generally in the country is far from abated.

The majority of the Skibbereen hospitals remained in use until the summer and autumn of the following year.

The Temporary Relief Act was successful in achieving the objective of ending starvation. It was however, never intended as anything other than one element, and a temporary one, in a wider scheme to deal with the continuing problem of Irish distress. The basis of the new policy was to be the Poor Law. Trevelyan described the background and the measures adopted in *The Irish Crisis:*

> To remedy this and other defects of the existing system, three Acts of Parliament were passed in the session of 1847, the principal provisions of which were as follows:
> Destitute persons who are either permanently or temporarily disabled from labour, and destitute widows having two or more legitimate children dependent upon them, may be relieved either in or out of the Workhouse, at the discretion of the Guardians.
> If, owing to want of room, or to the prevalence of fever or any infectious disorder, adequate relief cannot be afforded in a Workhouse, to persons not belonging to either of the above-mentioned classes, the Poor Law Commissioners may authorise the Guardians to give them outdoor relief in food only; the Commissioners' order for which purpose can only be made for a period of two months, but, if necessary, it can be renewed from time to time.
> ... After 1 November 1847, no person is to be relieved either in or out of a Workhouse who is in the occupation of more than a quarter of an acre of land
> ... an independent Poor Law establishment is constituted for Ireland.

Trevelyan's description needs some explanation for a modern reader, though the clarity of his style goes some way to explaining how he became head of the Treasury at the age of 32.

There was some debate about the suitability of using a system designed to minimise the cost of dealing with long term endemic destitution to deal with a period of short term, but widespread distress, but the attractions of the Poor Law system outweighed any theoretical difficulties.

The revised Poor Law system had a number of implications. It was to be funded directly from local property taxes (the rates) which meant a significant increase on an already burdened local finance system. It was not impossible that ratepayers would be bankrupted by the new system. The Government was aware of this possibility and was not unduly concerned. An Incumbered Estates Bill was introduced in March 1847 to facilitate the sale of bankrupt estates. This bill failed, but a similar bill followed in 1848. As far as the Government was concerned, the removal of the existing landholders could be a positive good. By their neglect, the larger landholders had allowed the catastrophe to develop in the first place. The smaller tenants were too small to be efficient. In both cases their removal would facilitate a great leap forward by introducing "men with capital" who could commercialise Irish agriculture in a way more amenable to English understanding. Trevelyan wrote in December 1847:

> Strike rate after rate to enable the poor to be supported, or dispose of their estates to those who will be able to do so.

Unsurprisingly, ratepayers did not view their imminent bankruptcy in the same positive light. Poor Law Guardians, mainly of the landowning class, protected their interests by minimising the numbers receiving relief. This had been anticipated by the Government. Another means for a landlord to reduce his rate burden was to remove all those with a rateable valuation of £4 or less from the land, as the landlord was liable for the entirety of those rates. A further pressure on the smaller landholders was the stipulation that nobody holding more than a quarter of an acre could receive relief of any kind. This was an amendment to the Act introduced by the Irish landlord, Sir John Gregory. The "Gregory Clause" was intended to minimise the burden on the rates by introducing an additional check on people applying for relief. It was introduced in association with a scheme for assisted emigration, and the implication was clear: it was preferable that the poor leave the country than they become a burden on the ratepayers. Few opposed the amendment.

The clause had the potential to force those who were temporarily distressed to make themselves destitute in order to receive relief, changing the Poor Law system from one designed to relieve the destitute to one where one had to become destitute to receive relief. The clause was unpopular. The Cork Examiner editoralised in February 1848:

> We may in one word express our opinion of it, and our horror of its working, and call it damnable.

For a severely distressed Union such as Skibbereen, the new relief system had significant implications. A high level of distress generated a high Poor Rate. This had to be met by ratepayers whose position had been weakened over the previous two years. While it was the poorest that suffered the worst during the Famine, the land-owners, middlemen and the large and middling farmers had also been affected. Rents went unpaid, corn that would have been sold on the market was consumed at home; lack of labour meant land went untilled. Despite the absence of blight, the shortage of seed meant that the potato harvest of 1847 was small. The resources to pay the Poor Rate were diminishing while the demands on that rate were set to increase significantly.

The new system had the potential to significantly impoverish the small and middling farmers while creating an incentive for the larger landholders to evict their smaller tenants. The predominance of the land-owning class among the Poor Law Guardians, who both set the rate and admitted to relief, further created an incentive for relief to be minimised. This was not how the official world saw the system. For Trevelyan, the Poor Rate was a tax on the propertied classes in favour of the poor.

> The necessity of self-preservation and the knowledge that rents can be saved from the encroachments of poor-rates, only in proportion as the poor are cared for and profitably employed, will secure a fair average good conduct on the part of the landed proprietors, as in England, and more favourable circumstances will induce improved habits.

Locally, there were many concerns at the new system, which were voiced at a meeting held in Skibbereen in mid-September, following a similar meeting for the east of the Union held at Ballydehob on the first of the month. The absence of local employment, the depressed local economy, the lack of room in the Workhouse, and, in particular, the poor state of the Workhouse Guardians' finances, were all among the issues discussed. Later that month a deputation met the new Lord Lieutenant, Lord Clarendon.

The delegation comprised of Cork MPs, local Anglican clergymen and magistrates. Rev. Richard Townsend pointed out the inability of the local rates to meet the anticipated need. Lord Clarendon said:

> ... that it was a very ordinary practice, on all these occasions, to call upon the Government, but gentlemen should first show what they had done themselves.

He was particularly interested in the arrears of rates that remained unpaid and in the local fishing and mining industry.

> His Excellency displayed the greatest condescension during the whole interview, which occupied more than an hour.

He held out no prospect of Government assistance; local resources were to be the primary source of funds. Despite its notoriety the previous winter, Skibbereen was not among the 22 Unions recognised as particularly distressed which received additional Government aid. In November 1847 the Guardians voiced their reservations about the new system to the Chief Secretary. They regarded the policy of emptying the Workhouse of the old and infirm as harsh, and disliked the lumping together of those chronically destitute and those temporarily distressed by the current conditions. In the expectation that the new system would impose a greater workload, the Guardians offered to resign in favour of Commission-appointed full-time Guardians.

Despite an initial attempt in November by the Guardians to distribute outdoor relief to able-bodied persons, the Inspector, Mr. Marshall, was able to manage the Workhouse in a manner approved by Government. By the end of November those unable to work were moved out of the Workhouse. Instructions were issued to prevent further admissions of such people. As much room as possible was to be reserved to the able-bodied to avoid the "ruinous alternative of giving outdoor relief to the able-bodied".

Lists of those in arrears of rates were made, a new book-keeper for the Workhouse was advertised and new rate books were prepared. Assistants to the Relieving Officers were appointed. Committees of local Guardians for the localities more than six miles from the town were established, though the Poor Law Commissioners refused to allow the local Committees to prepare lists of the needy. Weekly lists of the numbers in the hospitals were prepared. Additional accommodation, which catered for the children and gave sleeping quarters to upwards of 600 adults, was arranged. By 16 December, the boys from the Workhouse were moved to accommodation "about a mile from Skibbereen", which also functioned as a school. The girls were moved, to different accommodation, in February.

Schools were also established throughout the Union where the destitute children received daily rations:

8, 10 or 12 ozs (according to the age of the child) of rye bread, to which is added half a pint of warm broth, generally made from one of Soyer's [a chef well known for his famine recipes] receipts.

These rations were supplied by the British Relief Association. By early December 5,568 children (persons under 14 years of age) were being fed in 96 schools in this way. This number had risen to 12,000 by early the following month and it was expected that the number would rise to 15,000. By late January, Marshall was warning that he would need discretion to allow the figure to rise as high as 20,000.

> You can have no idea of the good the British Association bounty is doing to this Union; hundreds of lives have been saved by it, and were it not for this the scenes of last winter would have been witnessed in Skibbereen again.

Throughout the winter of 1847-48 and spring of 1848 Marshall continued along the lines he had established in November. In early February, advertisements were placed for a master and matron for an auxiliary Workhouse which had been acquired in Lowertown in the west of the Union. Additional accommodation for 500 to 600 men was to be made available. In a move typical of the mentality of the Poor Law, men from the eastern part of the Union were sent to this western depot. One hundred of the 400 sent refused to go, thereby making themselves ineligible for relief. New reception sheds, which could double as day rooms, were added to the main Workhouse.

Despite the difficulties at the outset, the Union's finances improved. A rate of 3s in the pound was struck in September 1848. Jeremiah O'Callaghan reported: "It is absurd to think that the landlords can pay it". Events proved him wrong. In the week prior to 20 January 1848, just over £1,000 had been lodged to the credit of the Guardians and Marshall reported that:

> Should more collectors be necessary, I have no doubt the Guardians will appoint them, as they are determined to carry out the orders of the Commissioners to the utmost; and from the advice and aid of the clergy in the collection of the rates, I have every reason to hope that little delay will occur in having them paid in.

By early February the Guardians had cleared their debts and were in credit. This was achieved without bankrupting the major landowners. Among Skibbereen landlords, it appears that only R.H.H.

Beecher (who was in financial difficulties before the Famine) and Alexander Taylor O'Driscoll applied to the Encumbered Estates Court when it was finally established.

From the Government's perspective, the picture in Skibbereen is of a system slowly becoming established, after some initial difficulties. The twin objectives of maximising the collection of the Poor Rate and ensuring that sufficient places were kept free in the Workhouse to test the able-bodied were met.

Despite Marshall's efficiency and the businesslike tone of his reports, distress remained. Fr. Fitzpatrick believed that "the distress in the district was much greater than the Guardians seemed to be aware of" and "vast numbers were applying for tickets to whose applications the Relieving Officers could not attend". One recurring difficulty was that of people recommended for admission by the local Relieving Officers arriving in Skibbereen to find no room at the Workhouse. According to Fr. Fitzpatrick:

> Hundreds of persons, widows, orphans, and able-bodied men had received tickets but, on application to the Workhouse, they were told there was no room. ... They were sent away by the Master without giving them a morsel to eat. They were so exhausted by hunger that they were unable to walk home.

An early cause célèbre was that of Curly Coughlan. Mr. Coughlan lived, with his wife and five children, at Kilmoe, 27 miles from Skibbereen. His father had held a farm from Lionel Fleming, a Poor Law Guardian. On the father's death, this was divided among the three sons, paying a total rent of £5. In the 1845-47 period Mr. Coughlan fell into arrears. He offered to give up his land to the landlord in November 1846 but the landlord would not accept without the other brothers' parts. He then gave his land to his brothers. In August 1847 he "left home ... to work at the harvest" returning with 10s, 7s of which he spent in support of his family. Now, in November 1847, destitute, he had received a recommendation from Fr. Fitzpatrick to enter the Workhouse with his family. On arriving at the Workhouse he was refused admittance until the Relieving Officer had seen his house. Coughlan then left his family in Skibbereen to walk home and await the Relieving Officer. According to Fr. Fitzpatrick (not explicitly denied by Mr. Marshall), when the Relieving Officer, William Williamson, arrived, he refused to issue a ticket to Coughlan as his family were not present. Coughlan had then to go back to Skibbereen and bring his family back to Kilmoe, whereupon he received the ticket. "Thus the man walked 135 miles and the wife, with a child on her back, 108 miles". Lionel Fleming believed that Coughlan was still in possession of land, in contravention of the Gregory Clause, and ought not to be admitted. Mr. Marshall believed that "no blame appears to be attached to any party but the man himself". Events such as these did not make the system popular. In December 1847 the Guardians again offered to resign.

The combination of funds from the British Relief Association and the relief from the Poor Law prevented death from starvation. The relief provided was not generous and this, combined with the disincentives to availing of that relief, ensured that distress remained. Newspaper reports are not as graphic or as frequent as the previous winter but they are persistent. In October the Cork Examiner reported on:

> ... hundreds of half-starved, wretched looking men and women, who collected outside the Board-room calling for admission to the house, employment or relief.

In January 1848 the Cork Examiner called attention to the distress in Kilmoe. In May, a correspondent from Kilmoe reported that:

> Deaths have been and are occurring in this parish from disease at a much greater extent than in other years under ordinary circumstances.

These indications are corroborated by the frequent references in Marshall's reports to dysentery, which, though not always fatal, is associated with poor diet. "Dysentery has been rather on the increase" Marshall reported on 9 November. This was repeated on 25 November with the note: "fever is not prevalent" and repeated again in late January. By then many of the children were suffering from dysentery, measles and smallpox. At the end of March he reported that: "dysentery prevails to a considerable extent". Again, in early April, he wrote that: "dysentery prevails in that district [Schull/Ballydehob] to an alarming extent at present, and not confined to the lower classes". Nor had fever disappeared. Captain Gordon, the Inspecting Officer in the Bantry Union was one who became "dangerously ill" from fever in February. He survived.

The Great Famine in Skibbereen

The case of Peter and Margaret Driscoll gives a particular insight into conditions in March 1848. Relieving Officer W.D. Williamson reported:

> The man named Peter Driscoll did apply to me for out-door relief, which I refused, knowing him to be in possession of a farm of land ... I then told him that on his producing me a certificate from the landlord of his giving up the possession, that I would give him outdoor relief, he being old and infirm. I heard nothing about him after till I heard that he was carried dead to the town of Schull ... immediately after Driscoll's death his wife, Margaret Driscoll did apply for out-door relief, and told me that her husband was dead. I then inquired if she or he had given up the land, to which she replied, that they did not, but that he went to give it up. I told her that she could not be relieved either inside or outside the Workhouse as long as she held the land.

At this point Mrs. Driscoll went to get the necessary paperwork from the landlord's agent, Robert Swanton, and Williamson heard nothing more from her. She had died from "old age, exhaustion and exposure to cold" according to the inquest jury.

The Driscoll case is also a clear instance of the operation of the Gregory Clause. Intended as an additional deterrent to prevent abuse of the system, the effect was to deprive people of the means to work themselves out of the need to get relief. As in many systems that depend on a deterrent element, once conditions arise where the deterrent does not work, the system can end up creating a situation worse than that which it was designed to address. In this case, the Gregory Clause increased destitution and the burden on the rates.

Despite all these difficulties, there were signs of a recovery in the agricultural economy in 1848. On 17 March 1848, Marshall reported that:

> Mr. Keane, the agriculturist, has had four meetings in the Union, which were well attended by farmers, from which I anticipate good results. On my way to and from Castletown I found a very general appearance of exertion among the farmers preparing the land for potatoes.

The following month he "was glad to find the people extremely busy in the western part of the Union planting potatoes and preparing the land for crops".

The figures for those receiving relief lend support to this general picture of improvement. At the end of the soup kitchens in

September 1847, 13,032 were receiving relief. By April 1848, the daily average was 8,299. The following months saw a steady decline: May – 8,553; June – 7,633; July – 7,685; August – 4,066; and September – 2,349, just 2.2 per cent of the 1841 population.

Some care needs to be taken with these relief figures; improvement in circumstances is only one reason for a person leaving the lists. Death, emigration or exclusion are others. Similarly, percentage figures for the 1841 population can be deceptive, as the population in 1848 was certainly less than that in 1841. Nevertheless, the reduction from 13,032 in September 1847 to 2,349 in September 1848 can reasonably be seen as a sign of improvement. Combined with the prospect of a good harvest, this boded well for the area.

Of course, it was not to be. In November 1848, Inspector Marshall reported to the Poor Law Commissioners on the prospects for the Union. A new outbreak of the blight had attacked the potato crop. The turnip crop had failed. The local fishing industry had collapsed. The British Relief Association, which had fed the children the previous winter, was discontinuing aid. Many small farmers had exhausted their resources in acquiring seed in the hope of a good harvest.

The relief figures rose again. By January 1849, over 20,120 were in receipt of either indoor or outdoor relief, though the figure had declined to 19,170 by March. However the scenes of the winter of 1846-47 did not recur. The relief system, with its many faults, did fulfil its fundamental objective. The Government had, at last, found a policy that averted famine and met its longstanding precept, i.e.:

> The landholders and other ratepayers are the parties both legally and morally answerable for affording due relief to the destitute poor.

Chapter 5
CONCLUSION

Archibald G. Starke, who had visited Skibbereen in 1844, returned to the town in 1850. In 1844, he found a town with "an air of roughness, comfort and growing prosperity".
In 1850 he wrote:

> ... my heart sank as the clatter of the horses' hoofs scarcely aroused the listless observation of a few straggling and half-starved people in the streets ... The houses on either side of the street seemed, with a few exceptions, to have been deserted by their tenants. A crowd of beggars surrounded the steps of the Beecher Arms ... The great barony of West Carbery, in which Skibbereen is situated, is in as wretched a plight as it can be ...

The 1851 census confirms that 11 per cent of the houses in the town had disappeared since 1841. "In another world only will stand recorded the number of lives that were lost" said Dr. John Jacob, the physician to the Queen's County infirmary. What was true then is true now. The total figures for population decline do not distinguish between emigration and death.

Starke remarked on his second visit to Skibbereen: "The population has been very much reduced by deaths and emigration within the last few years". Strictly speaking he was wrong, as the population of the town had increased by some 39 per cent due to the increased capacity of the Workhouse, but he was correct concerning the district as a whole.

In 1849 the Skibbereen Union was broken up, the western part forming the new Union of Schull and the Roscarbery part being added to the new Union of Clonakilty. This makes it impossible to compare the population of the 1841 Union in with that of 1851. James S. Donnelly has estimated a population decline of 36.1 per cent for the Schull/Skibbereen part of the old Union between 1841 and 1851. According to the 1851 census, the population of West

The Great Famine in Skibbereen

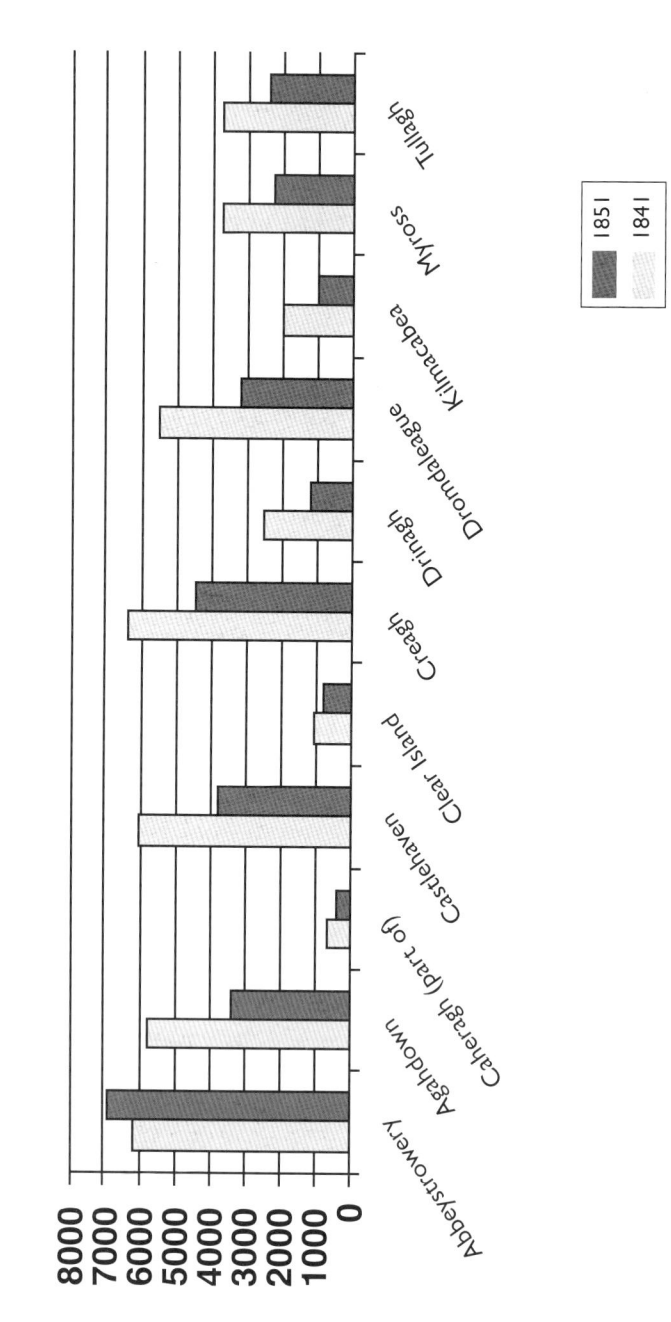

Figure 2. Population changes between 1841 and 1851: Carbery West, East Division

Conclusion

Carbery, East Division declined by 35.55 per cent between 1841 and 1851. A figure in the region of 35-36 per cent seems a reasonable one for population decline in the region. Establishing how much of the decline was due to excess mortality and how much was due to emigration is a more difficult task.

Emigration was clearly a contributor to the decline but it is impossible to be definitive about the rate of emigration from Skibbereen during the Famine. Passenger lists do not give the place of origin of those embarking. There is little evidence that large-scale emigration to places outside the country took place. Some 3,023 emigrated from Baltimore in 1845 and 1846, but this was before the collapse of the local economy. Dr. O'Donovan and Mr. Swanton organised a scheme of assisted emigration in 1846, but this was on a small scale. There are references in both official documents and local newspapers to emigration but these generally refer to the stronger tenants. This apparent absence of large-scale emigration from the Union is not in any way remarkable. It is accepted among commentators that there is a correlation between low emigration rates and high proportions of landless labourers in the population. Poor people do not emigrate. Skibbereen had 42 per cent of the population landless and another 16 per cent with property rated below £4, indicating a low probability of emigration. Nor did any local land-owner or public body, other than Dr. O'Donovan, create an assisted emigration scheme to offset this disability. The modern historian, S.H. Cousens, has suggested a 10-12 per cent rate of emigration for County Cork. Poor Law Inspector Marshall's figures for the West of the Union give an emigration rate of 2.4 per cent for 1847. Combining the two would give about 8 per cent p.a. emigration over the 1847-1850 period. Emigration can explain a quarter of the population decline, at the very most.

For population change, we are forced to rely on two sets of unrelated data. One is the census data, referred to above. The other is the data covering September 1846 to September 1847 produced by Inspector Marshall for the northern and western sides of the Union and published in October 1847. Close study of the census data is informative, but not especially revealing.

The changes in population for the civil parishes of Carbery West, East Division are illustrated in Figure 2. The Abbeystrowery increase is due to the presence of the Workhouse in the parish. The

The Great Famine in Skibbereen

remote Clear Island suffered a loss of 22 per cent while the eastern parishes of Kilmacabea and Drinagh, much nearer the centre of relief, both had declines of more than twice that, approximately 52 per cent. Castlehaven and Creagh have the first and second highest rateable valuation and are seventh and ninth respectively in the population decline list. Drinagh and Dromdaleague, on the other hand, are the third and fourth wealthiest parishes, yet suffered the second and fourth highest population decline. The figures illustrate the point that one needs to be wary in drawing conclusions on the factors affecting population decline during the Famine. The same point is apparent from the statistics in Figures 3, 4 and 5 below:

Parishes by per capita Rateable Valuation (% of £)	
Clear Island	.43
Tullagh	.47
Caheragh (part of)	.64
Aghadown	.65
Myross	.69
Kilmacabea	.70
Dromdaleague	.72
Drinagh	.73
Creagh	.76
Castlehaven	.77
Abbeystrowery	.82

Figure 3. Relative wealth of parishes

Parishes listed by % decline in inhabited houses (excluding Tullagh)	
Drinagh	48.02
Kilmacabea	47.75
Myross	43.71
Caheragh (part of)	43.68
Creagh	41.01
Aghadown	41.01
Dromdaleague	39.87
Castlehaven	38.03
Abbeystrowery	29.65
Clear Island	17.39

Figure 4. Decline in inhabited houses

Conclusion

Parishes listed by % decline in population (excluding Abbeystrowery)	
Kilmacabea	51.96
Drinagh	51.77
Caheragh (part of)	48.01
Dromdaleague	42.51
Aghadown	42.19
Myross	38.83
Castlehaven	37.87
Tullagh	35.9
Creagh	30.75
Abbeystrowery	29.36
Clear Island	22.14

Figure 5. Decline in population

Inspector Marshall's statistics were published in October 1847 and purport to give an analysis of mortality and migration in the northern and western parishes of the Union from September 1846 to September 1847; Goleen, Schull, Ballydehob, Kilcoe, Caheragh, Drimoleague and Drinagh. I am indebted to Fr. Patrick Hickey for the analysis of Inspector Marshall's statistics which follows.

Marshall shows 6,811 deaths between September 1846 and May 1847, a mortality rate of 16.49 per cent on the 1841 census figures. Almost 70 per cent of these (4,724) occurred in the three months of March, April and May. Adding the deaths from June to September 1847 (503) raises the percentage mortality to 16.95 per cent.

There is some evidence to support the suggestion that Marshall's estimates are underestimates. Marshall gives 349 deaths for the parish of Schull in January 1847; the Skibbereen Soup Committee reported a daily average of 24 for the same month, giving a total of 744, more than double Marshall's figures. Marshall gives 449 deaths for Schull in February. Dr. Sweetnam, the dispensary doctor, estimated that the average daily mortality was 35, giving a total of 980, again more than double Marshall's figures. The Cork Examiner, on evidence probably supplied by the parish priest, reported that 2,000 had died in Ballydehob by May 1847. Marshall's figure is 1,245. Marshall was not appointed until March 1847, though his data purports to describe events from September 1846. Keeping a record of

The Great Famine in Skibbereen

deaths does not appear to have begun until January 1847. Factors other than distress played a part in Skibbereen and Schull acquiring their reputations as "the two famine-slain Sisters of the South". But both locals and Government Relief Officers, which latter had a basis for comparison, believed that distress and mortality in the area were exceptionally severe. It may, therefore, be justified to raise Marshall's mortality percentage.

Although he may have erred on the side of caution, Marshall's figures have the great value of distinguishing between emigration and mortality. This allows a comparison of the mortality rate and the Poor Law valuation of the parishes (see Figure 6 below):

Parish	% Mortality	Per capita valuation
Goleen	18.8	11s.10d
Drinagh	18.4	£1.4s.0d
Ballydehob	18.0	14s.7d
Schull	17.7	12s.7d
Caheragh	15.8	19s.2d
Drimoleague	15.7	18s.5d
Kilcoe	9.8	£1.0s.7d

Figure 6. Valuation and mortality compared

This table goes some way to establishing a direct relationship between valuation and mortality. The wealthier parishes of Kilcoe, Drimoleague and Caheragh are in the lower range of mortality. The same phenomenon is apparent with the census figures in the case of Abbeystrowery. But Drinagh, the wealthiest parish, has the highest mortality rate. Drinagh had no resident rector or gentry nor, by February 1847, did it have a soup kitchen. Nor did Aghadown, yet distress there was not amongst the most severe. Clear Island is the most curious case; poor by rateable valuation but among the lowest in terms of depopulation and vacant dwellings.

A tempting hypothesis is that low rateable valuation is an indicator of increased mortality, but low emigration. This is consistent with Marshall's own figures on emigration (see Figure 7 below) and with Cousens. It would also explain phenomena like Clear Island.

Parish	% Mortality	Per capita valuation	% Emigration
Goleen	18.8	11s.10d	0.9
Drinagh	18.4	£1.4s.0d	2.6
Ballydehob	18.0	14s.7d	2.3
Schull	17.7	12s.7d	4.4
Caheragh	15.8	19s.2d	1.5
Drimoleague	15.7	18s.5d	1.2
Kilcoe	9.8	£1.0s.7d	4.1

Figure 7. Emigration figures

Migration to another Union, particularly into Cork City, certainly occurred but is even less well-documented than emigration out of the country. Fr. Mathew told a Commission in June 1847:

> No tongue can describe, no understanding can conceive, the misery and wretchedness that flowed into Cork from the western parts of the County.

He estimated that some 20,000 came from the west into the city. Some must have come from Skibbereen, perhaps even from Drinagh and Kilcoe, but it will never be known how many.

The final picture may be something as follows: there was a decline in population of some 35-36 per cent. Of these, perhaps 8 per cent left the country; others left the Union; 20 per cent died before September 1847 and a further 6 per cent in the years 1848, 1849 and 1850.

Declining birth rate is another feature associated with the Famine. The population of Carbery West, East Division was growing at an annual rate of 1.35 per cent per annum. Had that rate been maintained, the population in 1851 would have been 49,400 rather than the 28,035 that it was. Figure 8 below, showing the decline in births between 1845 and 1850, illustrates the change clearly. The collapse in the birth rate in the third and fourth quarters of 1847 is consistent with extreme distress at the end of 1846 and the first half of 1847. The later decline in the fourth quarter of 1849 and first quarter of 1859 can be associated with renewed distress in 1848-49 when some 56 per cent of the population were again in receipt of relief.

There are some curiosities. The pattern for Aghadown is unusual – there may have been some distinctive local characteristics explaining this.

The Great Famine in Skibbereen

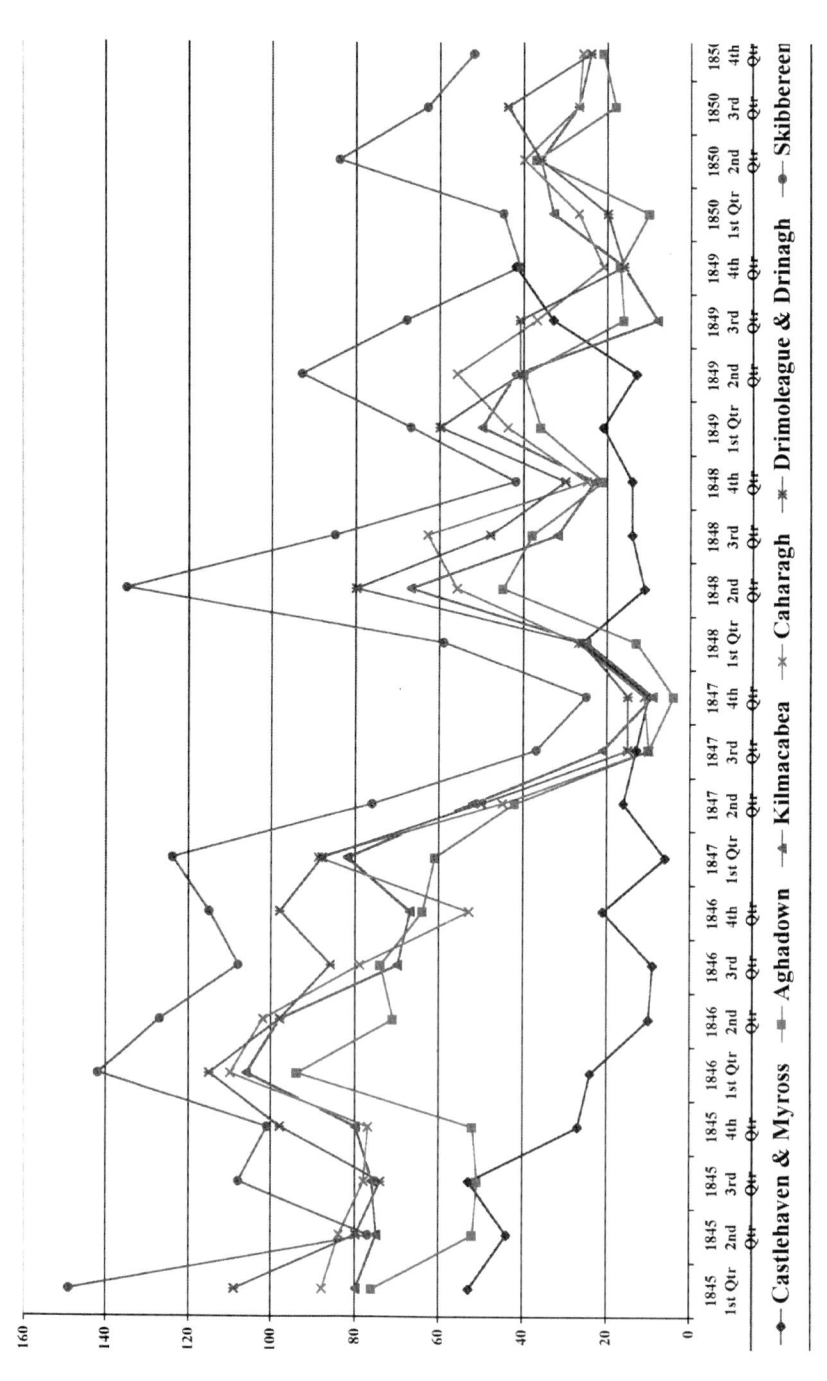

Figure 8. Births in Skibbereen Catholic parishes 1845-1850

Conclusion

High mortality and population decline were not the only effect the Famine had on Skibbereen. Patterns of landholding, and, by extension, the social structure changed. Existing land-owners, such as R.H.H. Beecher, were pushed into bankruptcy. Others, like the solicitor McCarthy Downing, became significant land-owners.

This changing pattern of landholding is apparent from the agricultural returns from 1847 to 1852 for the Skibbereen Union.

1845-1852 % of total holdings by size (actual numbers in brackets) and % increase/decrease

	1-5 acres	5-15 acres	15-30 acres	30 + acres
1845	13.73 (1,295)			
1847	6.469 (484)	32.375 (2,422)	27.62 (2, 067)	25.80 (1,930)
1848	6.729 (429)	27.07 (1,726)	30.68 (1,956)	34.35 (2,190)
1849	5.84 (332)	23.44 (1,332)	31.22 (1,744)	39.14 (2,224)
1850	4.93 (131)	23.66 (1,107)	29.46 (1,378)	40.42 (1,351)
1852	4.85 (224)	20.13 (930)	28.38 (1,311)	42.49 (977)
	-25%	-37.82%	+2%	+63%

Figure 9. Changing patterns of landholding

As can be seen, the smaller holdings of 1-15 acres are declining while the 30+ acre holdings are increasing significantly. The actual number of 30+ acre holdings is decreasing, suggesting an increase in the average size of holdings in this category.

This consolidation was effected in a number of ways.

Among the 5-15 acre holdings, decline is most marked between 1847 and 1849, during which there was a decline of 9 per cent. This period coincided with increased emigration from the area, which, as we have seen, was particularly associated with the stronger tenants. Declining income, escalating rate bills and the general malaise would all have combined to encourage emigration.

Destitution and mortality took their toll. The largest drop in the 1-5 acre holdings is between 1845 and 1847, the Famine years. The second largest is between 1849 and 1850, when the potato crop was again hit by another attack of blight. Both changes are consistent with the weakest being rendered destitute by the impact of the blight. The Gregory Clause accelerated the flight of the weakest from the land; Curly Coughlan and Peter Driscoll were both cases of tenants who were obliged to leave their land in order to receive relief (see Chapter 4).

The pressure of the Gregory Clause on tenants was accentuated by the pressure on landlords which was a consequence of a high Poor Rate. It was in the interests of the landlord to remove tenants whose holdings were below a rateable valuation of £4, as it was the landlord who was responsible for the entirety of the bill.

The evidence for forced evictions, or "exterminations" as Fr. Fitzpatrick called them, is unclear. No records from estates in the Union survive. As with emigration, we are forced to rely on limited evidence.

Neither the Cork Examiner, nor its West Cork correspondent, Jeremiah O'Callaghan, were friends of the landlords. Yet, despite a policy of actively seeking information, the Cork Examiner records the evictions of only some 200 families in the years 1847-1849. Of those, 154 families were evicted from the estate of the absentee landlord, Rev. Maurice Townsend. Even these were at the rate of 50 per year.

Against that, there remains the fact that the proportion of smaller holdings (1-15 acres) declined by 64.3 per cent between 1847 and 1852. In absolute terms 1,752 of such holdings disappeared. It would be surprising if all were the result of voluntary emigration or the handing up of land.

Evictions were a major concern for many people. In mid-November 1847 the inaugural meeting of the Tenant Protective Society of Skibbereen was held. The meeting was called to protect the tenants:

> ... from the repeated attempts of the landlords of this district on the unprotected tenantry of the locality.

Attendants told of "harrowing scenes of oppression daily witnessed" and that:

> The streets were, for some months the melancholy scenes of auctions – the skeleton cattle borne off by the landlords to be fattened on the waste desmesnes, whilst their wretched owners now seek admission to our overthronged Workhouse.

Conclusion

The family of O'Donovan Rossa was evicted when they fell into debt after the death of the father. Fr. Fitzpatrick told Archibald Starke in 1850 that evictions were "extensive".

To the extent that both population and the social structure of Skibbereen were affected by the Famine, Skibbereen was no different from much of the country. What distinguished Skibbereen was the magnitude of the calamity that created those changes.

APPENDIX

A note on the sources

This book is intended for the general reader, so the normal scholarly footnotes have not been used.

The correspondence of the Temporary Relief Commission in the National Archives is the main primary source for the 1845-1846 period. The list of this material is now available on the Internet at the National Archives of Ireland website. The eight volumes of Famine papers, extracted from the British Parliamentary Papers by the Irish University Press are essential reference works, including, as they do, the correspondence between the Treasury and the Relief Commission, the Board of Works correspondence and extensive correspondence and statistics concerning the Poor Law. The British Parliamentary Papers series includes the census material, the annual agricultural returns, the 1836 Poor Law Inquiry and the 1844-45 Devon Commission, all of which were used in the research for this work. The Catholic parish registers held in the National Library are an important source for demographic information. The correspondence of Rev. F.F. French gives a precise insight into the plight in the west of the Union.

Cork is fortunate in having three local newspapers in publication at the time of the Famine: the *Cork Examiner*; the *Cork Constitution*; and the *Southern Reporter*. I have made extensive use of the *Cork Examiner*. Extensive use of the *Southern Reporter* is made in Patrick Hickey's M.A. thesis on *'Four Peninsular Parishes in West Cork 1796-1855'* (UCC, 1980), which itself is invaluable for the western part of the Skibbereen Union. Since the preparation of this text, Fr. Hickey's work has been published as *Famine in West Cork: the Mizen Peninsula, Land and People, 1800-1852* (Cork, 2002). Hickey's 'Famine, Mortality and Emigration: A Profile of Six Parishes in the Poor Law Union of Skibbereen 1846-7', in P. O'Flanagan and C. Buttimer, *Cork: History and Society* (1993) is invaluable on the subjects of mortality and emigration in the west of the Union.

Older printed material includes: Horatio Townsend's 1810 *Statistical Survey of the County of Cork*; Samuel Lewis's 1837 *Topographical Dictionary*, now available in a specifically Cork edition, edited by Tim Cadogan; William Thackeray's *Irish Sketchbook* 1842; and Archibald Starke's *The South of Ireland in 1850*.

Material specifically associated with the Famine includes: Charles Trevelyan's 1848 *The Irish Crisis*; O'Donovan Rossa's *Rossa's Recollections* 1838-1898; Charles Northend's *Life and Labours of Elihu Burrett*; and the *Narrative of a Journey from Oxford to Skibbereen in the Year of the Irish Famine* which is an account by Lord Dufferin and Mr. Boyle of their trip to Skibbereen. This is available on the world wide web. Mgr. Rourke's 1898 *Great Famine* contains correspondence with those, including McCarthy Downing, who were active in the crisis.

Modern works consulted include: James S. Donnelly, *The Land and People of Nineteenth Century Cork*; Christine Kineally, *This Great Calamity*; Patrick Hickey's 'Famine, Mortality and Emigration' in *Cork, History and Society*, edited by Buttimer and O'Flanagan; *Famine 150 Lectures* edited by Cormac O'Grada; the same author's *The Great Irish Famine* and *Ireland Before and After the Famine*, *The Great Famine*, edited by R. Dudley Edwards and T. Desmond Williams; and *The Famine – Thomas Davis Lectures* edited by Cathal Porteir. Jean Dreze and Amartya Sen's *Hunger and Action* gives a contemporary perspective on famine.

Peter Foynes, M.A.,
Cork,
2004.

LIST OF BENEFACTORS

Sincere thanks to the following Benefactors of the Famine Commemoration Project:

A.O.H., 536 Therese St, Clayton, New Jersey, USA.
Bank of Ireland, Market Street, Skibbereen
David Barry, Coronea, Skibbereen.
Liam Barry, 9 Francine St, Australine, Western Australia.
J.J. Cahalane and Co. Ltd., Bridge St, Skibbereen.
Carbery Timber, Coronea, Skibbereen.
Casey's Cabin, Baltimore, Skibbereen.
Joe Connolly, Townsend St, Skibbereen.
Cork County Council, County Hall, Cork.
Brian and Ann Crowley, Coronea, Skibbereen.
Con Daly, 36 Ann Devlin Pk, Dublin 14.
Kate Doherty, 41 Fairlight Rd, London SW17.
Drinagh Co-op, Skibbereen.
Pat Joe Dwyer, Letter, Skibbereen.
The Late Mary Dwyer, Townsend St, Skibbereen.
John Field and family, Main St, Skibbereen
Jerry Geaney, Boston, USA
Michael Gill, Mardyke Street, Skibbereen
Johnny Goggin, 40 Wheatland, Hexton, Hounslow, England.
The Hazel family, Castletownshend Rd, Skibbereen.
John and Teresa Hickey, 12 Mardyke St, Skibbereen.
Peg Lennon, 90 Upper Bridge St, Skibbereen.
Jerry Lucey and family, North St, Skibbereen.
Michael Madden, 41 First St, Melrose 02176, Mass. USA.
Medical Centre, Market Street, Skibbereen
C.P. McCarthy and Family, North St, Skibbereen.

The Great Famine in Skibbereen

Teresa O'Connell and family, Curragh, Skibbereen.
The O'Donovan family, Hollybrook, Skibbereen.
Raymond O'Donovan, 54 Merrywood Lane, Short Hill, New Jersey, USA.
Cathal O'Donovan, T.C. and family, Baltimore Rd, Skibbereen.
Noel O'Driscoll, North St, Skibbereen.
Denis and Corney O'Driscoll, Phoenix, Arizona, USA.
The late Dr. John O'Keeffe, Baltimore Road, Skibbereen.
Gene O'Sullivan and family, Valentia, Co. Kerry.
Jerry O'Sullivan, Baltimore Rd, Skibbereen.
Donal O'Sullivan, Bridge St, Skibbereen.
Denny O'Sullivan, Dun Baoi, Coronea, Skibbereen
Lord David Puttnam, Old Court, Skibbereen.
Rossa College, Skibbereen.
Seamus Ryan, North Street, Skibbereen
The Late Annie Sheehan, North St, Skibbereen.
Sisters of Charity, Convent Station, New Jersey, USA.
Skibbereen Credit Union.
Skibbereen Town Council, North St, Skibbereen.
South of Ireland Petroleum, Cork Road, Skibbereen
St. Fachtna's De La Salle P.P.U., Skibbereen.
The Late Rev. John Walsh P.P., Castlehaven.
West Cork Education, Institute for Rural Development, Sutherland Centre, Skibereen.
West Cork Leader Co-op.
Finbarr and Ann Williams, Borodale, Coronea, Skibbereen.

INDEX

Abbeystrewery 3, 11, 32, 84, 85
Agahadown Relief Committee 60
Aghadown 59, 70, 84-87
Alcock, Rev. 9
Allridge 57
Amendment of Board of Works Act 22
Amendments of Drainage Act 22
Anderson, Charles 29
Armagh 57
Audeley, Lord 2

Baldwin, Thomas 20, 48
Ballydehob 1, 20, 39, 73, 77, 85-87
Baltimore 9, 31, 37, 54, 59, 83
Bantry 9, 11, 40, 42-43, 77
Bantry Local Relief Committee 40
Barley 45, 47
Barleymeal 45
Barony of Carbery West 3, 9, 27, 31, 53-54
bedding 10, 13, 46
Beecher, William 56
Beecher Arms 81
Beecher, Rev. M. 2
Beecher, R.H.H. Esq 2
Beecher, Richard 28
Bettsborough 14
biscuit 58-59, 63
Bishop, Assistant Commissary-General 59
blight v, 14, 19, 21, 23-25, 27, 29, 31, 33, 35, 37, 39, 41, 43, 73, 79, 89
Board of Health 69
Board of Works 21-22, 32-33, 38-39, 48, 51, 54, 56, 63, 65, 93
Bohane, Denis 47-48, 53
Boilers 34, 57, 60
Boyle, Honorable George 67
bread 30, 45, 49-50, 52, 58, 63, 75
Bridge Street 52
Bridgetown 51

British Relief Association 34, 57, 75, 77, 79
broth 75
Buckley, Curly 45, 47
Burke, Edmund 35
Burrett, Elihu 67, 70, 94
buttermilk 16

cabbages 13
cabin 10, 47, 51, 95
cabins 5, 9-10, 70
Cadogan, Tim 94
Caharagh 10, 70, 84, 85
Carbery, Lord 2
Cardiff 55
Carlow 7
Carrighue 59
Castlehaven 10, 52, 67, 82, 84-85
Castletown 59, 78
Castletownsend 9, 31
cattle 6, 32, 34, 53, 90
Caulfield, Rev. 54-55
Cavan 57
census, 1841 3, 9, 85
census, 1831 3
Ceylon 56
Chadwick, Edward 34
Charity Soup House 54
Chief Secretary for Ireland 56
cholera 36
Clarendon, Lord 73
Clear Island 82, 84-86
Clonakilty 39, 81
Coast Guard 21, 23, 31, 37
Coast Guard Stations 31
Coffin, Commissary-General 40, 42
Collins, John 3, 7, 15, 45, 47
Commissary General 23
Commission on Colonisation 4, 17
Commons 35

97

The Great Famine in Skibbereen

conacre 4, 6-8, 16, 32, 42
Constabulary 3, 23-24, 30, 32, 36, 53
Constabulary Force 24
Coolish 19
Coolnaclehy 45
Cork Butter Market 17
Cork Constitution 37, 93
Cork Examiner 17, 27, 29, 31-32, 40, 45, 50-51, 54, 72, 77, 85, 90, 93
Corn 1, 5, 13, 19, 26-27, 30-32, 41-42, 47-49, 55, 63, 73
Indian corn 27, 30, 41, 48, 63
Coughlan, Curly 76, 90
County Surveyor 24
Cousens, S.H. 83
Creagh 8, 16, 31, 54, 65, 82, 84-85
Crookhaven 19, 31
Cummins, Nicholas 52, 57-58
Custom House 1

Devon Commission 7-8, 11, 14-16, 93
Donnelly, James S. 11, 81, 94
Donovan, Michael 47
Dore, Fr. David 10
Dore, Dr. 53
Dreze, Jean 36, 94
Drimoleague 2, 4, 37, 60, 85-87
Drinagh 60, 82, 84-87
Driscoll, Mary 45-46
Driscoll, Peter and Margaret 78
Drishane 19
Dublin 24, 27, 30, 57, 64, 68
Dufferin, Lord 67, 94
Dunston, Tom 47
Durrus 2, 9
Dysentery 62, 66, 70, 77

Earl of Bandon 37
eggs 12-13
Emigration 15, 54, 72, 79, 81, 83, 86-87, 89-90, 93-94
Emigration, Assisted 54, 72, 83
Encumbered Estates Court 76
England 5, 10, 54-55, 73, 95

Estate Drainage Act 22

First World War 15
fish 1, 10-12, 48, 58, 68
Fishery Piers Act 22
Fitzmaurice, Col. 58
Fitzpatrick, Fr. 36, 47-48, 56, 76, 90-91
Fleming, Lionel 76-77
Fleming, R.S. 20
flour 1, 30-32, 58, 63
Free Trade 48
French, Rev. F.F. 2, 61, 93
fuel 47, 69

Glandore 28, 31, 53, 59
Goleen 3, 8, 85-87
Gordon, Captain 77
Graham, Sir John 24
Grand Jury Presentment Act 22
Grattan, Henry 57
Gregory Clause 72, 77-78, 89-90
Gregory, Sir John 68, 72
Grey, Sir George 55

Harrington, John 46-47
Hayes, John 14
Hegarty, Jeremiah 37, 39, 45, 47
Hewetson, Commissary-General 35, 50
Hollybrook 28, 96
Home Secretary 24, 55
Housing 9, 14
Huband, Captain 51, 53-54, 58
Hughes, Mr. 49-50, 59
Hungerford, Thomas J. 3, 27

Ilen 20, 27, 29, 54
Illustrated London News 67
Incumbered Estates Bill 71
Indian meal 31, 48-49, 59
Inglis, Assistant Commissary-General 56
Island Bridge 37

98

Index

Jacob, Dr. John 81
Jones, Lt. Col. 38, 48, 56, 59, 63, 67

Keane, Mr. 78
Kelleher, John 46
Kennedy, J.P. 24
Kiladerry 47
Kilcoe 59, 85-87
Kildare 57
Kilkenny 5, 7
Kilkerranmore 8
Kilmacabea 82, 84-85
Kilmoo 29, 70, 77
Kineally, Christine 94

Labouchere, Henry 56
Labour Rate Act 33
Lavis, Mr. S. 2
Leap 2, 70, 72
Lewis, Samuel 1, 94
Lick Road 46
Limerick 5, 7, 12, 45, 56
Limerick, John 65Lisheenassingana 39
Litter 46
Liverpool 49, 60
Local Relief Committee 27, 40
London 25, 34, 57, 67
Lord Lieutenant 22, 24, 26, 33, 63-64, 73
Lowertown 75

Mahony, Nelly 51
Marmion, Henry 19
Marmion, J.H. 17
Marmion, Thomas 3, 43, 54-55
Marquis of Sligo 49
Marshall, John J. 65
Mathew, Fr. 4, 8, 15, 17, 32, 61, 87
Maynooth 52
McCarthy, Charles ix,14
McCarthy, Daniel 1, 3, 14, 28

McCarthy Downing 3, 19, 28-29, 52, 89, 94
McCarthy, James 3, 8, 14
McCarthy, John 46-47
McKennedy, Denis 37, 39, 45, 53
Meath 57
Merrick, John 20
milk 10, 12, 45
Mill Cove 31
Minchin, George 3, 32, 36, 51, 53
Molony, James 69
Molton 57
Mowbray 57
Mulcahy, Fr. James 10
Myross 10, 29, 31, 37, 39, 52, 68-69, 82, 84-85

National Archives 93
National School 12, 30
Neal 51
Newman, Mr. Henry 2
North Street iv,48,56
Northend, Charles 94

O'Callaghan, Jeremiah 29, 66, 68, 75, 90
O'Donovan Rossa 47, 70, 91, 94
O'Donovan, Dr. 19, 36, 46, 51, 54-55, 83
O'Donovans, The 2
O'Driscoll, Alexander 19, 76
O'Grady, Mr. 45
O'Rourke, Mgr. 52
O'Sullivan, J.J. 31
O'Sullivan, James 21
oatmeal 31
Oldcourt 3, 7, 15, 29
Ordnance Survey map, 1841 3

Parker, Major 56, 58, 65-66, 70
pawn 46-47
Peel, Sir Robert 39, 68
Petty Sessions 21, 30
pig 1, 7, 11, 13, 16, 30, 40
Pole, Captain 17

The Great Famine in Skibbereen

Poor Law Commissioners 71, 74, 79
Poor Law Guardians 16, 21, 30, 64, 72-73
Poor Law Inquiry (1836) 4, 10, 93
Poor Law Union 1, 3, 21, 63, 93
Powell, Edward 29
Pre-Famine Skibbereen 2-4, 9, 13, 15, 17
Prendergast, Joseph Samuel, M.D 65
Public Works 20, 22, 24, 27-29, 31, 33, 37-40, 45-47, 53, 55, 65-66

Quakers 27, 57
Quakers, Cork 57
Queen's County 81

rateable valuation 2, 4, 13, 72, 84, 86, 90
Reenbeg 68
Regan, Daniel 11
Relief Commission 17, 20-21, 27, 29-30, 32, 35, 63, 65, 70, 93
road making 12
road sickness 66
Robinson, Mr. 29
Roscarbery 8, 14, 29, 81
Rosebank 3
Routh, Lady 63
Routh, Sir Randolph 24
Royal Agricultural Society 22
Russell, Lord John 40

salt 10, 48
Sen, Amaryta 36
sand 6, 15
Schull 1-2, 17, 19-20, 29, 61, 66, 70, 77-78, 81, 85-87
scytheman 14
seaweed 15, 67
sheep-stealing 53
Sheffield 57
Sherkin Island 37
Skibbereen i, iii, iv, vii, ix, x, 1, 2, 3, 4, 6, 7, 8, 9, 10, 11, 12, 13, 14, 15, 16, 17, 19, 20, 21, 22, 24, 25, 26, 27, 28, 29, 30, 31, 32, 34, 36, 37, 38, 40, 42, 43, 45, 46, 47, 48, 49, 50, 51, 52, 53, 54, 56, 57, 58, 59, 60, 61, 64, 65, 66, 67, 68, 69, 70, 72, 73, 74, 75, 76, 77, 78, 81, 82, 83, 84, 85, 86, 87, 89, 90, 91, 93, 94
Skibbereen Agricultural Show 17, 19
Skibbereen Poor Law Guardians 16
Sligo 49-50
Smithville 14
Society of Friends 57, 67
Somerville, Mr. 19
Somerville, Thomas 54
Soup 34, 48, 54-61, 63, 67, 69, 78, 85-86
Soup Committee 54, 56, 58, 85
Soup Kitchen Act 63
South Reen 52-53, 68-69
Southern Reporter 93
Starke, Archibald G. 81
Sullivan, Michael 11
Saunders, Mr. W. Herbert 27
Swanton, Mr. 54, 58-59, 83
Swanton, Robert 78
Sweetnam, Dr. 85
Swiney 51

task work 38, 53
Temporary Relief Act (1847) 63, 71
Temporary Relief Commission 63, 65, 93
Tenant Protective Society 90
Thackeray, William 1, 3, 9, 11, 15, 94
The Three Clerks 35
Thoughts on Scarcity 35
Times 10-11, 14, 27, 40-41, 43, 52, 57, 62
Tipperary 5, 7, 12, 14
Townsend and Wright, Messrs. 2
Townsend's Bridge 29
Townsend, Madame 48
Townsend, Henry 20
Townsend, Horatio 1, 3, 94
Townsend, Rev. Maurice 90
Townsend, R.B. 3
Townsend, Rev. Stephen 2
Townsend, Thomas 14
Townsend, Mr., White Hall 2

Index

Traill, Rev. Dr. 19-20, 70
Trevelyan, Charles 32-35, 38, 40, 48, 50, 55-57, 59, 61, 63-64, 67, 70-73, 94
Trollope, Anthony 35
Tuckey, Rev. Thomas 4
Tullagh 70, 82, 84-85
turf 4-6, 46
Turnip 79
Typhus 70

Union 1-4, 14, 21, 23, 58-61, 63-66, 68-70, 72-75, 77-79, 81, 83, 85, 87, 89-90, 93
Union of Clonakilty 81
United States 19, 26

Walsh, Michael 69
Waterford 7, 17
Webb, Rev. 20
Wellington, Duke of 52
Westport 49
wheat 15
Whitehall 25, 56
Wholane, Jerry 69
Whooley, James 69
Williamson, William 76, 78
Workhouse 1, 23-24, 26, 36, 47, 51, 55, 58, 62, 68-71, 73-76, 78, 81, 83, 90
Workhouse of the Union 23
Wright, Rev. John 16, 29, 31
Wrixon-Beecher, Sir William 2

GW01162485

HAROLD WILSON'S EEC APPLICATION

HAROLD WILSON'S EEC APPLICATION

INSIDE THE FOREIGN OFFICE 1964–7

Jane Toomey

UNIVERSITY COLLEGE DUBLIN PRESS
PREAS CHOLÁISTE OLLSCOILE BHAILE ÁTHA CLIATH

First published 2007
by University College Dublin Press
Newman House
86 St Stephen's Green
Dublin 2
Ireland
www.ucdpress.ie

© Jane Toomey 2007

ISBN 978-1-904558-69-9

All rights reserved. No part of this publication may be
reproduced, stored in a retrieval system, or transmitted in
any form or by any means, electronic, photocopying, recording
or otherwise without the prior permission of the publisher.

CIP data available from the British Library

*The right of Jane Toomey to be identified as the
author of this work has been asserted by her*

Typeset in Bantry, Ireland in Adobe Caslon and
Bodoni Oldstyle by Elaine Burberry
Index by Jane Rogers
Text design by Lyn Davies
Printed in England on acid-free paper by
MPG Books Ltd, Bodmin, Cornwall

To
John, Mary and Padraig

*

Contents

―

Acknowledgements
ix

Abbreviations
xi

INTRODUCTION
1

ONE
WAIT AND SEE
10

TWO
HAROLD, GEORGE AND PERSISTENT PRESSURES
27

THREE
NO ALTERNATIVE CIRCLE
45

FOUR
HOW TO GET INTO THE COMMON MARKET
56

FIVE
BY LITTLE STEPS TOWARDS THE CONTINENT
68

SIX
GO ON – HAVE A GO!
82

SEVEN
AN APPLICATION AND A VETO
100

EPILOGUE
117

Notes
122

Bibliography
140

Index
143

Acknowledgements

—

I would like to thank a number of people in the School of History at University College Dublin. I am grateful to colleagues for inspiring my interest in history and for the opportunities to tutor and lecture in such an engaging environment. For encouraging and supporting my doctoral thesis, I have nothing but fond memories of Albert Lovett my original supervisor who sadly passed away in my first year of the PhD. Special thanks must go to Richard Aldous who not only took over supervision of my thesis at short notice but who has been a source of constant support and advice and who has read countless drafts of this book. Without his encouragement this book would still be a work in progress! I am also very grateful to the Irish Research Council for the Humanities and Social Sciences and its chairman Maurice Bric for a postdoctoral research fellowship.

Ronan Fanning, Paul Rouse, Kathleen Bourke, William Mulligan and Bob Boles all read a full draft of the book and devoted much time and energy to improving matters of style and structure.

Thank you to Barbara Mennell and all the staff at University College Dublin Press for their hard work and co-operation. It was a pleasure to work with Barbara and her advice and enthusiasm were invaluable.

I am also indebted to the numerous politicians and civil servants I had the pleasure of interviewing. I am grateful for their time and memories and the extent to which they enhanced my knowledge of the period. In particular, special thanks must go to Robin O'Neill who read a full draft and provided plenty of advice.

Thanks must also go to the staff at the National Archives in Kew, whose efficiency made my job easier.

I would also like to thank the National University of Ireland who awarded me a grant with regard the publication of my work.

I have dedicated this book to three people, without whose love and constant support it would not have materialised. My parents, John and Mary who encouraged me through five years of my PhD and who always told me to 'aim for the highest brick in the chimney pot'! Finally, I owe a huge debt of thanks to my partner Padraig for his patience in reading numerous drafts of the book and providing solutions to intractable problems. Ava, my daughter, was no use as a proofreader, but always managed to put everything into perspective.

JANE TOOMEY
Dublin, September 2007

Abbreviations

BBC	British Broadcasting Corporation
CAB	Cabinet Papers
CAP	Common Agricultural Policy
CBI	Confederation of British Industry
CC	Cabinet Conclusions
DEA	Department of Economic Affairs
ECSC	European Coal and Steel Community
EDC	European Defence Community
EEC	European Economic Community
EEOD	European Economic Organisations Department
EFTA	European Free Trade Association
FCO	Foreign and Commonwealth Office
FO	Foreign Office
FTA	Free Trade Association
GATT	General Agreement on Trade and Tariffs
GNP	Gross National Product
NAFTA	North Atlantic Free Trade Association
NATO	North Atlantic Treaty Organisation
NFU	National Farmers Union
OECD	Organisation for Economic Co-operation and Development
OEEC	Organisation for European Economic Co-operation
PREM	Prime Minister's Papers
TNA	The National Archives, Public Records Office, Kew
WEU	Western European Union

Introduction

—

On 27 November 1967, the French President Charles de Gaulle vetoed Britain's second application for membership of the European Economic Community (EEC). The veto came as no surprise either to those directly involved in the application or those observing from the sidelines. Only a few months earlier at a press conference on 16 May 1967, de Gaulle had issued what the British media referred to as a 'velvet veto'. It was not a categorical 'non', but it was a clear indication that he had no intention of allowing Britain to join the EEC. De Gaulle maintained that British membership would upset the EEC and that it would only become a possibility when 'this great people so magnificently gifted with ability and courage, should on their own behalf and for themselves achieve a profound economic and political transformation which could allow them to join the six continentals'.[1] The French had put an end to Britain's hopes of joining the EEC for the second time in less than a decade.

This book sets out to examine the dynamic relationship that existed between British Foreign Office officials and Prime Minister Harold Wilson's Labour cabinet of 1964–7, when it came to formulating and executing Britain's second application to join the EEC. The following chapters trace that application and look at how those in Downing Street and the Foreign Office teased out various policies in an attempt to succeed where the government of Harold Macmillan, Conservative prime minister (1957–63), had failed.

It is a narrative that analyses British attitudes, British policies, British tactics and British disappointment. Extensive research of recently released archival material has been enriched by the generosity of some of the leading participants in Britain's second application. Interviews with both of Harold Wilson's private secretaries, members of his cabinet and senior Foreign Office officials all shed further light on this fascinating chapter in Britain's relationship with mainland Europe in the 1960s.

In order to appreciate fully the circumstances facing Harold Wilson when he sat down in his office in 1964, it is necessary to look back on what his predecessors had encountered when it came to Britain's European policy.

I

The man who has often been referred to as the 'father of Europe' – the first to call for the creation of a 'United States of Europe' – Winston Churchill, was also the man who encapsulated Britain's foreign policy in the era after the Second World War. Speaking in Paris in November 1944, Churchill discussed the importance of a solid Anglo-French relationship:

> For so many years past have these two nations shared the glories of Western Europe, that they have become indispensable to each other. It is a fundamental principle of British policy that the alliance with France should be unshakeable, constant and effective.[2]

In conversation with Konrad Adenauer, the West German chancellor, on 4 December 1951, Churchill drew a diagram of three concentric circles, with Britain being the only one to inhabit all three. Churchill envisaged a world made up of these three circles: the British Empire, America and Europe, with Britain standing at the point of intersection of all three. This concept of the 'three circles' determined the extent to which Britain would immerse herself in the third circle, that of Europe. Until the late 1950s, Britain believed it could participate in all three circles, and not give priority to any one in particular.[3]

Between 1945 and 1957, Britain chose not to join the Europeans formally for a variety of reasons. Britain chose not to participate in the Schuman Plan in 1950 or in the Messina Conference in 1955, which later led to the creation of the EEC in 1957.[4] Oliver Wright,[5] who was a prominent Foreign Office official at the time and who would later become Harold Wilson's private secretary (1964–6), gave a candid portrayal of the period:

> Britain at the time took no notice, was perhaps even contemptuous at times, unwisely perhaps, but had other things to do. First of all, the British thought that the European idea would not succeed, and secondly they thought it was a ludicrous plan.[6]

However, Britain's policy of 'co-operation without commitment' allowed it to participate in the Marshall Plan in 1947, sign the Brussels Treaty in 1948 and join NATO and the Council of Europe in 1949.

In 1956, the Suez crisis followed Colonel Nasser of Egypt's nationalisation of the Suez Canal, which led to British and French retaliation owing to the loss of the Suez Canal Company. This retaliation was not supported by the United States or the international community and the British and French were therefore forced to withdraw. In addition to jolting the British psyche, the fallout from Suez also contributed to Britain's questioning the continued feasibility of the 'three circles' approach to foreign policy. It also contributed to the realisation that the 'special relationship'[7] was not immortal.

The other critical factor that contributed to the change in policy was the success of the European idea on the continent. The acceptance of a new path was highlighted by Harold Macmillan in October 1959, when he stated:

> For better or worse, the Common Market looks like being here to stay at least for the foreseeable future. Furthermore if we tried to disrupt it we should unite against us all the Europeans, who have felt humiliated during the past decades by the weakness of Europe. We should also probably upset the United States, as well as playing into the hands of the Russians. And, of course, the Common Market has certain advantages in bringing greater cohesion to Europe. The question is how to live with the Common Market economically and turn its political effects into channels harmless to us.[8]

II

Britain's first application to join the EEC, made by the Macmillan government, was not born out of any genuine Europeanism. Indeed, had there been another way for him to buttress Britain's world role, to counter economic realities, or to compete with the 'Six' it is certain that an application to join the EEC would not have been made while Macmillan was in office. The negotiations, which began in Paris on 10 October 1961, were arduous and complex. In his memoirs, Macmillan likened them to a steeplechase, 'in terms of length and severity of the obstacles it made the perils of the Grand National look like a local point-to-point'.[9] It was a conditional application, its success riding on the successful conclusion of a number of issues, particularly British commercial relations with the Commonwealth and British domestic agriculture.

Apart from the detail of negotiation, the issue of Franco-British relations was crucial. The possibility of British entry threatened the foundations of what de Gaulle had been adamantly protecting: de Gaulle's unassailable position amongst 'the Six' and his blueprint for the future of Europe would be extremely vulnerable if Britain were to gain entry into the EEC.

The man who perhaps spent the most time analysing de Gaulle's vision, and in particular Britain's place in it, was Michael Butler, a British embassy official in Paris in the 1960s. Butler spent his time sourcing out attitudes and opinions amongst officials at the Quai d'Orsay and other circles in Paris. It was during these years that Butler came to the conclusion that the accepted view of de Gaulle in British circles needed a closer assessment and, if necessary, a serious adjustment of tactics:

De Gaulle was intent on emptying the European Community of its supranational content. This included keeping Britain out. De Gaulle believed Germany, Italy, Benelux were the stooges of the Americans. Given that the Americans in his eyes were determined to dominate Europe and Britain would help them to do this, if he allowed Britain to join, it made it much harder to drain out the supranational content from the Treaty of Rome.[10]

He also commented that:

> The General was quite devious, and proceeded to play one against the other [the other five]. De Gaulle would report and mis-report to the prime minister of whatever country about what another had said. When I realised what was happening, I began to make a record of these statements, not exactly to call him a liar but to expose the perversion of the truth. By April 1962 I had managed to persuade those around me of my thesis. I sent a dispatch to the Foreign Office, pointing out that the General was trying to keep us out.[11]

Nevertheless, Butler was adamant in his convictions and persevered, sending another dispatch to the Foreign Office in September 1962, outlining de Gaulle's behaviour and the various power relations of the other five and that between Britain and France. It was unfortunate that this dispatch was not taken more seriously, for it is clearly evident that his descriptions of de Gaulle's foreign policy and his attitude to the other players were all too accurate. Butler remembers the aim of the dispatch 'was to warn the Foreign Office what was going on in the general's mind; however at the time it did not have much effect'.[12]

What frustrated some officials was the fact that Macmillan had refused to read the signs and ultimately made the whole idea of a veto much easier for de Gaulle to execute. Reflecting on a meeting between Macmillan and de Gaulle at Rambouillet in France in late 1962, Butler pointed out that 'the General had more or less told Macmillan he was going to veto a British application, but wrapped it up a little. Macmillan did not believe it.'[13]

According to Oliver Wright, de Gaulle knew that France could have the leadership of Europe and the Six and he did not want Britain to threaten this. Also, de Gaulle did not want an Atlanticist Europe and did not want a 'Trojan horse' inside the Community.[14] In de Gaulle's eyes, Britain had not presented him with sufficient evidence that she had in fact chosen to respect his chariot and run alongside it.

De Gaulle's vision of Europe was somewhat along the lines of what Macmillan referred to as 'L'Europe à L'Anglais, sans L'Anglais', and he shared the same aversion to the idea of supranationality as the British did.

It is ironic that de Gaulle's vision had so much in common with the British, yet he would be the one to refuse their application. He chose in many ways to model the future of Europe on earlier British blueprints, while at the same time guaranteeing British exclusion.

On 14 January 1963 de Gaulle put a stop to any hopes of Britain joining the 'Six', with his veto. The following day Macmillan made a broadcast on the breakdown of the Brussels Negotiations: 'I am afraid that (despite assurances to the contrary), the only explanation for what has happened is that the French government hoped the negotiations would fail in one way or another.'[15]

III

De Gaulle played a pivotal role in Britain's journey towards Europe and it is therefore necessary to examine how the Foreign Office viewed his attitudes and innate fears on the subject. In particular, two key questions emerged that perplexed politicians and Foreign Office officials during the 1960s as they endeavoured to persuade de Gaulle to allow them to enter the EEC. What type of Europe did de Gaulle want? And how did Britain fit into this view?

The consensus that began to emerge in the Foreign Office was that de Gaulle's attitudes and most certainly his prejudices were shaped by events in the past. In addition to this, the Foreign Office began to recognise that de Gaulle's ultimate goal was to make France great again. James Marjoribanks was the Ambassador and Head of the UK Delegation to the EEC from 1965 to 1971. His private notes in preparation for a documentary in 1990 on de Gaulle's vision of France's place in the international political structure are noteworthy: 'De Gaulle's idea of France was inseparable from grandeur. France must always be at the centre. This attitude brings conflict with Britain and other nations who do not always share this preoccupation.'[16]

For de Gaulle, France's greatness was closely intertwined with the future development of Europe. De Gaulle advanced the idea of a 'Europe for the Europeans' whereby through unity of forces they would be able to look after their own defences and, ultimately, become less dependent on outside (i.e. American) help. This desire to make mainland Europe more independent was not new. There has been a long tradition in continental quarters of regarding mainland Europe as a balance to Britain, the Soviet Union or the United States. Napoleon had set out to rival British supremacy and build a continental blockade of mainland Europe in the early nineteenth century. Yet to British officials at the time, not all of de Gaulle's actions here were born out of a noble desire. According to Robin O'Neill, who was working in the Foreign Office at the time:

He was an extremely old-fashioned thinker, and not the far-sighted visionary he thought himself. His aim was French hegemony within Western Europe, including French domination of Germany. The Franco-German partnership has always in French eyes meant that Germany must do what it is told.[17]

Macmillan maintained that 'He talks of Europe and means France'.[18] For de Gaulle, Europe was the vehicle that was vital to steering his country back on course. The whole concept of European integration was fine, insofar as it did not impinge on France's sovereignty or independence. The only way to ensure such an outcome was to create a 'French-led Europe', one in which the direction and pace of the European vehicle was controlled by France.

'Between France and the Soviet Union, there are no matters in direct dispute. Between France and Great Britain, there always have been and there always will be'.[19] This candid utterance from de Gaulle reveals much about how he viewed Britain and perhaps goes far in explaining why he continually sought to limit their involvement in Europe. Crucially, events were not the only element that constituted this complex backdrop – de Gaulle's personal relations with a number of Britons added further weight to his hypothesis. Charles de Gaulle noted in his *Mémoires de Guerre* what Winston Churchill had said to him: 'Chaque fois qu'il nous faudra choisir entre L'Europe et le grand large, nous serons toujours pour le grand large. Chaque fois qu'il me faudra choisir entre vous et Roosevelt je choisirai toujours Roosevelt.'[20]

As much as de Gaulle admired and was indebted to Churchill for all his help during the Second World War, this famous outburst, made in 1944, was never far from his mind when dealing with the British. Furthermore, his efforts to forge some sort of Anglo-French alliance late in 1944 came to no avail. De Gaulle, hoping unison would create a louder voice for the two countries, was again left desolate as Britain made its preference for the transatlantic connection clear. Dealings such as these clearly shaped his impression of the British and underlined most of his post-war policies.

Where would Britain fit into de Gaulle's grand scheme of things? The easiest way to assess the situation is to weigh up the advantages and disadvantages of British entry for France. Clearly, in de Gaulle's mind, two overriding disadvantages won out over any supposed advantages voiced by any other fellow Frenchmen or European neighbours. Firstly, de Gaulle wanted to be the sole navigator of Europe's destiny. With the inclusion of Britain would come another heavyweight, and as the much-quoted phrase points out, 'there was only room for one cock on this dunghill'. De Gaulle enjoyed his dominant position and was willing to go to any lengths to guarantee this dominance. Secondly, one of the main explanations presented for de Gaulle's obstruction of British entry was the Trojan horse theory. If one of the fundamental aims of his policy were to make Europe less dependent on American support and involvement, then why would he admit a country that had made no secrecy of its faith in an Atlantic Alliance? As one of his biographers Jean Lacouture wrote:

> Since his British visitors did not agree to exchange 'more Europe' for 'less America', since they wanted both the protection of Kennedy and the keys to Europe held by de Gaulle, since they were clearly hoping to win on both tables, the General would be pitiless.[21]

According to Robin O'Neill:

> His anti-Americanism was pathological, but in a sense well founded in the equal American mistrust of him, and indeed of France. Britain was perhaps seen as a Trojan horse for US influence. For de Gaulle, Britain would have had to detach itself from the chariot wheels of the United States, and run beside his instead.[22]

Fearful of American domination, supranational organisations, and clearly unconvinced of Britain's suitability to join the EEC, de Gaulle was an insurmountable obstacle in the early 1960s. The question now circulating in the Foreign Office was what would be the best way to proceed given the magnitude of the obstacle. At the beginning of February 1964, Michael Palliser, who was working in the Foreign Office at the time and who would later become Wilson's private secretary in 1966, wrote to Jeremy Thomas, who was the French desk officer from 1963 to 1967 and said that:

> General de Gaulle is a short-term phenomenon and however much he may at present be exploiting the negative elements in the French character, I do not personally believe that when he disappears, France will, for long, pursue his present policies. In essentials we have to try to keep the lines open to the French, in our common interest and even while General de Gaulle is still there, to the extent that this is possible.[23]

Crispin Tickell, who was working in the British embassy in France at the time had already highlighted this fact to Palliser in his Foreign Office minute entitled 'Two Scorpions in a Bottle: Prospects for Anglo-French Relations', Tickell maintained that 'General de Gaulle is and has always been the main impediment to the third alternative – the resumption of the Entente Cordiale', and Tickell like many others at the time admitted in private that 'there is little we can do about him'. Tickell's concluding comment to Palliser who subsequently agreed with him was: 'There may well be ways of influencing the general but not surely enough to shift him from attitudes compounded more of emotion than logic'.[24] Only time would tell whether the words and actions of British officials, politicians, and prime ministers would be convincing enough to influence de Gaulle and the only question now facing politicians and officials was what to do next.

IV

This was the dilemma Harold Wilson inherited when he replaced Macmillan as prime minister in October 1964. However, little is known about Harold Wilson's views on Europe as he wrote very little about Europe, and even his close cabinet colleagues found it hard to decipher his views on the subject. One of the most reliable accounts is that of Bernard Donoughue one of his close advisers, who maintained that:

> Wilson was always mildly anti-Europe, in the sense that he seemed not to like Continental Europeans; their style of life or their politics. He was basically a north of England non-conformist puritan, with all the virtues and the inhibitions of that background. The continental Europeans, especially from France and southern Europe, were to him alien. He disliked their rich food, genuinely preferring meat and two veg. with HP sauce. For holidays the furthest he could usually be tempted was the Scilly Isles, which enabled him to go overseas and yet remain in Britain.[25]

Wilson's attachment to the Commonwealth remained constant. Philip Ziegler, his official biographer maintained that:

> His love for the Commonwealth was romantic and traditional; he relished the idea of Britain at the heart of this great international network; he believed that it represented the surest way by which his country could remain among the foremost powers.[26]

It was this personal attachment to the Commonwealth and the belief in Britain's power that led him to declare in his first major speech on foreign policy as prime minister: 'We are a world power, and a world influence, or we are nothing'.[27] Britain was now being led by a man who, when shadow foreign secretary, had shared the opposition of the then Labour Party leader, Hugh Gaitskell, towards the idea of Britain joining the EEC. While in opposition, Labour had increasingly moved towards a negative stance when it came to the question of Europe. Hence, Gaitskell's speech to Labour's annual conference at Brighton in 1962 epitomised the anti-European direction in which the party was heading, when he declared that British entry into the EEC would signal 'the end of a thousand years of history'.[28] The definitive 'anti' stance alienated the likes of Roy Jenkins, George Brown and ardent pro-Europeans; however, it struck a chord amongst party supporters, yet when it came to the 1964 election campaign, the question of Europe barely featured. The Labour Party were keen to cling to the past, with their manifesto stating 'though we shall seek to achieve closer links with our European partners, the Labour Party is convinced that the first responsibility for a British Government is still the Commonwealth'.[29] With no detailed strategy on Europe, inevitably a policy of 'wait and see' would be adopted given the slim parliamentary majority.

ONE

WAIT AND SEE

—

I

The Labour Party under the leadership of Harold Wilson won the general election in October 1964, with a thread-like majority of five seats. It was the first Labour government since Clement Attlee had left office in 1951 and marked a watershed in British politics. Wilson's biographer, Ben Pimlott, highlighted the sense of occasion:

> It was a remarkable victory. It was the first occasion in peacetime since 1906 that an incumbent Conservative administration had been displaced by a non-Conservative party with an absolute majority. It was also the first result since the 1920s to put in office a party leadership largely lacking in ministerial experience. The 1945 victory had followed a period of coalition, in which the public had become accustomed to Labour ministers; and the 1950 result, numerically similar to 1964, had followed five years of Labour in office. By contrast Labour's 1964 success had been preceded by the Tory triumph of 1959, when the Conservatives had a majority of 100.[1]

In February 1965, *The Observer* wrote that Britain's influence on its European neighbours was 'at its lowest point since 1066, when another Harold was in charge'.[2] Whether *The Observer*'s charge was accurate and whether Wilson's administration worsened the already fragile relations which existed after the failed first application will dominate this chapter. Con O'Neill was one of the leading architects of Britain's European policy in the Foreign Office during the 1960s. On 25 July 1964, he wrote: 'What then should Her Majesty's next Administration do? And still more important, since in fact there will be little it can do to change the existing situation, what should it say?'[3]

According to Robin O'Neill:

> The Wilson Government in October 1964, without a clear foreign policy, was probably instinctively anti-Community. For a few months the alternatives were looked at (e.g. the Commonwealth or a Free trade area), partly through reluctance to join, and partly because de Gaulle was standing across the road.[4]

This is echoed by Michael Palliser who recounted that 'The Labour Government of 1964–6 were merely exploring, wondering what to do, how to play the hand. The planning staff were more concentrated on East of Suez than with Europe, but they still had to keep the flame alive.'[5]

Before de Gaulle met with Wilson after Churchill's funeral in January 1965, Pierson Dixon, Britain's ambassador to France, was granted a short farewell interview with de Gaulle on 23 January 1965, as Dixon was soon to be replaced by Patrick Reilly. According to Dixon, 'On this valedictory occasion he [de Gaulle] seemed to be speaking with more than usual openness – no doubt in reaction to my own frank and personal approach.'[6] De Gaulle stated:

> Mr Macmillan had almost convinced him that we were ready to come into Europe. It was the Nassau Agreement that had finally convinced him that we were not ready, since it showed that we continued to rely on the United States.[7]

Not only did de Gaulle state his aversion to any American domination of Europe, but he also outlined his conception of the EEC: 'The EEC was merely a convenient commercial arrangement, it did not amount to more than a customs union'. Finally, with regard to Franco-British relations, de Gaulle assured Dixon that he believed there were no serious problems in this area and advocated that 'The most useful thing we could do would be to develop practical ways of working together, by building a great modern aeroplane or driving a tunnel under the channel.'[8] Aside from the fact that the practical programmes resulted in both Concorde and the Channel Tunnel eventually being built, three striking themes stand out: de Gaulle's unshakeable anti-Americanism; his sceptical view of the EEC's future; and his emphasis on practical and technical co-operation with Britain as opposed to any other co-operation. Jeremy Thomas, French desk officer at the Foreign Office made the Western Department of the Foreign office aware of de Gaulle's view:

> One is left with an overpowering impression of the General's scepticism, almost cynicism about Europe's future development; the EEC – merely a convenient commercial arrangement which France would leave if she were ever voted down; European political integration – unlikely to develop; and a common defence policy ridiculous.[9]

The later evolution of de Gaulle's – and France's – policy is evident. The French were increasingly of the opinion that the Labour Government had little interest in Europe, as Drew Middleton wrote in *The New York Times*:

the French have got the impression that the British Labour Government is profoundly disinterested in Europe and no longer harbours any grudge against France as a result of the Macmillan's government unsuccessful bid to join the Common Market; the way is therefore clear for a real improvement in relations between Paris and London.[10]

However, de Gaulle had set out on his path paying diminishing attention to sentiments across the water and no place was given to Britain in the evolution of his grand design. The British Embassy in Paris concluded that de Gaulle believed the Labour administration would pose no serious problem when it came to the EEC. It further offered the view that warmer Anglo-French relations should not be equated with a desire to see Britain pursue a place at the European table.

In an interview on BBC Television on 15 February 1965, the recently appointed (January 1965) secretary of state for foreign affairs, Michael Stewart, tried to avoid committing the Labour Party to a definite policy. With regard to the question of joining the Common Market he stated:

> There's not so far been any concrete evidence that the French Government has changed from the position it took up when it in effect prevented our entry into the Common Market – whatever our views might be – some time ago. So until there is concrete evidence of that kind, there's not much point in discussing the question in those terms.[11]

Stewart focused on the 'here and now', the various avenues of co-operation that Britain was pursuing, such as the Western European Union, the Council of Europe, and joint aircraft projects, and described the speech of Alec Douglas-Home, the Conservative Party leader, as based on 'generalities'.[12] Later in the month, Duncan Sandys from the Conservative Party met Maurice Couve de Murville, the French foreign minister (1958–68), at the Quai d'Orsay. Couve was quite encouraging about the prospects of British entry at this stage and declared to Sandys that:

> If the British government declared their readiness to sign the Treaty of Rome and to accept the decisions on prices and other matters, which have already been taken by 'the Six', he maintained that 'nobody could prevent Britain from joining the Common Market in five minutes – not even General de Gaulle'.[13]

This was not the case, for de Gaulle ultimately had the power to decide on Britain's fate. Sandys asked whether the French government would genuinely like to see Britain in the Community. Couve replied: 'My answer is yes and no. Yes, if we are convinced that you will act as good Europeans, otherwise, no.'[14] Officials in Whitehall believed that:

> It was not the creation of political institutions which he had in mind. What he was concerned to know was whether Britain could be relied upon to look at the problem of defence and the question of relations with the United States from a European standpoint.[15]

In March 1965, Michael Butler was forced to leave the British Embassy in Paris and was sent to Harvard University in the United States as it was felt that he was not helping the British case. In the autumn of the previous year de Gaulle had commented to friends that Butler was awkward and too vocal in his views. Policy was now concentrated on attempts to placate de Gaulle, and to improve bilateral relations. Butler's removal from the British Embassy and his relocation in the United States emphasise the desire in the Foreign Office at the time to avoid any confrontation with de Gaulle.

II

On 3 March 1965, Michael Stewart sent a minute to the prime minister, emphasising his concern over the way things were developing in Europe and warned the prime minister that:

> Our present attitude and policies are not enough to prevent General de Gaulle achieving his object of making this unit into a 'closed shop'. There can be no question of renewing our application to join the Common Market as things stand. But one day we may wish to, and it is very much in our interest that we should keep the option open.[16]

By now the focus of attention was on the forthcoming meeting between Wilson and de Gaulle, due to take place at the beginning of April. Harold Caccia was the permanent under-secretary of state between 1962 and 1965; he had been Britain's Ambassador to America between 1956 and 1961. On 1 March Patrick Reilly, the British Ambassador to France (1965–8), wrote to Harold Caccia at the Foreign Office about possible topics for discussion. In particular, Reilly cautioned against any discussion of 'association':

> I would, with respect, have thought it unwise for the prime minister to pick up the possibility of some association for Britain with the European Community. If we were to raise it now, the French would seize on it as evidence that we had finally

abandoned hopes of full membership and were no longer pressing to participate in any political developments amongst the Six.[17]

Then, on 12 March, Stewart followed this up with another letter to the prime minister, this time including a report, which Caccia had brought from Vienna, detailing the views of Dr Bruno Kreisky, the Austrian foreign affairs minister, about the forthcoming talks. According to Kreisky, 'As things are, the President of France still owes Britain an answer'.[18] Stewart hastened to add a further word of caution:

> If the prime minister were by chance not to raise this issue with President de Gaulle during the course of his visit, the effect might be most serious. The French would be more than likely to use any such silence and not only with the other members of the EEC, adding the gloss that the silence was a witness to what they had always claimed, namely that Britain was more interested than she was ready to join Europe.[19]

A letter from Patrick Reilly to Michael Stewart on 18 March 1965 made a number of very relevant points in relation to the imminent meeting with de Gaulle. In this dispatch Reilly attempted to outline the French government's attitude towards the visit:

> It is clear from the way the government are briefing the press and from our own conversations at the Quai d'Orsay and with members of General de Gaulle's staff at the Elysée that the French are not expecting indeed do not want any far reaching results to emerge from this visit.[20]

The very fact that the British prime minister was visiting French soil once again would allow de Gaulle to claim that his tactics in the past had not lost him friends or allies:

> Provided that this visit can be said to have passed off in a friendly manner, French propaganda will be able to represent it as effectively putting an end to the period of coolness in Franco-British relations resulting from British hard feelings after the Press Conference. The French would like to be able to add that the Labour Government is sufficiently pragmatic and realistic to accept the justice of the General's action.[21]

Two other French objectives included the exploration of technological and other forms of bilateral co-operation and the opportunity to drive a wedge between the British and their two principal allies, the United States and

Germany. Referring to the latter objective Reilly was keen to point out that 'the French are no longer among those close friends to whom we can speak with confidence that what is said will not be exploited in repetition to others for whom it was not intended'.[22] With these French objectives in mind, it was felt that there were two possible ways in which to approach de Gaulle at the forthcoming meetings. The first would be 'to accept the French version of Franco-British relations and make the best of it, tacitly accepting the French claim that we are no longer anxious for membership of either economic or political Europe'.[23] Or the alternative route would have been to emphasise Britain's concern over the political, military and economic effects of the current division of Europe, while avoiding direct confrontation with de Gaulle.

While the British were attempting to judge how best to approach the talks, de Gaulle was clear about his ambitions. Having received criticism both at home and abroad for the manner in which he had treated Britain's application in 1963, de Gaulle was now determined to remedy the situation, without making any concessions to the British. De Gaulle wanted to show that the much-revered 'entente cordiale' still survived, but at the same time hoped that his 1963 verdict would become accepted as the best outcome, especially in the minds of the newly elected Labour Party. De Gaulle was subsequently reported by Reilly to have questioned Britain's future path and to have commented that they were at a difficult point in their history, and 'were rather groping to find which way to turn'. De Gaulle thought it was a pity, but 'it was neither their fault nor anyone else's; but until they made their choice nothing could be done'.[24] However, writing to Caccia on 30 March, Reilly spoke about again about de Gaulle's intentions towards the British and warned that 'General de Gaulle may seek to use the present weak financial position in order to bring pressure to bear on the prime minister'.[25] Furthermore, he had probed some French sources on what exactly de Gaulle would want of the British, with the supposition being that 'he is after a free hand in Europe'.[26]

Wilson and Stewart travelled to France early on 1 April 1965, where they met with de Gaulle later that day. Their previous meeting had taken place after Churchill's funeral in January 1965, and de Gaulle had indicated to those close to him that he was much impressed to find that 'old England is still herself'.[27] That morning in April in the Elysée Palace, Wilson and de Gaulle discussed some of the larger issues overshadowing the European question, such as the growing crisis in Vietnam, the growing rift between the Soviet Union and Communist China, the Middle East, and Africa. Writing in his memoirs Wilson recounted how he was received by de Gaulle at the Elysée Palace:

> He invited me into his study and we sat down on his settee, each of us flanked by an interpreter, his being the multilingual Prince Andronikov, and on my side,

Oliver Wright, Foreign Office Private Secretary at No. 10. In the event the prince translated both ways leaving Oliver free to take a very full note.[28]

After an agreeable lunch they then went on to discuss financial questions, with Georges Pompidou, French prime minister from 16 April 1962 to 13 July 1968, Maurice Couve de Murville, and the Minister of Finances and Economic Affairs (1962–6) Valery Giscard d'Estaing all present. Again Wilson recounts how:

> The General presided benignly from the settee, saying nothing. I remembered the story of the banker who had urged the President to take a closer interest in certain economic developments as being vital to the future of France, and the General replying by dismissing the whole of economics as 'quartermaster stuff'.[29]

This remark highlights again the primacy of politics in de Gaulle's thinking. Yet when it came to the question of relations with America, economics were of significant importance, and could not be relegated to the 'quartermaster'. After dinner the economic questions and the debate surrounding gold recommenced:

> We assembled in one of the anterooms for coffee, but I suddenly found myself being piloted by one of Couve's secretaries through long corridors, across an enormous salon, and then away to the right, far from any visible human being. The inevitability of my abduction reminded me of one of the more frightening inter-war French films. Not a Briton in sight.[30]

In the event, Wilson recalled how it was 'clear that I had failed to pass the examiners. I had not, at least not yet, shown the degree of economic perception qualifying me for entry into the anti-American, anti-liquidity gold club'.[31]

The following day the question of Anglo-French relations was raised and President de Gaulle invited the prime minister to open the discussion. Wilson began by stating that 'he had come to Paris in the genuine hope and desire that relations between the United Kingdom and France would improve'.[32] Wilson then maintained that 'there was one aspect of Anglo-French relations which he particularly wished to stress, namely the possibility of establishing a greater degree of functional co-operation between the two countries, particularly, perhaps, in the field of aviation'.[33] Here, perhaps, he was taking on board Reilly's point about the French desire for bilateral co-operation, and ultimately hoping to find something to offer de Gaulle to soften his attitude towards the British. Slightly more than 'functional co-operation' was discussed between the British foreign secretary and the French foreign minister as a side meeting at the Quai d'Orsay, with Couve asking if Britain did indeed wish to join the Common Market. Michael Stewart retorted that it 'would depend on the attitude of France: did the French Government wish Britain to join?'[34]

The one thing that stands out from examining these exchanges is the extent to which Britain under the premiership of Wilson was at the mercy of the French with respect to relations with the EEC. The man who had said no to Macmillan's application could just as easily do the same to a future British application, and Wilson and his party were quickly beginning to realise this. Furthermore, considering the Labour government had still not decided on a definite approach to the Common Market issue, it was considered best to placate de Gaulle to a certain extent. By Stewart throwing the question back at Couve, he attempted to shift the focus away from the lack of certainty surrounding Britain's European policy. Wilson, wrote to de Gaulle after his visit that he had 'found our talks immensely stimulating and valuable, and I think that we now have a good basis on which to develop our relations'.[35] Developing Franco-British relations, however, remained no straightforward task.

III

The opening of the Calais Fair in France on 10 July 1965 witnessed the French minister of information, Alain Peyrefitte, encouraging the development of a warmer phase in Anglo-French relations. He claimed that the two countries were, 'Fated both through sentiment and through reason, to develop that which unites them more than that which separates them, to draw progressively closer to each other, and together to build a future based an exchanges, co-operation and friendship.'[36]

Peyrefitte went on to describe the Channel Tunnel as marking the end of Britain's isolation. It would 'mark the end of British insularity and would at last firmly anchor Britain to the continent'. It would finally 'mark the end of the struggles and discord which have in the past separated our two peoples'.[37] Peyrefitte's remarks were not the only warm remarks; similar sentiments were expressed by Monsieur Bourges, under secretary in charge of scientific research, nuclear and space affairs, who at the inauguration of the Channel Fair in Dieppe said:

> That everything which could maintain, confirm and reinforce the traditional ties between France and Great Britain was highly desirable, just as it is desirable that the Europe of tomorrow should not ignore Great Britain who very naturally finds her place in it.[38]

So what was it that lay behind these unusually warm remarks? The French propaganda machine was constantly trying to portray France in the best possible light. Both to domestic and foreign audiences alike, there was an underlying desire to show that France was not alone, that Britain did in fact share its vision of the Common Market's future, that the two countries did have a great bilateral future ahead of them and, finally, to illustrate to the French public that, contrary to what many believed, France was not in fact isolated.

On 14 July 1965, Jeremy Thomas wrote:

> The rumour is going around that General de Gaulle wanted to rebuild the alliance between Britain and France; and that he might propose some unspecified deal with us; perhaps British adherence to an un-supranational sort of enlarged Common Market, and that he might float some such idea at his next press conference.[39]

Despite the speculation, Thomas urged that caution should be observed when reading Peyrefitte's statements and that they should not be taken at face value:

> In a word the French propaganda machine is trying to convince the world that the British, having belatedly come to their senses, and having decided to overcome the disadvantages of their geographical insularity by creating an umbilical link with mother France in the shape of a Tunnel, are at heart good Gaullists.[40]

Certain commentators believed that it was necessary for Britain to make a choice between the United States and the EEC. Yet although many adhered to this proposition, this choice between two of Britain's 'three circles' contradicts many underlying tenets of Britain's foreign policy during this period. One of the contributory factors in the decision to make an application to the EEC was to follow persistent American advice.

The minutes from the Western Department and the European Economic Organisations Department (EEOD) illuminate the sense of frustration amongst the British policy-making elite at the time, as they had no choice but to watch de Gaulle dictate to the other five and follow his lead. Frank Roberts, ambassador to the Federal Republic of Germany 1963–8, reported from Bonn that *Die Welt* had a cartoon portraying the British lion making up to an arrogant de Gaulle and disregarding a German who bandaged the lion's injured foot. Nevertheless, he maintained that 'reports of German reactions do not suggest that anyone here suspects Britain of trying to woo de Gaulle', and that 'the Federal Government is reported as welcoming any moves that bring Britain closer to Europe but Parliamentary opinion is said to see de Gaulle's remarks as designed simply for internal consumption in connection with the election campaign'.[41] It is clear that de Gaulle approached relations with Britain with one eye on the forthcoming election on 5 December 1965.

A paper discussing the dangers of a French victory was written in the Foreign Office on the 28 December 1965. The paper stressed that:

> The principal reason why we think it would be 'dangerous' for French conditions to prevail within the Community is because we believe General de Gaulle's concept of European unity and of the future relationship between Europe and the United States to be fundamentally opposed to our own.[42]

This raises the question of how these two competing visions could ever be reconciled. The words 'fundamentally opposed' are indicative of the problem. Why would de Gaulle allow a country 'fundamentally opposed' to his own vision enter into the EEC? With hindsight this question should have been given more attention, but was downplayed owing to the dynamics of British foreign policy.

It was also felt that de Gaulle's approach failed to stand up in the real world, and grand idealistic visions about a 'third force' were not the way Britain intended to handle international relations. Referring to de Gaulle's attitude the paper stated that:

> His basic purpose is to force an American withdrawal – military as well as economic – from Europe so that the Continent may be 'independent' of the United States and be able to play a balancing role between the United States and the Soviet Union. We believe this to be a dangerously conceived approach.[43]

IV

Addressing the 'Committee for Belgian-Netherlands-Luxembourg Co-operation' in The Hague on 14 January 1966, Con O'Neill talked about 'Britain's Place in Europe'. Three years to the day that de Gaulle put an end to the British negotiations, O'Neill emphasised the degree to which Britain's relations with Western Europe had been debated, and as a result 'over the last six or seven years we have discovered a thousand reasons for joining it, and a thousand against'.[44]

One of the men who signed the Treaty of Rome commented to one of the British negotiators: 'that if in his own country, so long and deep and passionate a debate had raged about the question – to join or not to join – as in England, then they would never have made their minds up at all'.[45]

Having acknowledged a warmer attitude in Britain towards the question of closer connections with Europe, O'Neill highlighted the two problems which he felt had been blown out of proportion on the continent – namely that of the 'special relationship' and that of 'supranationality'. Contemplating that United Europe would be a partner and not a rival of the United States, O'Neill felt that there was no real problem:

> Some people outside Britain believe it is our determination to cling exclusively to that relationship which makes us reluctant to commit ourselves fully to Europe. Whether our relationship with the United States is 'special', I do not know. It is certainly important to us and will remain so. But few people in Britain now believe that a deeper commitment to Europe would harm it.[46]

Turning to the second perceived problem on the continent, that of supranationality, he felt that the British had been misrepresented as it was indeed a problem for every member state, not just Britain. Furthermore he maintained that:

> The problem lies more in the practice than in the principles; and I venture to express the purely personal view that, should we ever succeed in joining the Community, we may well be found to be the champions rather than the opponents of its 'supranational' aspects.[47]

O'Neill's considerations remained detailed thoughts as opposed to a specific programme of action. The Foreign Office was obviously constrained and its officials could only take things so far, having at all times to await the signal from the political elite. Given Wilson's slim parliamentary majority in his first administration it is not surprising that the signal could not be given and instead a policy of 'wait and see' had by then become the established policy.

Wilson's European policy must be further seen in an economic context. The Labour Party inherited an economic situation described by Michael Stewart as 'grave but not critical'.[48] Upon taking office in 1964, the Wilson government inherited a balance of payments deficit of roughly £800 million, a situation which dominated Britain's foreign policy. Any mention of devaluation was denounced: Wilson again was fearful of a repetition of past events, as the Labour Party was frequently remembered as 'the party of devaluation', as a result of experience in 1931 and 1949.

What could be done to aid Britain's recovery? The answer lay in the unveiling of a National Plan, initiated by George Brown who was now in charge of the Department of Economic Affairs. Published in September 1965, it was heralded by all involved as the panacea to slow economic growth. Setting ambitious targets such as sustained growth at four per cent per annum for the next five years, it was not surprising that the majority of economists and various ministers viewed it as overly simplistic and overly optimistic.

According to James Callaghan, the chancellor of the exchequer between 1964 and 1967, 'over optimism was a basic mistake which damned the plan from the outset'.[49] Yet, criticisms aside, within the cabinet economics was the overriding concern, the priority to which all other policies were subordinate. The National Plan, economic decline and the possibility of devaluation will all be examined in further detail later on.

Nonetheless, on 25 January 1966, Michael Stewart gave a speech at a conference on Britain and the European Community, held by the Federal Trust for Education and Research. He stated that there was a far greater interest and concern for the EEC in Britain at the time and that there was 'the much more willing recognition that we in Britain form part of Europe'.[50] However, Stewart went on to point out that there would be no contradiction between this and maintaining traditional links with Britain's other two circles:

> There is, I think, a growing recognition that we in Britain form part of Europe. There is, I think a growing understanding that to feel this way and to desire a closer relationship with Europe is not at all incompatible with our continuing attachment to British ideas and British ways or with our continuing close ties with partners, allies and friends abroad – particularly in the United States and the Commonwealth.[51]

The following day, the new leader of the Conservative Party, Edward Heath, made a speech to the Federal Trust, entitled 'The development of Europe: the next stage'. In this, he emphasised the political motivations for seeking entry into the EEC. Seeking to dispel some of the myths surrounding the 1961–3 negotiations, he maintained that not only were the political reasons for applying more important, but that in the process the British people had been exposed to the dynamics of integration and had been somewhat converted to the merits of joining:

> I hope it is absolutely clear to everybody that the main reason why we entered these negotiations was the political reason of creating a greater political unity in Europe. And I believe – perhaps again those who doubt will go back to the records of the time – that in fact we did light a flame in the hearts and minds of the people of the country during those years and a flame which is still burning strongly and, in fact, I think stronger than ever before today.[52]

In an address by Stewart to the Imperial Defence College on 26 January, the issue of the Common Market and the Commonwealth was dealt with. Posing the question as to whether there was a choice to be made between the Commonwealth and Europe, he first uttered a word of caution:

> I should perhaps say first of all that while suggestions are being made in some quarters that there should be a new British initiative to join the Common Market, it seems to me that there is a strong element of wishful thinking in this. In practice, there is very little indication that the circumstances which led to a breakdown of the negotiations in 1963 have changed to any significant degree.[53]

Yet, leaving prudence aside, it was hoped that the future might herald different circumstances ultimately more conducive to British membership:

> Some of the problems that faced the British negotiations during the Brussels negotiations may become easier as time passes. I do not therefore regard the question of membership of the European Common Market as a choice between Europe and the Commonwealth.[54]

Perhaps one individual who saw the merits in examining the close similarities between Britain's and France's visions for the future of Europe was the Hungarian economist and economic adviser to the cabinet Thomas Balogh. Balogh was known for his continued criticism of the Foreign Office handling of the whole question. Balogh wrote to Wilson on 31 January 1966: 'It is exceedingly unfortunate that the Foreign Office should be consistently egging the Government on towards an anti-French posture.'[55] Balogh felt that Britain had a lot more in common with France than the other five when it came to issues such as majority voting and the Commission's power, and did not see why Britain should not pursue a closer alliance with France.

Britain's former Ambassador to France, Gladwyn Jebb, or Lord Gladwyn,[56] as he was commonly referred to, outlined the changing British attitude towards Europe in a lecture delivered in Hamburg and Bonn, on 2 and 3 February 1966. He highlighted the watershed that had taken place in Britain's history in 1961:

> In the classic phrase of Lord Macauley, every schoolboy knows, that from the reformation until 1961 the European policy of England, and then of Great Britain, was, if necessary, to throw her weight first on one side and then on the other, and to prevent any one European nation from achieving the mastery of the Continent. This policy was ruthlessly, and invariably successfully, pursued for a period of some four hundred years.[57]

However, this policy seemed to have come to an end in 1961 with Britain's decision to seek membership of the EEC. Between 1957 and 1960 'the British government brooded over the situation . . . in other words it became clearer and clearer that the game which had been played for 400 years could no longer be played now, and that the whole situation had changed profoundly'.[58] There was no longer any purely continental balance to preserve. Germany and France had created a United European bloc, which was in a sense Britain's nightmare. Gladwyn added:

> It is quite true that for so long as the economic situation in Britain remains perfectly tolerable for the ordinary Englishman, there may not be any great popular pressure on Her Majesty's government to change their present attitude of careful 'wait and see'.[59]

V

Again, the backdrop to Anglo-French exchanges cannot be forgotten. In the summer of 1965, de Gaulle boycotted EEC institutions as he was opposed to plans to increase majority voting in the EEC. The crisis was averted in January 1966 with the introduction of the 'Luxembourg compromise' – to safeguard a country's veto on important issues. However, until the issue was resolved it caused chaos throughout the EEC and has been subsequently referred to as the empty chair crisis. In light of this it is not surprising that de Gaulle would wish to keep the British on his side, or at least silence their criticism. It was events at the heart of the Community such as these which had made the 'five' more aware of the desirability of having Britain on board.

Even after this internal crisis in the EEC was resolved, things did not return to normality overnight. In January 1966, de Gaulle threatened to withdraw French forces from NATO and one of the founding fathers of Europe, Paul-Henri Spaak, the Belgian statesman at the time, cautioned Britain when it came to any overtures from France. Spaak had been the president of the General Assembly of the ECSC (1952–3) and was the minister of foreign affairs from July 1965 to March 1966. He stressed 'the need for us to handle very carefully any approach – whether direct or oblique – that may come to us from France, particularly if General de Gaulle is at the same time attacking NATO'.[60]

Headlines in the French press such as 'Mr Stewart considers that the French Veto against the entry of Britain into the Common Market has been raised' (*Le Monde*); 'A New Step by Britain Towards the Common Market' (*France Soir*); 'de Gaulle today opens the door to the British whom he did not want in the Common Market' (*L'Aurore*) implied that significant hurdles had been overcome by both sides. However, the articles also contained varying degrees of scepticism. The fact that Britain's membership of the EEC had become an election issue, that no real concrete change in attitude on the French side had taken place, and the fact that America and the Commonwealth still loomed too large on Britain's horizon to make it suitably 'European' were just some of the factors cited to dampen the hopes of many on both sides of the channel who had obviously been deluded into thinking that there were signs of a real breakthrough. Perhaps the most telling statement was issued by André Guerin in *L'Aurore*, who pointed out that:

> It would be as remarkable for de Gaulle to have changed his mind fundamentally about British entry as it would be for him to decide in favour of integration in NATO, as he has hitherto been equally opposed to both concepts.[61]

This comment while pessimistic, is telling of the French assessment at the time. With the Conservatives having recently declared their intention to take Britain into the Common Market at the next possible opportunity, Wilson gave a memorable speech in Bristol on 18 March 1966. He told the election audience that:

> The government's position, as we have stated again and again, is that we are ready to join if suitable safeguards for Britain's interests, and our Commonwealth interests, can be negotiated. Given a fair wind, we will negotiate our way into the Common Market, head held high, not crawl in. And we shall go in if the conditions are right.[62]

'Ready to join', 'negotiate', 'go in' – were all seized upon by those looking for evidence of a shift in the Wilson administration's policy. These words were, however, surrounded by much more cautionary phrases:

> We believe that given the right conditions, it would be possible to join the EEC as an economic community. But, we reject any idea of supranational control over Britain's foreign and defence policies. We are in Europe but our power and influence are not, and must never be, confined to Europe.[63]

While Wilson slowly began to embrace the turn towards Europe, it was neither whole-hearted nor immediate. One must bear in mind that it was delivered practically on the eve of the election. Having kept the door to Europe ajar for the period of Labour's first administration, here was the first real suggestion that Wilson might in fact want to proceed through it. Michael Palliser recounted how the speech caused considerable confusion to Wilson's opponents and also to his party: 'Wilson made it because Barbara Castle would be making a very anti-European speech. So it was very clear to me at this stage that he was intent on following the same line as Macmillan.'[64]

The prime minister's Bristol speech was the subject of much criticism in Germany, where Frank Roberts reported that 'In particular his rejection of any idea of supranational control over foreign policy and defence was described as sheer Gaullism, and amounted to a repudiation of the basic inspiration behind the community'.[65] At a time when Wilson needed to muster support for British entry amongst the 'five', comments such as these were detrimental. Roberts then went on to add that there was further disappointment expressed 'at the enthusiasm with which anti-European statements and references to a German finger on the trigger had been received by electoral audiences'.[66]

Roy Jenkins, the home secretary (December 1965–November 1967), in a press conference the following day reiterated the folly in reading too deeply into de Gaulle's words at a time when he was already embroiled in disputes with NATO:

> We have got to be very careful indeed that de Gaulle doesn't merely want us in Europe in order to serve his purposes of separating Europe from the United States, and I think Mr Heath ought to be extremely careful indeed that, for the purpose of trying to snatch a short-term electoral advantage, he doesn't allow himself to be turned into a tin on a Gaullist's cat's tail.[67]

Oliver Kemp,[68] deputy head of the UK Delegation to the European Commission 1965–7, met with Edmond Wellenstein,[69] formerly a senior official in the European Commission and ECSC high authority secretary, on 21 March and referred to the French initiative towards British EEC entry: 'it had been made at this particular time in order to minimise the serious effect of the French declaration on NATO, and to influence us to react less vigorously against the declaration than was in fact the case'.[70] On the other hand, Wellenstein did put faith in the French desire to achieve some form of rapprochement with Britain and its entry into the Common Market.

In an article entitled 'The British must decide whether to catch the EEC Bus', the London Correspondent of *Corriere Della Serra*,[71] Alfredo Pieroni, took a distinctly critical view of Harold Wilson's approach:

> Mr. Wilson had said that Britain wants to be free to continue to buy food and raw materials in the cheaper markets. This is understandable, but he is just like a man refusing to pay his subscription to a club offering very substantial advantages. As for Mr Wilson's words that British power and influence should not be confined to Europe, Labour's own *Daily Mirror* asked what power and what influence he was referring to.[72]

The article concluded stating that, 'It should also be understood that Britain is not conceding anything or doing anyone a favour by entering'.[73]

VI

Analysis of the communication across the channel during these years demonstrates that the British were hesitant: unsure of exactly how they wanted to pursue their European policy. Throughout this period the French sent out signals that were difficult to interpret. Encouraging yet evasive, the French government made a number of statements that could be interpreted as a willingness to see Britain join the Community. However, at the same time, British politicians were continually warned not to read too much into these revelations, for fear of a false sense of optimism permeating their thoughts and actions.

Numerous British civil servants urged their politicians to be conscious of the timing of these statements. Was the underlying motive altruistic or merely a clever seizure of opportunities, such as the French elections, the empty chair crisis, and the ensuing problems with NATO? Furthermore, they also emphasised the importance of differentiating between what de Gaulle said, and what his ministers said. One only needed to look back to the 1963 veto, to see that in the end almost all power rested with de Gaulle.

Labour's handling of these vital exchanges was clearly not the performance of a party firmly committed to taking Britain into Europe. Europe was low on the list of their priorities, the subject of vague and non-committal statements, with the emphasis on the here and now as opposed to long-term strategies. The Labour government were content at this stage to keep a foot in the door rather than racing to put two through it.

Operating with a majority of less than five seats, it would have been very difficult for Labour to say or do more in their dealings with de Gaulle and the French in those days. It is not surprising that Wilson and his colleagues' main aim was to keep the door to Europe open. What they would then do and whether they would want to enter through this door were questions that would certainly not be answered until their second term of office with a hoped for bigger majority. Robin O'Neill recalls: 'During these years, Wilson worked his way through it slowly. What we were doing was putting our foot in the door and keeping it there and it was very important it was not kicked out.'[74]

For the time being, they were content to have established relations with de Gaulle and his government, to have sent out a few informal feelers regarding the intentions of the French, and ultimately to have paved the way for future developments with regard to this increasingly pertinent issue. As the months progressed, Britain's policy developed from improving Anglo-French relations to a policy of 'wait and see'.

TWO

HAROLD, GEORGE AND PERSISTENT PRESSURES

—

The fact that Labour chose to apply for membership of the EEC surprised many. The party was clearly regarded as even less European than the Conservative Party, and it is therefore intriguing to examine Labour's motivations. The dominant question is whether it was a decision motivated more by political, economic or ideological factors, and ultimately why it was decided to make a second application to join the EEC. The purpose of this chapter is to explore the attitudes and influence of Harold Wilson and George Brown when it came to formulating European policy and examine the myriad of pressures which led again to seeking membership of the EEC.

I

In April 1965, Harold Wilson categorically stated to the House of Commons that 'There is no question whatever of Britain either seeking or being asked to seek entry into the Common Market in the immediate foreseeable future'.[1] Yet in just over a year and a half, this position was turned on its head, with Wilson telling the House of Commons: 'I want this House to know that the government are approaching the discussion with the clear intention and determination to enter the EEC if essential British and Commonwealth interests are safeguarded. We mean business'[2] Evidently Wilson had no strong feelings on the subject either way, for no one possessing a deep conviction could complete such a u-turn in just over a year.

Wilson's conversion to joining the EEC was laid bare at a meeting in Chequers on 22 October 1966, when he declared his intention to undertake a probe of the capitals of Europe. By 14 November, he was ready to declare that 'There is no future for Britain in a "Little England" philosophy'.[3] The man who had once disagreed over the very nature of the EEC and its political unity was now prepared to travel to the continent to see if Britain could be accommodated in this European body.

Time and the experience of office had combined to point Wilson in the direction of Europe. Some commentators believe Wilson's metamorphosis as a pro-European was initiated as early as before the 1964 election. However, most evidence points to Wilson becoming more pro-European in 1964–6. The question of when Wilson finally made up his mind to take the European option has perplexed politicians, officials, and his biographers. Oliver Wright asked Trevor Lloyd Hughes, Wilson's press secretary, when it was that Wilson decided to go for the European option and make that application. Hughes replied: 'it was when Harold Wilson was on the train, where a lot of his ideas came to him, when he had time to ponder, to think on his own, and this took place gradually during the period from late 1965 until early 1966'.[4] Wilson epitomised mainstream British establishment thinking: slow to realise the erosion of other alternatives; slow to realise the only viable option was in fact the European circle. Moreover, Wilson's turn towards Europe, like that of his predecessor Macmillan and numerous successors, revealed a determination to enter the EEC, but with no evidence of any deep-seated belief or trust in the whole European idea.

Party politics also determined the development of Wilson's European policy. It was much easier as an inhabitant of 10 Downing Street to press ahead with a bold policy initiative and hope to carry previously dubious or sceptical passengers with him:

> Thus we have seen the Labour Government since 1964 successfully persuading their followers to stomach, if not to like, foreign and economic policies which the same followers fought bitterly in opposition. Power is a mighty solidifier in politics.[5]

Although Wilson was free to navigate policy, he still had his hands tied when it came to maintaining unity amongst his ministers. The party had a large number of both pro and anti Europeans and Wilson tried to appease each side. Any move in the direction of Europe would then quickly have to be tempered with some concessions. Ultimately what governed the entire process were the tactical skills with which Wilson handled the whole question, and Robin O'Neill testifies to this. He recalled how:

> It was typical of Wilsonian policy in general to take time over it, to let others talk themselves into the decision he wanted to adopt. I saw this in the 1970s as well – with renegotiation (it was clear from the outset that he wanted to stay in), therefore let them talk themselves into the ground. Wilson always paid a great deal of attention to holding the party together, one must always remember the great deal of suspicion and reluctance that was in the party when it came to the question of Europe.[6]

II

Having examined Harold Wilson's turn towards Europe it is important to acknowledge the role of George Brown in facilitating and supporting a second application to the EEC. He stated in his memoirs 'How much I believe that in every political sense, Europe's future, as well as our own, depends upon our succeeding in joining, and as I think thereafter leading, the Community of Europe',[7] and he went on to say 'I have always quarrelled with Dean Acheson's much repeated remark about Britain's having lost an empire and not found a role. We have a role: our role is to lead Europe. We are, and have been for eleven centuries since the reign of King Alfred, one of the leaders of Europe.'[8]

As an unswerving advocate of British entry into the EEC, Brown, in contrast to Wilson, never wavered in his attitude towards Europe. Brown's vocal support of entry into the EEC was one dominant factor amongst many which had alienated him from some in the Labour Party after Hugh Gaitskell's death,[9] allowing Wilson to befriend both camps. It was Wilson rather than Brown who succeeded Gaitskell as the party leader. According to Robin O'Neill: 'George Brown's vigorous advocacy of membership of the EEC was important, both because of his influence with Wilson and because of his standing within the Labour Party, and his leading position within an important group of the Party.'[10]

At the same time, although considered too fond of alcohol, Brown was extremely popular with colleagues and voters, as the joke, 'Better George drunk than Harold sober' illustrates.[11] Yet even his behaviour did not allow his influence on this issue to be diminished. As Jeremy Thomas has pointed out: 'Though mercurial in attitude, and though Harold Wilson often suspected his motives and was exasperated by his behaviour, George Brown was probably decisive in nudging the prime minister and Cabinet towards the EEC.'[12] Even de Gaulle was reported as having a soft spot for him: 'I rather like him – in spite of the fact that he calls me Charlie'.[13]

The move of Brown from the Department of Economic Affairs to the Foreign Office in the Summer of 1966 was related to a desire to put an end to the inconsistent policies that had characterised Britain's European policy. With Brown at the helm of the Foreign Office, a new dispensation brought a policy which headed out on a straight line in the direction of Europe. In contrast to Michael Stewart's reticence to take a direct lead, Brown was determined to leave his mark on British foreign policy. Only a week after his appointment, Brown was quick to point out that 'so long as I am foreign secretary, Foreign Office policy will be made in the Foreign Office. That's what a Foreign Office is for'.[14] To Brown, being the foreign secretary was not a job; it was '*the* job'.[15] Essentially the man who was now in a position to do this 'job' was someone of strong convictions. A vocal pro-Marketeer even when Gaitskell had adamantly opposed it, Brown had a distinct vision of the future of Europe and, moreover, of Britain's place in it. Believing that Western Europe should be integrated, he envisaged an ultimate situation whereby the whole process of European integration would 'stop the polarisation of the world around the two Super-Powers'.[16] This was almost identical to de Gaulle's vision of Europe. Stressing from the outset that he did not want to be swayed from his beliefs, Brown commented:

> The Foreign Office is equipped to give the best of information, the best of briefing on any international issue one cares to mention. But what bothered me, made as I am, was the thought that it was they who were deciding the areas I should be briefed about, and I quickly became aware that, unless I was very determined, I would inevitably become the purveyor of views already formed in the Office.[17]

Outspoken anti-Europeans at the time such as Thomas Balogh, could not begin to dent his intellect. Eric Roll, who was appointed permanent secretary of the Department of Economic Affairs refers to Brown as 'the best untrained mind he had come across'.[18] Although the Foreign Office was instrumental in guiding Britain towards the three applications to the EEC, and will be discussed in more detail later, Wright was adamant that it was the politicians who ultimately determined events:

> We hire our brains to the government of the day. We advise on policy, we execute policy, but we do not decide on policy. The government decides on a set policy and the Foreign Office then carry out their instructions . . . one must keep in mind that everything ultimately depends on the political direction from the top.[19]

It was Brown who gave that lead, who advocated that the best way forward for Britain at this time was to follow a European path, and by putting him at the helm of the Foreign Office, it is clear that Wilson by this stage knew that too. In his memoirs Brown wrote that: 'I get rather irritated sometimes when people talk of Britain's "joining Europe", and I want to ask, "In what other Continent has Britain been over the past few thousand years?"'[20] This remark by Brown epitomises the origin of his pro-European sentiments. Idealism fuelled a great part of his attitude, believing in the natural evolution of Europe as a union of states, and with the British ultimately taking lead. The ostrich-like mentality of ignoring the changing environment would no longer suffice if Britain were to remain great, and it was Brown's recognition of this that would lead him to point others in the direction of Europe. Wilson wrote in his memoirs how:

The Foreign Office, at the same time, could do with a shake-up and a little more dynamism. We seemed to be drawing nearer to the point where we would have to take a decision about Europe, and George Brown seemed to me the appropriate leader for the task which might lie ahead.[21]

George Brown illustrates this commitment in his own memoirs:

> High on the list of things I wished to press the button and hoped the bell would respond comes the integration of Europe. I have devoted much of my political life to that and had to work very hard in the Labour Government to persuade the prime minister of the tremendous importance of this for British interests – economic, industrial, strategic and defence. With the help of my friends I didn't do too badly at this.[22]

Douglas Jay, president of the Board of Trade between 1964 and 1967 and a vocal anti-European was keen to point out that: 'The application to join the Market would probably never have been made if Brown had carried out his threat to resign during the July 1966 financial crisis.'[23]

A vocal and vehement advocate of entry into Europe was exactly the type Wilson needed at the helm of the Foreign Office if he was to make any headway in a pro-European direction. Therefore, it was no surprise to many that when Wilson had made up his mind and had the room to manoeuvre, that he chose Brown to replace Stewart. Indeed, it may well be that George Brown's move from the DEA to the FO on 12 July 1966 was more than a symbol of the change in emphasis from national planning to the attempt to call the old continent in to redress the stagnation of the British isles.[24] Perhaps two of the people most qualified to comment on Brown's influence are Sir Nicholas Fenn[25] and Sir Derek Day,[26] both assistant private secretaries to Brown in the 1960s. Recalling the influence of Brown on Wilson's attitude to Europe, Fenn stated that:

> This influence was immense, consistent and sustained. George came to the Foreign Office already a convinced European. Harold Wilson attached great importance to the Anglo-American relationship and to the Commonwealth . . . On the central issue facing British foreign policy at the time – namely out from East of Suez and into Europe – he [Brown] was one hundred per cent right; and only George could have picked up Harold Wilson, and thrust him into Europe.[27]

Day supported this view:

> There is no doubt that George Brown was always an enthusiastic advocate of Britain's involvement in the development of European integration at a time when

the Labour Party and Harold Wilson had, to say the least, serious reservations. It may be going too far to assert that George Brown converted his Party and Harold Wilson to a European vocation, but I would argue that his commitment and determination did much to persuade the Government to make the Second Application.[28]

Brown was often miscast as no more than a bumbling buffoon, but his role in Britain's journey into Europe was an important one. He was one of the leading actors in this story. By the end of the second application he had emerged as a much more sophisticated operator, and certainly not as the often portrayed buffoon of the Labour Party, but rather a deep thinker and a clever political operator.

Ideologically, his influence can be seen when one looks at both what Wilson and ultimately Whitehall had to say on the matter. Brown's ideas percolated through Whitehall, and the way he viewed the whole process of European integration inevitably rubbed off on Wilson. It was this gradual percolation of ideas that resulted in Wilson declaring in January 1967 to de Gaulle that:

> The task of France and of Britain was not to be mere messenger boys between the two great Powers. They had a bigger role to play – and other nations wished them to play it – than merely waiting in the anterooms while the two great powers settled everything direct between themselves.[29]

In a similar vein, discussing the whole question of European integration and unifying the continent, Brown had advocated 'getting common policies – financial, commercial, external and defence – so that we can stop the polarisation of the world around the two Super-Powers'.[30] One cannot fail to see how Wilson's statement is in fact inimical to Brown's vision for the future of Europe. Brown's impact on Britain's European policy did not stop with the shaping of it, for he was instrumental in pushing the policy of entry as far as he could. 'I am rather inclined also to think that a general debate – possibly a day at Chequers – could usefully precede a more detailed discussion of the material the officials had prepared.'[31] On a practical level it was Brown who was the first to raise the possibility of assigning a full day to serious debate on the issue. Acknowledging the merit of George Brown's advice, Wilson did in fact convene a meeting at Chequers on 22 October 1966, the first time the cabinet met formally to discuss the matter in detail. In conclusion, one can only contend that Brown's timely move to the Foreign Office, his passionate pro-European sentiments and their influence on Wilson, and his constant manoeuvring towards the European path, ensured that he was without doubt the strong battering ram to Wilson's knock. As David Ratford, second and later first secretary at the Foreign Office, 1963–8, recalled: 'The strength of Brown's own pro-European convictions was palpable as were his fears that Wilson might back-slide.'[32]

Wilson's influence on Britain's European policy did not relate to personal convictions or prophetic solutions, but lay in his role as facilitator. The agnostic was always open to advice from others; he was slow to come to a decision, but when he had made such an informed decision, was committed to the policy of taking Britain into Europe. According to James Callaghan:

> The approach of Harold Wilson was very realistic. In my view, he was basically in favour of membership of the European Community, but he was more measured in assessing whether it would be an advantage to join at the time, or not.[33]

Therefore while Brown was the innovator, Wilson was the facilitator who allowed the policy to germinate and develop in the Labour Party in its own time.

III

Le Monde stated in October 1967 that 'Mr Wilson's volte-face was even more surprising than Macmillan's ... but it was also more complete'.[34] The fact that Wilson's conversion was 'more complete' was due to a complex web of intertwined factors. These ranged from the dynamics of party politics and mounting pressure from the Foreign Office and interest groups, to the stark economic situation and the threat of devaluation. Wilson's opposite number, Edward Heath, who had a fervent approach to Europe conditioned Wilson to reappraise his party's position on Europe. He calculated that the pro-European Heath would undoubtedly make EEC membership a key issue at the following general election. From the middle of 1966, Wilson was determined to seize the advantage. As Leonard Beaton in *The Guardian* pointed out at the time, Wilson had 'a large interest in depriving the Tories of any clothes in which they may cut a dashing figure'.[35] By applying to join the EEC, by seeking to concentrate on the European circle, Wilson could counter initiatives by the Conservatives. At this stage the application carried a high possibility of being vetoed by de Gaulle for a second time, so it was not as if Wilson was committing himself to a predetermined outcome.

Wilson realised that an application to Europe would add impetus to a rapidly flagging government. With other policies in ruins, a fresh innovative approach could divert attention from them and at the same time in some ways lessen the damage. If the National Plan was not working, why not emphasise the link between economic and foreign policies, and highlight the need to follow the European path in order to reverse previous decline? Similarly, if Britain was forced to cut back on its world role, such as narrowing its defence commitments overseas, why not counter this with the argument that Britain's power would be bolstered by a concentrated involvement in Europe? Both will be discussed in further detail later, but need to be raised at this point to illustrate the extent to which tactical advantage could be extracted from a fresh application to the EEC.

Finally, some would suggest that it was not just inter-party politics but also intra-party politics that added to Wilson's ultimate decision. Determined to remain in the driving seat, always on the lookout for potential threats, it is not surprising that Wilson also took the position of some of his rivals into consideration. 'Harold is obsessed by the feeling that the Common Marketeers, led by Michael Stewart, Roy Jenkins and Tony (George Brown's deputy in 1964, he then went on to become secretary of state for education in 1965 and president of the Board of Trade in 1967) are ganging up against him. I think he exaggerates.'[36] Richard Crossman, who was at the time lord president of the council and leader of the House of Commons, may be right in his evaluation that Wilson perhaps exaggerated the issue, but that is irrelevant here. What was of paramount importance was that Wilson himself was feeling the pressure. The constant exposure to Brown's persuasive argument, the presence of the passionate pro-European Heath as his opposing number, and his inability to dismiss a growing faction within his party, ensured that party politics undoubtedly contributed to Wilson's turn towards Europe.

Political parties were not the only agents exerting pressure on Wilson when it came to the question of Europe. The constant flow of opinion from the Foreign Office was also at play. Occupied by a younger, more outward-looking breed of officials and marshalled by such pro-Europeans as Michael Palliser, Con O'Neill, John Robinson, who was first secretary in the UK's delegation to the EEC between 1962 and 1967, and Paul Gore-Booth, who was permanent under secretary of state for foreign affairs between 1965 and 1968, they sought to forward their vision of Britain in Europe. With apathy and agnosticism characterising the majority of the cabinet's view of the European issue, an obvious vacuum existed. Poised in a perfect position to exploit this vacuum was the Foreign Office. Many have attested to the significant role of the Foreign Office, including Robin O'Neill, who concluded that 'but for the Foreign Office it might all have petered away. The Board of Trade was pretty sceptical if not hostile; the Commonwealth Office was very backward. The Foreign Office kept things going. Con O'Neill and John Robinson kept the thing alight – the fire burning.'[37] The gradual reassessment that had been initiated as a result of the Suez crisis a decade earlier, was now beginning to bear results.

No longer was the head in the sand mentality prevailing, now an energetic group of officials had pragmatically weighed up Britain's options, and the consensus that emerged clearly pointed in the direction of Europe. Not only did their vision divest from past policy, but they were determined at all costs that their nascent strategy would not be stillborn. In order to convert others to their way of thinking, all possible pro-European avenues were meticulously investigated.

John Robinson, who was one of the foremost engineers of Britain's European policy at the Foreign Office, testifies to this:

> I wrote a paper after the veto, pointing out how many telephones, how many refrigerators, how many washing machines there were per 100,000 inhabitants of France. Things we'd been absolutely convinced we were superior in. But we were not superior. Nobody troubled to look them up, but I looked them up. My figures were accepted.[38]

On the other hand, departments such as the Treasury, the Ministry of Agriculture and the Department of Economic Affairs were not only reticent, but at times hostile to a wholehearted embrace of the European option. One of the most vocal sceptics of joining the EEC was Thomas Balogh: 'Those who were against it, like Tommy Balogh, saw the "hand of the Foreign Office" behind all advocacy of British EEC membership. There is something in that though not in the sense in which he would have meant it.'[39] Oliver Wright believes that 'Tommy was very good on everything but judgement, he always got it wrong.'[40] Another official pointed out the dynamics of such a clash:

> Con O'Neill and Robinson were an effective team. Politicians look to the officials to identify the way in which a policy should happen. There are also others advising and Balogh was particularly influential with Wilson. Therefore, you have the usual battle between advisers like Balogh and other officials. Balogh resented the fact that he was not the only voice being listened to.[41]

Writing to the prime minister in January 1966, Balogh outlined his fears and he cautioned against the adoption of a rigid anti-French stance:

> The French position on a whole range of matters – majority voting, the powers of the Commission, the composite reserve unit scheme for increasing international liquidity – is much more in line with our interests than is the attitude of the Five. This being so, it is exceedingly unfortunate that the Foreign Office should be consistently egging the Government on towards an anti-French posture.[42]

These points were again reiterated a few months later in July 1966, when Balogh observed that joining the EEC, contrary to widespread belief, might not be the panacea to all Britain's economic ills. In particular he felt that Britain 'would have to give up a large part of our present economic armoury, and might therefore not be able to deal as effectively as we can now with any problem which might arise after entry'.[43] In relation to the long-term consequences and the shorter-term problem of the weakening of the balance of payments, he concluded that 'It would be a grave responsibility for officials if these problems which have been discussed, albeit tangentially, by the Economic Advisers were not fully reported to the Ministers.'[44] Not just concerned with the economic details of an application, Balogh was also distinctly dissatisfied with the way in which the whole issue was being handled. Referring to the Foreign Office's shortcomings in this area, he believed:

> It is obvious that the impression will inevitably be given that the problems have been studied far more thoroughly than they have actually been and that ministers have had time to consider the consequences of the study which they have not . . . I feel that we are being committed to policies without due consideration.[45]

Admonishments from Balogh were, however, consistently outweighed by the constant stream of pro-European arguments emanating from the Foreign Office. Robin O'Neill maintained:

> There is no question that Con O'Neill and John Robinson, in the Foreign Office, played a critical part in keeping the importance of EEC membership before ministers in both Conservative and Labour governments in the 1960s. There was no comparable interest on the part of officials in other British Government Departments.[46]

Furthermore, he recognised the significance of keeping this vibrant pro-European pressure group together:

> It was in a sense generous as well as far-sighted of the Foreign Office to keep the O'Neill/Robinson team together at a time when the prospects for another application looked very dim; but ministers never questioned the preservation within the Foreign Office of this tiny pressure group.[47]

Officials such as Con O'Neill were quick to emphasise the appealing allure of pursuing the European option. One such Foreign Office minute was sent by Con O'Neill to David Mitchell at the Department of Economic Affairs in June 1966:

Our desire to join the EEC can be seen as an effort to strengthen the base from which we exert world influence so that we can exert that influence more effectively, whether to strengthen the Commonwealth by strengthening its leading member, or to have a better say in the formulation of U.S. policy, or to influence (and contain) Germany, or not to be denied playing a part in the eventual east–west settlements, or to increase our trade overseas.[48]

In order to counter any negative arguments that might take root, Con O'Neill pointed out that 'in the current state of the economy, all economic officials and advisers tend, wherever there are alternatives, to plump for the gloomier view. There is a strong atmosphere of pessimism, not to say defeatism.'[49]

Not willing to sit back and wait for events to unfold, the Foreign Office was instead busy initiating new policies. Referring to the paper produced solely by his office entitled 'How to get into the Common Market', Con O'Neill openly admitted to Wilson's private secretary in August 1966 that 'some of the conclusions drawn in the paper as to the kind of action that may be necessary in order to enter the Community go well beyond existing government policy'.[50]

Well aware that the balance of payments arguments had swayed some against rushing to lodge an application, Con O'Neill was determined that the mention of the inevitability surrounding British entry would spur others in the opposite direction. The germ behind the creation of such an innovative paper was that 'as time passes the difficulty and the price of entering the Community will both grow greater'.[51] When one looks closely at Wilson's attitude at this time it is clear that the pressures and influences emerging from the Foreign Office were having the desired effect.

On the eve of the Chequers meeting (22 October 1966), Harold Wilson was quick to dismiss many of Balogh's accusations that the foreign secretary's document were somewhat 'inconclusive' and 'inconsistent', and by now could see no merit in exploring either of his suggested alternatives – that of an 'Atlantic Alliance' or 'The Little England Approach'.[52]

If the prime minister's office had any lingering inhibitions or doubts, they could only have been further eroded by statements such as those written by Con O'Neill the day before the Chequers meeting:

> For the last 20 years this country had been adrift. On the whole, it has been a period of decline in our international standing and power. This has helped to produce a national mood of frustration and uncertainty. We do not know where we are going and have begun to lose confidence in ourselves. Perhaps a point has now been reached where the acceptance of a new goal and a new commitment could give the country as a whole a focus around which to crystallise its hopes and energies. Entry into Europe might provide the stimulus and the target we require.[53]

To those undecided or easily swayed, tempting bait such as 'a new goal' and 'a new commitment',[54] were utterly more appealing than the pessimistic prophecies put forward by the likes of Balogh, no matter how real at the time.

IV

Outside government and the civil service, the Confederation of British Industry (CBI) and much of the British press exerted varying but visible pressure to join Europe. The single voice of industry, often regarded as the 'middleman' between business and government, the CBI, carried a certain weight in issues pertinent to EEC membership. As the 1960s progressed, the CBI became more pro-European and established the 'Steering Committee' under the chairmanship of Gerry Norman (Chairman of the De la Rue Co.) that sought to examine the various economic implications of membership of the EEC. It was felt that in relation to Macmillan's application, British industry had no clearly defined opinion and voice and therefore, if the opportunity for another application arose, it would need to have a more coherent position. As the *Sunday Times* pointed out:

> Additional support for a new investigation into the possibilities of the market has come from those industrial leaders who feel that, during the last negotiations for Britain's entry, British industry as a whole did not seem to be able to commit itself one way or the other to definite views on the pros and cons of joining.[55]

No longer prepared to appear ambiguous on the subject, the CBI was now actively exploring the benefits of joining the EEC. On 27 and 28 October 1966, A. J. Stephen Brown, President of the CBI, led a 14-strong party of British businessmen to talk with their French counterparts, the Conseil National du Patronat Français. The *Financial Times* reported that:

> The feeling in London is that French industrialists, although perhaps not as enthusiastic about British participation as some of their counterparts in other Common Market countries, are by no means hostile to British entry. In addition, it is believed that economic considerations might soon make General de Gaulle more receptive to the idea. Clearly the Paris talks should help clarify the picture.[56]

Referring to the penultimate draft of the CBI study on potential membership, Robinson wrote to Norman Statham, Head of the European Economic Integration Department 1965–8, and concluded:

The study is whole-heartedly in favour of the earliest possible entry of Britain into the Community. It adopts a very confident attitude on the ability of British industry to hold its own . . . .. In taking the line repeatedly that we should join quickly, in order to play our part in formulating Community policy, the report at no stage suggests that our purpose would be to prevent things being done, but, rather to develop the Community.[57]

The prime minister met representatives of the CBI on more than one occasion in 1966 and 1967, and was left in no doubt as to their determination and desire to join the EEC. Discussing the need to maintain the momentum, once the decision had been taken, John Davies, Director-General of the CBI pointed out that 'the CBI had set its face against studying any alternative to our joining the EEC because of the obvious dangers of diverting attention from the main objective'.[58]

Where the CBI was the 'middleman' between business and government, the British press was a vital link between the public and the government. In the context of examining the various forces influencing the decision to make a second bid, the pro-European outlook of much of the British press throughout Wilson's administration was particularly significant. During the premiership of Harold Wilson, considerable pressure was brought to bear by much of the British press to embrace quickly and decisively the European option. In particular, Cecil King, proprietor of the *Daily Mirror* was determined that Britain should join the EEC and made no secret of this view. He felt it was his duty to adopt the mantle of educating the British public, an idea that was particularly well received by foreign observers. King discussed steps such as these in a meeting with some of the founding fathers such as Walter Hallstein, who was the first president of the Commission of the EEC, and who also opposed de Gaulle's view of a Europe of the states and Paul-Henri Spaak, in May 1965.[59] In the course of this conversation with Hallstein, and without any emphasis or appearance of vanity, King had thrown out incidentally the remark that if Wilson did not get himself a sensible European policy in the near future, King's newspaper would cease to support him and that meant that he would not win the next election.[60] Not only were media magnates such as Cecil King eager to inform the general public of their views, but they were also determined to ensure that politicians, and in particular the prime minister, understood the message. With a constant flood of pro-European arguments being transmitted to the public via the press, it is no wonder that popular opinion began to look more favourably on the European option.

In October 1966, a Gallup poll undertaken for the *Daily Telegraph* revealed an unprecedented level of support for entry into the EEC. Sixty-eight per cent said that they would approve if the government decided to join the EEC,

14 per cent disapproved, and 18 per cent did not know.[61] This led the *Daily Telegraph* to declare:

> Support for British participation in the European Common Market has been mounting steadily over the past two years. It is now substantially higher than it was at any time under Conservative Governments either before, during or after the unsuccessful period of negotiation.[62]

Burke Trend, who was cabinet secretary from 1963 to 1973, wrote a paper to the prime minister on the 28 October 1966. He referred to this support and pointed out that:

> The general climate of domestic public opinion appears to be favourable to a renewed attempt to see whether we can 'get into Europe' – not least because people seem to feel instinctively that the sort of Europe which we should now try to enter is perhaps rather different from the sort of Europe which we tried, but failed, to enter nearly four years ago.[63]

It is clear that evidence of such a favourable public mood was yet another factor propelling the Wilson administration in the direction of Europe. Added to this was the Foreign Office's skilful manoeuvring of ministers, the prime minister's own attitude towards Europe, George Brown's forceful advocacy, and the energetic pushing from the CBI and much of the British press. This all amounted to persistent pressure that undoubtedly played a role in motivating the Wilson administration to make the second application for membership of the EEC.

V

Looming even larger on the horizon was the clash of policies that would inevitably lead to the National Plan's demise. Fundamental to a favourable outcome was the need for investment and expansion. However, with the need to maintain the value of the pound came the required restrictive economic policy. The two policies were incompatible. Add to this the inherent institutional handicaps and one is immediately struck by the degree to which the programme was indeed hampered. Set up to keep a close eye on the Treasury, it was not surprising that the Department of Economic Affairs was regarded with suspicion. The fact that each department was headed respectively by long-time rivals Brown and Callaghan [64] would leave one wondering how the policy expected to remain devoid of an antagonistic air. For a plan of such magnitude to solve the ailing Britain economy, a strong degree of co-operation and consensus would need to have been present from the outset.

In July 1966, a national seamen's strike combined with deteriorating economic factors to produce a severe run on sterling. The pound fell to its lowest level since November 1964, forcing the government to choose between deflation and devaluation. With the rise in the interest rate to seven per cent, the National Plan was effectively suffocated. According to Eric Roll, the influence of Brown here was immense: 'Brown was certainly responsible for the July measures – George was the leader on this.'[65]

Eric Roll remembered that Wilson and Brown kept arguing over the timing of entry: 'do we dig a hole first and then apply, or apply and then dig a hole'.[66] There was not much left of the National Plan, and it faded from the economic horizon, quickly abandoned by all who had only recently placed their faith in economic planning. 'With the death of that idea vanished forever Labour's short-lived reputation, which Wilson had done much to cultivate, as the party of efficiency and modernity.'[67]

Having been blown off course, the Wilson administration needed to navigate a new course that would remedy those economic ills and also heal the wounds left by a failed economic policy. That course was to Europe, but it was chosen for more complex reasons than simply being seen as a quick replacement for the National Plan. As James Callaghan reflected:

> I do not think that the failure of the National Plan in any way affected opinion about the application, especially as it was believed by several of those concerned that the National Plan, with its projections, was too optimistic for it to succeed.[68]

To suggest that Wilson and his cabinet were prepared to replace one ship for another is to oversimplify the issue and to ignore the whole issue of devaluation. Devaluation was soon to re-emerge as not only a viable option, but as the seemingly inevitable one. Wilson, Brown and Callaghan had all rejected the option to devalue the pound at the beginning of their respective first terms in office. However, by the summer of 1966, Brown was adamant that this bitter pill would have to be swallowed if Britain was not to decline even further. Acknowledging the short-term impact, he felt it was the key to long-term success. James Callaghan verified this when he maintained that Brown:

> Was strongly opposed to a voluntary devaluation of sterling, from the time we were first elected until the early summer of 1966, when he became convinced that devaluation was a necessary condition for membership of the Community, and therefore changed his attitude towards sterling. He became a fervent advocate of early entry and undoubtedly had a strong influence on Harold Wilson's tactics.[69]

One can see the extent to which Brown's famous declaration that 'we've got to break with America, devalue and go into Europe',[70] was an apt summation of both his style and substance.

Brown, however, failed to mobilise his cabinet peers and the deflationary measures were regarded as adequate in addressing the economic crises. With James Callaghan content to opt for the deflationary package, the wrath of Brown was unleashed. After hearing of this unwillingness of the cabinet to embrace his policy of devaluation, Brown resigned, though he was tactfully ignored by the prime minister. The episode is often regarded as the moment when Wilson should have taken his secretary's advice and devalued, but that is to admonish Wilson with the advantage of hindsight. The sterling crisis of 1966 was to become the catalyst for further change, forcing the premier, ministers, politicians and officials alike to address some of the most pertinent questions of the day. The case for devaluation, and its exact consequences, were now becoming frequent topics of debate, thereby stimulating previously suppressed attitudes and approaches not only to Britain's future economic policy, but also to its place in the world.

The harsh economic situation ensured that both Wilson and Callaghan were increasingly receptive to altering now outmoded beliefs and objectives. With unprecedented post-war unemployment levels, and the unbearable price of further deflating measures, it is not surprising that Wilson was ready to acknowledge the case for devaluation. Yet, instead of taking a sharp u-turn and reneging on previous promises, it would be much more acceptable to both the domestic and foreign audiences to present it as an alternative route. Furthermore, to devalue inside the Community would also provide some sense of insulation and would certainly be received in a more favourable light by the domestic audience and the external markets.

It is clear that possible devaluation was a significant impetus not only to joining the European Community but also in ensuring that this transpired as soon as possible. Wilson's change of gear, from the patient agnostic to a determined advocate of entry testifies to this. To mix the question of devaluation with that of Europe not only allowed the Wilson administration to mask past mistakes and failures, but also injected a new vitality into a deflated government. Devoid of serious success at this stage, and unwilling to admit defeat when it came to past attempts at resuscitating the economy, the European experiment presented itself in many ways as a welcome alternative, a chance for the Labour government to redeem itself. With the government's economic platform dismantled and abandoned there was an urgent search to replace it:

> In the vacuum this created, entry into the EEC was seen as an alternative route to economic salvation. In psychological terms, Europe provided a strategic goal previously offered by the National Plan.[71]

As Robin O'Neill pointed out: 'The unsatisfactory economic situation of Britain was one of the relevant factors in the Wilson government's attitude towards EEC membership'.[72] Jeremy Thomas reiterated this point when he contended that, 'our economic weakness affected our tactics. We had become more realistic about our inability to go it alone.'[73] Again, it was timing and tactics that were affected by domestic politics rather than the principle of the decision or the overall strategy.

As a result of the sterling crisis in November 1967, the pound was devalued by 14 per cent. Yet what is important here is not the actual mechanics or milestones along the way to this eventual occurrence, but the interplay between devaluation and Britain's European policy. The whole devaluation debacle was part and parcel of the wider evolution taking place in Britain's economic and defence policies, and ultimately the way in which Britain was beginning to gain an altogether clearer picture of its standing in the world. Tony Benn, who was postmaster general in Wilson's government reflected on the time: 'The Tories had tried and had left in the balance of payments crisis in 1964. We had tried and had had to put the brakes on in 1966, and we were now looking for solutions to our problems from outside and somehow we were persuaded that the Common Market was the way of making progress.'[74]

It was perhaps the economic variable more than any other that managed to galvanise support for a decisive turn towards Europe. Ministers previously uninterested and even dismissive of this option now had to examine its merits. Excluding the vehemently anti-European ministers, the rest of the cabinet were left with little or no choice but to acknowledge that in the present climate the arguments in favour of seeking entry outweighed those against. The case of Wilson and Callaghan epitomises this contention. Neither possessed any strong European convictions; both were forced into accepting that Europe was the only possible route to follow at the time. In a sense, economic variables sealed the fate of the second application. Lord Gladwyn had astutely pointed out in February 1966 to audiences in Hamburg and Bonn 'that for so long as the economic situation in Britain remains perfectly tolerable for the ordinary Englishman there may not be any great popular pressure on Her Majesty's Government to change their present attitude of careful "wait and see"',[75] is relevant here.

Economic reasons for joining were both positive and negative. Offering a market of millions of consumers in close proximity to Britain was a tempting pull on its orientations. No longer could the statistics be sidelined and dismissed as illusions, because the reality was confronting the British year after year. Not only referred to by Konrad Adenauer as 'an old man who has lost all his possessions, but does not yet realise it', Britain now had to watch her poorer cousins prosper and ultimately outpace her. One of the fundamental arguments against joining the European countries during the 1950s was the economic realpolitik. With Britain consistently trading more within the Commonwealth area than with Western Europe, there was no incentive to immerse itself in a customs union with the European powers. As we have seen, Britain's pattern of trade was increasingly being conducted with Europe, favouring an even closer inspection of the relative merits of membership. Likewise, it was becoming apparent that the attempted 'bridge-building' exercises between EFTA and the EEC were pointless. The nucleus of Europe's economy was the EEC, and slowly but surely the British were beginning to realise that 'bridges' only carried one so far. To remain outside Europe was depriving Britain of the large market and accompanying economic advantages.

Ultimately the pressure from the Foreign Office, the advocacy of George Brown, the significant reorientation of Britain's trade and the changed nature of the communities themselves united in nudging the Wilson administration down that European path. As Michael Palliser put it, the realities around them could no longer be ignored:

> Fundamentally I think after the traumas of two World Wars and loss of Empire, Britain had to find a solid economic base and there was the European Community. The rate of growth in the years after 1958 was more visible and more vital amongst 'the Six' than in this country and Wilson intrinsically recognised that.[76]

THREE

NO ALTERNATIVE CIRCLE

—

Wilson's European policy was played out against the backdrop of a changing world and economic crises. In essence this was a time for re-evaluation, and Britain's decision to apply to join the EEC was part of that process. John Darwin, in his study of British decolonisation since 1945, compares Britain to:

> The image of an impoverished grandee, whose hereditary mansion becomes slowly uninhabitable room by room as, in apparently random sequence, the floors give way, the plumbing fails, the ceilings fall in. But however dilapidated the mansion became, it was not to be given up because no other mode of life was tolerable and an address is, after all, an address.[1]

Alun Chalfont, who was one of Wilson's junior ministers (foreign affairs) declared to an audience in October 1967 that: 'You've only got to look around and anyone in Europe has only got to find that in recent years ... the trend and the drive of our foreign policy has been less to do with the affairs of the world as a whole – less global in nature and more European.'[2]

The simile of the 'impoverished grandee' illustrates how Britain's status on the international stage had changed. Two of the famous 'three circles' had been 'shrinking' rapidly. Once at the hub of these 'three circles', Britain was now forced to concentrate on one in particular – Europe. Chalfont's utterances indicate the 'shifting' emphasis, the retreat from things global and the consequent embrace of things European. One could not attempt to discuss the motivations that lay behind Britain's second application to the EEC, without a thorough examination of the various external factors. It was ultimately international relations rather than domestic politics that would ensure a distinctive change in Britain's foreign policy.

I

It would be folly to suggest that Wilson ushered in a wide array of sweeping, unprecedented changes in Britain's external relations. However, the slow revolution that had begun with the Suez crisis in 1956 was later fuelled by

Macmillan's 'Grand Design'[3] and would be further facilitated and nurtured under the Wilson administrations between 1964 and 1970. What was unprecedented was the extent to which Britain's interests were now viewed from a purely national as opposed to global standpoint. Finally, accepting the need to cut its coat according to its cloth, Britain embarked on a serious reduction of its overseas commitments and moved away from an exclusive embrace with the Americans. Britain, in 1967, was in a position to embark on a European path, with a lot less baggage than had been the case a mere four or five years earlier, albeit still under the shadow cast by de Gaulle.

Britain's inability to maintain Great Power status was clearly recognised. What has not often been acknowledged is the Wilson administration's role in attempting to redefine its role. Although many of the decisions taken, such as devaluation and the withdrawal from East of Suez, were the result of limited options, the end result is what is significant here: Britain was becoming increasingly free to make rational choices based solely on its immediate needs. Macmillan had declared to the House of Commons in August 1961 that: 'We must all agree . . . that the problems involved in the future of our relations with Europe are among the most difficult and the most important that the nation has ever had to face'.[4] By 1967, events and reactions had certainly transpired to produce a situation markedly advanced from that in 1961. It was only through the dilution of Britain's Commonwealth relationship and a consciously changed Anglo-American relationship that European relations could be strengthened and further developed. In the words of the French desk officer, Jeremy Thomas: 'External factors certainly pushed Britain towards the EEC. The illusion of being at the centre of the famous three concentric circles had withered. There was the disillusion about the Commonwealth; and Labour, with its hostility towards US policy over Vietnam, didn't take to the 51st State idea.'[5]

In 1964, Miriam Camps, writing about the first application, concluded that 'The Commonwealth aspects of the question overshadowed all others, politically, economically and emotionally'.[6] A mere three years later, the Commonwealth could certainly not be said to be dominating any discussion in this area: at best it was briefly referred to. Yet this was not born out of any pre-meditated desire or plan on the part of the Labour government, rather out of a particular set of circumstances. The Labour Party was even more firmly attached to Commonwealth links than its Conservative counterpart. Roy Jenkins correctly predicted in June 1964 in an article in the *Daily Telegraph* that 'If a Labour Government came in during the Autumn it would make an attempt at closer Commonwealth unity, but that when this faltered it would be ready to make another application to Europe'.[7] To all intents and purposes it looked as though Jenkins had penned that comment in 1974, not in 1964.

The Commonwealth link was one of the cornerstones of Labour's foreign policy, with many of its prominent figures, especially to the left of the Party, displaying particularly strong emotions towards it. Wilson, for one, was known for his deep affection for the Commonwealth. Speaking to the House of Commons in August 1961 on a debate regarding the question of Europe, one of Wilson's few sceptical comments concerned that of his devotion to the Commonwealth: 'We are not entitled to sell our friends and kinsmen down the river for a problematical and marginal advantage in selling washing machines in Düsseldorf'.[8] This firm attachment to the Commonwealth link can be seen when Wilson wrote to Stewart regarding the type of 'Europe' that Britain might contemplate joining one day. Uppermost in his mind was that it would be a 'Europe' that did not threaten existing relationships in any way:

> Unless it is outward looking and not autocratic it must be inimical to Atlantic and more particularly Commonwealth links. The real test is the Agricultural policy, which in its present form is autocratic and would deal a deathblow to Commonwealth trade.[9]

Stewart declared 'As to our Commonwealth interests, these are of course neither homogeneous nor static'.[10] A prophetic statement when one looks at this in hindsight, but Wilson was to cling fervently to his loyalty to the Commonwealth for a while longer.

Labour's 1964 election campaign, notable for the absence of any significant debate on the European question, placed substantial emphasis on the whole issue of Commonwealth trade and propounded an expansion of this trade in the hope of solving some of Britain's persistent economic problems. Rebuking the Conservatives for allowing Commonwealth trade to decrease from 44 per cent to 30 per cent,[11] Wilson set about reversing this trend. However, his wish failed to materialise and by 1967 Wilson's musings on the subject had become a lot more realistic, acknowledging the long-term decline in British Commonwealth trade.[12] According to Stewart, Labour's ambitious pledges in this area amounted to nothing more than a pipe dream.[13]

Changes to the political value of the Commonwealth also highlighted Britain's altered relations with the rest of the world. According to Michael Wheaton, 'The Indo-Pakistan war had clearly demonstrated the British government's impotence in dealing with inter-governmental disputes within the Commonwealth'.[14] By opting for Soviet mediation over British, the adversaries sent a clear signal that could not be ignored. However, it was the crisis over Rhodesia that really highlighted the problems within the Commonwealth and consequently lessened the appeal of this circle. The problem of Rhodesia was one that haunted Wilson for most of his time in office. Under constant pressure to deal swiftly and effectively with Ian Smith's undemocratic regime, and dismissing the use of force, Wilson opted instead to employ economic sanctions to put an end to the illegal regime. At the Commonwealth prime ministers conference in Lagos in January 1966, Wilson maintained that such measures would see results in weeks as opposed to months. Criticism from the rest of the Commonwealth, in particular from South Africa, had steadily been mounting, resulting in the most disastrous Commonwealth conference to date. Doubts about the nature of the Commonwealth were now beginning to surface, leading members to look for alternative partners. The Labour Party, which had vowed to resuscitate the Commonwealth link in 1964, had by the beginning of 1966 practically pronounced it dead after the turbulent Commonwealth conferences in 1966. As Oliver Wright contended, 'The repulsion from the Commonwealth to a certain degree made Harold Wilson go for the European option. The African members of the Commonwealth clobbering the prime minister really was a very unpleasant experience.'[15]

The South African premier, General Smuts, had in 1943 warned the Empire Parliamentary Association – an audience unaccustomed to shock – that 'in the post-war world to come Great Britain would be compelled to make a choice between Empire and Europe'.[16] According to Dennis Judd: 'By the time the Labour government under Wilson came to power in October 1964, there seemed comparatively little that could be salvaged from the wreck of imperial decline and dissolution.'[17] Twenty years after General Smuts had outraged his audience, that choice between Empire and Europe had been made. Two years after the Labour government took office they too realised the fact that the days of presiding over a sprawling empire were gone. Determined to play a 'world role', but clearly unable to sustain this position– this was the dilemma which had faced successive British prime ministers and politicians throughout the 1950s and 1960s. 'In fact the triumvirate of Wilson, Callaghan and Denis Healey (at the Ministry of Defence) did try to chuck excess ballast over the side of the keeling ship of state, only to find that every time more water came back over the gunwales.'[18]

The Defence White Paper of 1966 marked the real watershed, in declaring that 'The United Kingdom would withdraw from Aden Colony and the South Arabian Federation, regardless of local circumstances, in 1967 or 1968'.[19] It had become obvious that Britain was financially and militarily incapable of sustaining its East of Suez presence. Finally, in July 1967, the process was completed with another Defence White Paper declaring the end of Britain's presence East of Suez to be achieved by the mid-1970s.

By acknowledging the realities of the day, Britain was now able to look closer to home to find the much-needed lodgings to replace its dilapidated estate:

With the political and military engines of neo-imperialism all but turned off, a reassessment of Britain's role could produce only one conclusion. Whether or not she entered the Common Market, it was in her local region, grappling with her age-old neighbours, under the umbrella of NATO but also in some kind of new political and economic alignment, that her future was bound to lie.[20]

II

By 1964, Britain was facing some serious decisions. To continue with the traditional 'three circles' policy of dipping in and out of all three circles, but not concentrating on one in particular, was becoming increasingly fraught with danger. Concentration on the Atlantic link held limited potential, owing to the unequal distribution of power between the two countries. Old policies were steadily being eroded, while new ones were rapidly taking shape. Pierson Dixon outlined some of his fears in a paper entitled 'Europe and Atlantic relations': 'My major worry has been lest Great Britain should end by finding herself isolated both from Europe and from the United States', and went on to say that: 'We might join the United States but could not hope to lead it. We could hope to lead Europe, and must try to join it'.[21]

According to Oliver Wright, Dixon's dispatch went 'right to the heart of our dilemma about Britain's future in the world'.[22] In the mid-1960s sentiments such as these were steadily gaining currency, especially in the Foreign Office, and by the time Wilson had vacated 10 Downing Street in 1970, they had become the accepted orthodoxy. When Heath became prime minister, there was a definite metamorphosis in Britain's foreign policy. Wilson had built on, and in many ways accelerated, Macmillan's reorientation of foreign policy with regard to its reflecting more and more interest in the European circle and less emphasis on the Commonwealth one. Wilson also played an important role in the reorientation of Britain's Atlanticist urges, but this is not to say that Wilson succeeded in radically reorientating Britain's foreign policy, or that he turned his back on the United States, moving rapidly in the direction of Europe. What Wilson did was look at all the available options: accept that Britain could never be an equal partner to the United States, and embark on the same European path as Macmillan, albeit reluctantly at first.

Less than two months after taking office, Wilson made his first trip abroad as prime minister to Washington, a trip indicative of his Atlantic leanings. Talking informally about Wilson's forthcoming visit to Washington, the Paymaster General stated that: 'the visit is regarded as of unusual significance. One eminent American official referred to it soberly as 'potentially the most important political event of the century and much is made of the feeling that you and President Johnson are likely to find a great affinity, both personally and in political approach and method'.[23] Robin O'Neill recounted that there were: 'frequent exchanges and visits on Wilson's part. The 'special relationship' did seem to be important especially with regard to defence, and made sense when Britain was not a member of the Community. She could not drop one and not have the other.'[24] Furthermore, 'interests remained the same, reliance on weapons the same. Wilson himself never shared the kind of instinctive anti-American feelings that marked the left of the Labour Party'.[25]

Writing to President Johnson in November 1966 in relation to Britain's decision to again seek entry into the Common Market, Harold Wilson was keen to point to 'the firm determination of my colleagues and of myself that there shall be no change in the fundamental relationship between our two countries and in our own basic loyalty to and belief in the Atlantic concept'.[26] Wilson clearly recognised the importance of the Atlantic connection, and was keen not to jeopardise it in any way. Reflecting on the Anglo-American relationship, James Callaghan pointed out that

> Wilson, like others of us (as de Gaulle rightly surmised), was concerned with the Anglo-American relationship and that the Atlanticist tilt in our policy should not be in any way undermined. Harold Wilson regarded the American relationship as a rock that must not be weakened.[27]

Yet, at the same time, Wilson did not have any illusions about the nature of the relationship and had said as much to the National Press Club in 1963. He was not so sure what was meant by a 'special relationship'. He said he was:

> more interested in a close relationship based on a common purpose, common objectives and as far as could be achieved community of policy. There was nothing so irrelevant in nature as a poor relation and if Britain's relationship with the United States were based on that status the sooner it was ended the better.[28]

It was this sense of realism that re-emerged when Harold Wilson maintained a detached stance over the Vietnam War. Undeterred by American disapproval, Wilson recognised the need to reduce Britain's defence commitments, signalling the end of the joint world policing role the two countries had adopted after the Second World War. Many were led to talk about the 'cooling' of the 'special relationship'. As Michael Palliser recalled: 'Wilson was sceptical of relations with America, and in some ways got on well with France, and was also seen as not so under the American thumb as his predecessor.'[29] Again, to equate Wilson's pragmatism and practical approach with an intent to lessen Britain's ties with the Americans is both inaccurate and unfair. What was happening was perceived as inevitable, Britain began to act in a manner more in tune with its genuine capabilities. This in turn would have a significant impact on Britain's European policy. For only through a certain dilution of its relations with the United States and the Commonwealth could a more concentrated approach be set in motion with regard to the European circle. Talking about this very subject of Anglo-American relations and Europe on Independent Television News on 9 October 1967, Alun Chalfont commented:

> I don't think this is a change in policy – this is simply a change in the facts of life. We've got to get this thing into perspective. The so called special relationship with the United States has been for some time now changing in character as our foreign policy is changing in character – as we have come to concentrate more on the affairs in the future of Europe.[30]

Indeed *The Times* went on to add that Chalfont's speech was completely in line with what the Foreign Office had been saying for quite some time:

> In the diplomatists' view, Britain's links with the United States – arising from language, common law, and many traditional attitudes in common, will always be close, but the idea of any organic special relationship has long since been misleading and the phrase itself is widely regarded as something of a millstone, hampering a sound appreciation of the real relations of Britain both with the United States and with Europe.[31]

This redefinition of the 'special relationship' was not confined to the British, for the Americans too were well aware of the altered balance of power. Propping up their British counterparts was doing the British no favours in the long term. There had to be an alternative solution, and the State Department was becoming increasingly conscious of the need to help Britain find it:

> It is basically unhealthy to encourage the UK to continue as America's poor relation, living beyond her means by periodic American bail-outs. We must redefine the so-called special relationships . . . Britain by itself is unlikely to adjust to face the facts of a new world environment . . . She needs the pressure of a determined US policy . . . We should shut the door on financial support to Britain's chronic financial crises, but should be prepared to provide Britain with financial supports it might need to adapt to the EEC.[32]

IV

It was obvious to both sides of the 'special relationship' that Britain's deteriorating economic position necessitated some sort of fresh alternative and this was to manifest itself in the considerable push that came from the United States with regard to Britain's decision to seek entry into the EEC. Reflecting on the period, Robin O'Neill later recounted that: 'American support in 1967 for the second application, though less openly expressed, was as strong as it hadbeen for the first'.[33] Patrick Dean, Britain's ambassador to America from 1965 until 1969 reiterated this point when he wrote to the Secretary of State on 12 January 1967: 'There is no shadow of doubt that the Americans regard it as being wholly in the United States' national interest that the momentum towards European economic (and ultimately political) unification should be maintained, that this "Europe" should include Britain and the sooner we can join the Common Market the better!'[34] Robin O'Neill's assessment is accurate. The Americans were well aware of the fact that to become too involved, push too hard, or shout too loudly at de Gaulle and his five officers would have been an imprudent mistake. As the Trojan horse theory was cited as one of the main obstacles to Britain's entry in 1963, then one obviously had to tread a very delicate path in 1967. The Americans made sure the British were left in no doubt as to their advocation of this path, but at the same time had no choice but to retreat somewhat.

According to Michael Palliser, the Americans 'had been discreet in expressing support for the prime minister's present efforts because they thought they could be counter-productive'.[35] 'Discreet' indeed, as Dean Rusk, the American secretary of state (1961–9) again made clear in April 1967: he 'asked whether there was any way in which the United States could help. On the whole they . . . thought it better to be reserved', and he concluded that the British 'should let them know if they could do anything to help. But they did not want to complicate things.'[36]

Eager not to complicate things, and determined to adopt and maintain a reserved position, George Ball, President Kennedy's under secretary and a keen European, is quoted in the *Sunday Times* on 7 May 1967 as saying: 'America will be watching the forthcoming discussions with enormous interest and silently cheering from the sidelines'.[37] Robin O'Neill highlights the consistency of American support for British entry into the EEC:

From at least July 1955, immediately after the Messina conference, the United States, which was all for the Europeans avoiding the mistakes of the first half of the twentieth century, consistently urged Britain privately to play a strong and positive part in the process of closer European integration. Therefore all of Wilson's pro-Community policy was very welcome in Washington and not seen as a threat.[38]

Patrick Dean wrote to Con O'Neill on 13 January 1967 that 'If we are unsuccessful on this occasion, the Americans are quite unwilling to contemplate that this would be the final parting of the ways. They are firm in the view that our entry into Europe is, as they often put it, "in the logic of history".'[39] 'Logical' is exactly how the Americans perceived this option – in their eyes it was in both Britain's and America's interest that Britain would seek membership of the EEC. According to Michael Palliser:

> The Americans were tremendous supporters and thought that the best role for Britain was to go in. The Wilson years were the maximum period for pressure, when there was the most encouragement to go in. Reasons again were a mixture of economics and politics.[40]

It was felt that it would be distinctly advantageous if Britain communicated with the United States from inside Europe as opposed to outside:

> In spite of our economic weakness we still had considerable clout (politics and defence) around the world, and this clout could be best exercised inside the European Community. The Americans were torn a bit, wanting Britain to stay East of Suez, but it was generally accepted that the best way to keep Europe on the American side was if Britain was inside it.[41]

In a telegram to Harold Wilson on 23 May 1966, President Johnson wrote that the Americans could not:

> risk the danger of a rudderless Germany at the heart of Europe . . . In the long pull, I am sure that the one best hope of stability and peace lies in the inclusion of Germany in a larger European unit . . . I am sure, also, that you and your country hold the key to this possibility and that you can play a role of great leadership in Europe. When all is said and done, no one has come up with a better formula than that of European unity and the Atlantic partnership and I doubt that anyone will.[42]

That Britain would significantly help unify and strengthen the West as a whole, was one of the main driving forces behind America's push. As Patrick Hancock, superintending under-secretary of John Robinson, pointed out in a minute on the American attitude to British membership:

British membership of the EEC would in some respects run counter to United States economic interests. The reason why the United States Government nevertheless want to see us in is that they see our accession to the EEC as contributing to European stability and promoting an 'outward looking' attitude in Europe.[43]

Richard Powell, the permanent secretary to the Board of Trade, visited Washington in November and further confirmed the unswerving support of the Americans for British entry. Reflecting on his visit he stated that: 'it is significant that in none of these discussions was the desirability, and indeed the long-term inevitability of British entry questioned on the American side. Nor was there any mention of possible alternatives.'[44] As far back as July 1966, George Ball had urged the British to apply without conditions. He also outlined the reasons why a Common Market with the United States was not really viable:

> The political consequences would be grave, there would be an Anglo-Saxon line-up against the Continent and democracy and Western orientation were not so firmly established in Germany that they would necessarily survive in these circumstances. Britain needed to join the Common Market to keep Germany safely tied to the West.[45]

If these were the underlying reasons behind the push from America, then what drove Britain to take heed of this persistent pressure? Michael Palliser recounts how Brown and Wilson responded differently to the American push: 'George Brown quite welcomed it, whereas Wilson resented it, he did not like too much American pressure'.[46] Nevertheless, 'while not decisive', the pressure from America did have 'a considerable impact'.[47] Perhaps what had initially influenced Macmillan was now exercising the same power over politicians and officials in 1966, namely the chance to bolster Britain's power and status in the world. George Ball, in a conversation with Patrick Dean and George Thomson (minister of state in the Foreign Office), on 16 May 1966, advocated that Britain play 'a much more prominent part in Europe and was willing to make it clear that she regarded herself as primarily a European Power and intended to play a full role there'. Ball 'recognised the difficulties, psychological, political and economic which such a policy posed for Britain but, he thought, that unless Britain could adopt such a policy she could never realise her full potential vis-à-vis the United States.'[48] To this end Patrick Dean wrote a letter to Con O'Neill on 13 January 1967, which was shown to Wilson the following day. Dean put forward a clear picture of American thinking on the subject and ultimately left no doubt in anyone's mind over the absence of any real alternatives to entry to the EEC. Emphasising the fact that there was no real support within the American Administration for any alternative solutions (for example institutional arrangements linking Britain with North America) Dean stated that 'A senior member of the White House staff put it to us frankly, if not brutally, the other day, that the value to the United States of the British relationship and with it our influence would largely disappear if we were to become the 51st State.'[49]

One need only contrast George Ball's suggestion to 'realise their potential vis-à-vis the United States' with Dean's cautionary warning that their 'influence would largely disappear if we were to become the 51st State'. If Ball's words were the carrot, then no doubt Dean's were the stick, which would both serve the same goal namely to push Britain further in the direction of Europe:

> The thought of our acquiring the status of a 51st state is as repugnant to them as they assume it to be to us. They seem to think, however paradoxically, that our influence over their own policies, which they see as a good thing, would be diminished rather than enhanced if we become too firmly linked to their chariot... The continuing value of our relationship to them will depend largely on the degree to which we can act as a force for stability, reason and responsibility, within the region in which our power is centred – Western Europe.[50]

FOUR

HOW TO GET INTO THE COMMON MARKET

—

Europe played a prominent part in the election campaign in 1966. Wilson's stance during the election was that Britain would make another application only if there was a good chance of succeeding – and his Bristol speech on 18 March 1966 epitomised these feelings. Although the question of Europe and the possibility of another application were a dominant theme in the election campaign, they had little impact on the election result. The British public, concentrating almost solely on the economic issues and the personality of Harold Wilson, spent little time assessing Britain's European policy. The polls had predicted an overall majority of 120 for the Labour Party and this turned out to be only marginally inaccurate. Wilson in fact won a majority of 97 seats. Labour had 363 seats, the Conservatives 253, the Liberals 12, and Republican Labour one seat.

Wilson was now in a position to implement bolder and more daring initiatives without the constant fear of defeat that had loomed large on the horizon in his 1964–6 term of office, when his majority was just five. With the obvious change in the tone and mood of the government after the election came a tangible change in the direction of Britain's European policy. There was little doubt about what Britain would attempt to do now. With the cabinet, albeit with some exceptions, the Foreign Office, the CBI, and most of the press all pointing towards entry, the question had been transformed from 'whether?' to 'how?'

I

On 5 May 1966, the foreign secretary, George Brown, gave a speech in Stockholm on European problems in a world context. Commencing with a line penned by the historian H. A. L. Fisher thirty years before, that 'ever since the first century of our era, the dream of unity – that is European Unity – has hovered over the scene and haunted the imagination of statesmen and peoples',[1] Brown went on to state that 'it would be quite wrong to suppose that our responsibilities which go beyond Europe in any way diminish our interest in and preoccupation with European affairs'.[2] Eager to convey the newly elected government's position on the issue, he categorically stated that he wanted to 'make it quite clear that Britain stands ready to enter the EEC provided that our essential interests are safeguarded. The political will to join the community exists in Britain today. There is no doubt about that at all.'[3] Brown concluded that: 'the attitude of the British people and of the British government towards membership of the EEC is only half the story. The other half is the will of the member countries of the EEC.'[4] Having said that, he did acknowledge that the process would take some time and reiterated what Harold Wilson had said: 'there is a lot more probing, a lot more exchanges before anyone can start rushing fences'.[5] Again, we see the vital presence of George Brown, constantly adopting a persistent but at the same time pragmatic stance.

Those close to Wilson were also fearful of losing momentum on the issue. After the election, Oliver Wright was succeeded as private secretary by Michael Palliser. Upon meeting Wilson, Palliser was frank about his view on Europe, stating 'I am pro-European',[6] to which Wilson quickly responded, 'We shall not have any problems over Europe'.[7] Labour's second term of office was inaugurated with another series of ambiguous statements by the French: 'At the WEU meeting on 17 March, the French Under Secretary for Foreign Affairs Monsieur de Broglie said that France had often stressed the desirability of resuming negotiations with Britain on the basis of the Treaty of Rome',[8] This optimistic note was then dashed by the Quai d'Orsay, which made it clear that 'Monsieur De Broglie had gone further than he had intended, and that in fact, there had been no change in the French position'.[9] Again, the familiar pattern was established, where a welcome encouraging statement was made, only to be knocked down soon after.

Commenting on *The Whitehall History of the Brussels Negotiations*, an FO publication documenting Britain's EEC negotiations, Norman Statham pointed out that 'the history reminds us that throughout the negotiations we were never able to fathom what General de Gaulle's true position was. Our situation now is no different'.[10] Furthermore, Statham supported moves to gain a clearer description of the French government's position vis-à-vis British entry, but again the same conclusion was voiced, that ultimately 'we are not likely to get much change out of the French'.[11]

Eric Roll firmly believed that 'The General can be outflanked'.[12] Thomas Balogh was concerned that Roll was ill advising Brown 'in the sense that France could be made to accept us irrespective of what our policy is'. When it came to dealing with de Gaulle, Balogh advised Wilson that such a position was 'completely misguided and such a view might well put us in a position of repeating our mistakes of 1963'.[13]

Brown wrote to the prime minister on 16 May, and urged that they accept the Treaty of Rome and then deal with the specific arrangements and regulations, for it was from those that the obstacles emanated: 'Hence I believe that we could make clear our acceptance of the Treaty of Rome at an early stage without prejudicing our important interests',[14] and concluded that 'I well understand the political complications of this course'.[15] Indeed it was the political implications that worried the prime minister, and it is therefore not surprising that he maintained his prudent stance when it came to accepting the Treaty of Rome:

> Until we have a considered recommendation of this sort before us, I should continue to be reluctant to invite the political controversy that would undoubtedly be aroused if we gave any public indication that we were prepared formally to accept the Treaty.[16]

On 20 May 1966, the German Chancellor Ludwig Erhard gave an informal briefing to some British correspondents in Bonn, referring in particular to relations between Britain and the EEC. In a letter to John Snellgrove, of the European Economic Organisation Department (1963–6), John Galsworthy (counsellor in the embassy in Bonn, responsible for economic affairs including the EEC) reported on the briefing and began by noting that 'The Chancellor said the sooner Britain could be brought into the Common Market the better. The question was not now "if" but "when and how".'[17] Furthermore, it was reported that Chancellor Erhard said that 'The Foreign Secretary's speech in Stockholm had increased his optimism, and assured the correspondents that there was no lack of will (on the Chancellor's part) to do everything possible to enable Britain to join.'[18] Germany was one issue, but France was another.

On 25 May, Patrick Reilly in a telegram to the Foreign Office, referred to de Gaulle's remarks in his presidential campaign, where he categorised 'Britain's involvement in Rhodesia, Aden, and Malaysia being stumbling blocks to Britain's entry into Europe'.[19] These were not the only stumbling blocks according to American observers. In an article in the *Herald Tribune* Ronald Koven stressed that the French president had not altered his fundamental hostility to Britain's entry. Michel Debré, the minister of economics (1966–8), was concerned about Britain's 'privileged links' with the USA and the Commonwealth and the pound's special position as a reserve currency. Koven maintained that 'The French feel Britain has to rid itself of its extra-European commitments before it can join the six nations.'[20]

For most avid observers of the situation it was becoming increasingly clear that while the French climate was apparently warming to the idea of British entry, the general consensus remained that there was very little chance of de

Gaulle admitting Britain into the Common Market for much the same political reasons as in 1963. Having spent a weekend in Belgium with Paul-Henri Spaak and a small group of Eurocrats in May 1966, Michael Palliser was able to verify this. Writing personally to Wilson, he summarised his impression:

> It was agreed by everyone, including the two Frenchmen, that General de Gaulle has no intention of allowing Britain to join the EEC, for the same political reasons as before; but that informed opinion in France is now much more favourable to our entry than in the past, seeing it as a necessary counter-weight to German influence.[21]

To which Wilson noted in the margins 'This is most useful'. [22]

II

As the visit of the French prime minister and foreign minister approached, Michael Stewart sent a minute to the prime minister in which he outlined the French attitude to British membership of the EEC. Stewart also noted that he had received a letter from Patrick Reilly in which he set out what he thought to be the French preconditions. These included: an acceptance of the Treaty of Rome; an acceptance of the Common Agricultural Policy; and an improvement in Britain's economic situation and balance of payments.

Having read the foreign secretary's minute of 21 June 1966, Brown, who would soon take over, commented to the prime minister that 'As far as the French are concerned they are in a very strong blocking position, both vis-à-vis us, and vis-à-vis the Five'.[23] He then went on to mention that the political obstacle that obstructed Britain's road into Europe (the alliance with America) was 'still as powerful as it always was'.[24] Brown was quite candid in relation to his concerns over co-operating with the French, and pointed out that it was not only in the political sphere that the French could employ reasons to block Britain's entry. The economic and financial problems that beset Britain were also a ripe target for de Gaulle to hone in on, as Brown warned Wilson 'they can shift the argument from one to the other as seems tactically opportune, and according to whom they talk'.[25] More than that, Brown warned against the danger of becoming 'suppliants' once again:

> Even if we succeeded in getting a discussion going, either with them or with all the Six, this would put them in the strongest possible position for protracting the examination of our 'Minimum Requirements'; and they would still be as they were in the last negotiations, on a 'double option': if they want us in they can press for the toughest possible terms, if they don't want us in, they can always break on political grounds.[26]

It is in this respect that he strongly advised the prime minister against taking the economic route and instead urged him to concentrate on the political field, to attempt to get the Germans onside and support a more Atlanticist Europe. Upon reading Brown's minute, it emerged that the prime minister was not interested in narrowing down tactical options and he dismissed Brown's political approach of 'outflanking the general'.

Speaking in June 1966 on the television programme *Britain in Search of a Continent*, Brown had been adamant that the whole process should be consistently pushed forward: 'I think it's up to us to carry the process forward and not allow ourselves to be paralysed by one veto'.[27] Brown also emphasised the economic factors behind Britain's decision to seek entry. Denying that it was ever 50–50 in terms of the balance between economics and politics, he categorically stated that 'I certainly think that the whole development of the world since then makes the economic argument very much stronger, very much stronger indeed than 50–50.'[28] Those willing to persuade Britons of the merits of joining the EEC have always found it easier to disguise politics in an economic cloak when it comes to the question of Britain and Europe. Regardless of how strong the political reasons might be for or against joining the European projects, it was invariably believed more palatable for the British to have them presented in economic terms. Brown's statements on the primacy of economics were clearly directed at the British public. By contrast, his firm belief in the political argument is advocated much more strongly in his memoirs.

During that debate on television, Brown and Heath disputed Britain's bargaining position. Brown claimed 'we are not going in from weakness. We have considerations, interests, concerns, that must be taken care of, and we must be ready to stand up and argue for those, negotiate for those'.[29] Heath's concluding comment was that Brown was effectively deluding himself:

> We have an adverse balance of payments, we have pressure on the pound, we have constant problems with the pound, we have a thousand millions of additional indebtedness. This is a far worse position than when I was negotiating. It is not facing up to the facts to say that the situation at the moment isn't a weak one internationally, and everybody in Europe knows.[30]

For all the debates on television programmes in Britain, the main obstacle to Britain's application was the reaction of France. Michel Gabrysiak in the *Sunday Times* wrote that there was considerable support in France for Britain joining the Six, and he maintained that 'Monsieur Pompidou will, I am told on the highest authority here, urge that bilateral talks should take place between France and Britain to precede any new formal negotiations by the

UK to join the Common Market'.[31] Brown, however, still remained adamant about the perils of pursuing bilateral talks with the French, but conceded that in order to keep things moving, risks must be taken, adding 'If Pompidou and Couve in the course of their visit next week give us any hint of a desire to talk, and if, *a fortiori*, there is an actual invitation, we should respond positively.'[32] Before the Pompidou meeting, Patrick Reilly sent a telegram to the FO, in which he pointed out that while de Gaulle considered British entry inevitable, he was in no hurry to see it materialise:

> The General almost certainly wishes to extract for it a political price, in terms of severance of British ties with the United States and of nuclear co-operation in the defence field, which her Majesty's Government could not pay without a major reversal in their foreign policy.[33]

Oliver Kemp, who was stationed in Luxembourg, was keen to point out the dynamics at play amongst the Six: 'Whereas the other five think of political union in terms of genuine collaboration on an equal basis between Western European countries, the French are obsessed with the political dominance of France.'[34]

Commenting on the forthcoming visit of Pompidou and Couve de Murville, a Foreign Office Guidance Telegram stated:

> In several respects the visit is bound to be something less than a love feast. Over the past year General de Gaulle has withdrawn France progressively from the work of the North Atlantic Treaty Organisation and his determination to rid France of every form of United States 'domination' (except of course the ultimate reassurance of the continued American nuclear umbrella) has become more pronounced...[35]

The conversations that took place with Couve and Georges Pompidou, the French prime minister, on 4 July 1966, threw further light on the French attitude. According to Terence Prittie, one of the British correspondents, 'Couve came out with all sorts of complaints and accusations'.[36] Consequently, he reported Couve as saying that 'Everybody is against the French and we get blamed for everything that goes wrong'.[37] In this mood, it was not considered likely that there would be any friendly gestures emanating from the French side of the channel in the near future. Eric Roll who was present at the meetings in July later recalled:

> The British had in front of them this huge pile of documents whereas the French in contrast had not a single piece. From this it was obvious to me that de Gaulle

and Pompidou were not going to change the French position. I remember vividly thinking that this is not going to work.[38]

On 8 July 1966, Pompidou met with the Harold Wilson at the French Embassy in London. Also among those present on the British side were Brown, Stewart, Thomson, Reilly and Palliser. One of the crucial questions that Wilson raised concerned the failure of the previous negotiations in 1963. The record of this conversation went as follows:

> It was generally felt in Britain that our relations with the Commonwealth and our close association with the United States had been in part the cause of that failure, because, for at least one of our negotiating partners, they had resulted in our being regarded as insufficiently 'good Europeans'. Did the French attitude to Britain (and he was not referring to the attitude of the Six as a whole) remain the same as at that time?[39]

Stressing that they did not want any eventual negotiations to end in a repeat of the 1961–3 ones, Wilson wanted to know if there remained any French 'arrières-pensées', when it came to the question of Britain being sufficiently a 'good European'. Furthermore, he wanted to establish:

> Whether, if we remained close to the United States and to base our defence on NATO, this was to be considered a bar to our entry. In short did the French regard membership of the Common Market as we did, namely as an economic enterprise, though clearly with certain longer-term political implications? At the end of the day, would we have to choose between the United States and Europe?[40]

Pompidou answered this frank question and began by stating that:

> He feared that he must be rather naïve, since this question was one that he always found difficult to understand. Britain was a European country and he failed to see why Britain, or indeed any other European nation, should feel that they were confronted with a choice between Europe and the United States. It was as if one asked a country on the American Continent to make a choice between America and Europe.[41]

Pompidou's response was an echo of Brown's consideration – Britain is already 'in Europe'. In response to this Wilson agreed that Britain was indeed geographically a European power, but at the same time she had specific roles and responsibilities outside Europe and wondered if these roles and close relations with the United States would hinder relations with Europe. Brown supported Wilson's line of questioning and asked whether there was a need to abandon such connections. Pompidou at this stage declared that he could not understand why the links with America were such a big factor in the equation.

Intent on gaining further insight from the French, Wilson then reverted to the Nassau Agreement and asked whether there had been a causal relationship between it and the breakdown in the Common Market negotiations. To which Couve de Murville retorted that it was a coincidental as opposed to a causal relationship. Discussing the existing British foreign policy, Douglas Hurd, who was a British diplomat stationed in Italy at the time reported that Wilson and Brown felt that 'if we entered a negotiation to join the EEC, the French would still at some point adduce as an argument against our entry that Britain was too outward looking – outward looking towards the Commonwealth and towards the United States',[42] and stressed that 'the basic issue was whether we should at the end of a further negotiation be told that because of our foreign policy we were back in a Rambouillet/Nassau situation'.[43]

Pompidou and Couve maintained that this would not be the case. Evidently de Gaulle clearly disapproved of Britain's 'outward-looking' foreign policy; his ministers were not allowed to disclose such personal reservations. However, Wilson still felt that progress had indeed been made as a result of the talks, and commented how 'Monsieur Pompidou left our shores in an atmosphere of goodwill'.[44] Wilson's account is all the more intriguing when one looks at Michael Palliser's reflections on both the dynamics between men and the meetings. 'Wilson's relationship with Pompidou was not a happy one. A bit cavalier – a jumped up politician, was how Wilson saw Pompidou. It was clearly a misjudgement.'[45] The relationship was also further soured when at one stage Wilson had arranged to hold a dinner in Pompidou's honour, and arrived not only extremely late owing to a debate in the House of Commons, but also 'extremely scruffy',[46] according to Michael Palliser. Palliser also remembers sitting behind Wilson at the meeting in July:

> In political terms it was a significant disaster. Pompidou had a pretty poor view of the British Labour government. Wormser, Baucher, Brumer, George Brown and Wilson were present. The French at that time were doing very well. Sitting behind Wilson I could feel the mood of self-satisfaction coming from the French side. At long last they were gloating at us, and that day it was palpable.[47]

Palliser went so far as to contend that the dynamics of the personal relationship would always have hindered the outcome:

> Pompidou and Wilson were not on good terms at all. Although Pompidou and France could and should no longer veto British membership and let us in, I am not

at all sure it would have worked. Pompidou did not trust Wilson, and therefore I am not at all sure we would have succeeded under Wilson. Personal relations do play an extremely important part in history, and the genuine respect for Heath and relations there played a significant part in the French decision to let us in.[48]

Another critic of Wilson's handling of the talks with Pompidou was Eric Roll. He maintains that:

Harold Wilson was indeed an extremely intellectually clever man; however, his intellectual apparatus was not adequate for economic negotiations. Wilson was too narrowly based, and in the talks was to come up against Pompidou – and here Wilson was definitely inadequate. You had a man like Pompidou with a grand vision and then you had Wilson with his narrow view.[49]

III

From the British Embassy in Rome, Douglas Hurd wrote to Anthony Snellgrove, the assistant in European Economic Organisations Department, about Britain's entry into the EEC. It was noted in Italian circles that:

The prime minister continued to say that the EEC was essentially an economic organisation, although they understood the reasons for this emphasis and although European political union was obviously a long way off, nevertheless Signor Fanfani and his colleagues as we knew, were anxious that the political side should not be forgotten.[50]

On 18 August, Con O'Neill wrote to the Foreign Secretary George Brown and enclosed a Foreign Office paper entitled 'How to get into the Common Market', a paper which went right to the heart of the matters at hand. Discussing the prospects of getting into the Community, the paper maintained that 'The French attitude is the basic obstacle', and stated that 'the conclusion is that *at present* the French attitude is an absolute bar and that we could only get in now by changing it'.[51] Having posed the question of whether they could bring about a change in the French attitude, the paper concluded that in this regard '[w]e shall have to rely on time and circumstances which are the most effective agents of change'.[52] Clearly the French obstacle was the key, the pivot on which the whole enterprise would succeed or fail.

George Brown's private secretary, Nicolas Fenn, deciphered his scrawl beside these comments: 'This is jolly negative. What nonsense – otherwise why are we here?'[53] In a letter to Con O'Neill, Nicholas Fenn pointed out that: 'The

Secretary of State found this paper disturbingly negative and in particular defeatist about the French attitude',[54] and asked that Con O'Neill and the office study Brown's marginal comments. Eric Roll remembered this period vividly, recounting that 'on the British side, there was a lot of heart-searching – whether to keep going or not'.[55] Again there was a fracture between political and diplomatic analyses, with Brown and Wilson maintaining a far more optimistic stance than the more pragmatic officials in the Foreign Office.

Increasingly, there were many in the Foreign Office who doubted a successful outcome. As Jeremy Thomas later pointed out: 'My own opinion was that the old man did not want us in his club, but for all sorts of reasons we needed to work with France; and he would not be around forever. "Can you be sure of that?" asked the more suspicious of my colleagues.'[56] Ultimately, it was felt that the only possible way to buy French acquiescence would be to weaken links with America and its policies over Vietnam, NATO and nuclear energy, but it was acknowledged that 'to do so would, however, be fundamentally opposed to Her Majesty's Government's present policy', and furthermore:

> It would also involve a revolution in our view of the Common Market itself, which we see at present as part of the Atlantic complex, designed to strengthen that complex, and not as something separate from or opposed to it. A revolution would also be involved in our relationship not only with the United States but also with Canada, Australia and New Zealand.[57]

And so the core problems of distinct visions of the Common Market, distinct visions of a place in the world and distinct visions of American influence remained unsolved.

Thomas Balogh was particularly critical of 'The brief on the EEC', a paper for the forthcoming prime ministers' Commonwealth Conference. He claimed:

> Paragraph six tries to fudge the consequences of our joining the EEC because of the obvious impossibility of squaring the circle, that is protecting the Commonwealth interests and getting into Europe on terms acceptable even to the five, let alone the Six.[58]

Furthermore, Balogh concluded that:

> The brief seems to me a changeless repetition of the posture of the Conservative Government, which you so effectively and devastatingly criticised and I wonder whether it is a posture which is really compatible with our policy.[59]

In another Foreign Office paper on the American attitude to British membership, Patrick Hancock noted: 'It is perhaps worth mentioning that the case in which we would really need American support (but as things stand, could not rely on getting it) would be if Her Majesty's Government took a firm decision not to join the Common Market.'[60]

Anniversary celebrations commemorating the Battle of Hastings on 10 September 1966 were the occasion for more ambiguity and debate over France's real stance concerning British entry. According to the *Financial Times*, Jean-Paul Palewski, the president of the finance committee of the French National Assembly, gave a speech to a meeting of French and British Parliamentarians in Caen that represented 'at least a very powerful strand of opinion at the top of the French political machine'.[61] Palewski was adamant that Britain would not be able to join the EEC in the near future, owing to the lack of a European spirit and Britain's economic difficulties.

Patrick Reilly sent a telegram to the Foreign Office, and was keen to point out that the *Financial Times* classification of the speech as a 'chilling rebuff' was in fact starkly negative. Instead, he felt that the speech was indicative of a more general 'puzzlement' concerning Her Majesty's Government's position with regard to the question of accession. In conclusion, Reilly added that 'he did not think that Palewski's statement need be regarded as indicating a hardening of the French position against British entry'.[62] However, a covering note by Wilson is perhaps closer to the point, when it states: 'this perhaps slightly misses the point. France's line remains constant – and hard'.[63] This is significant, for at the highest level the French attitude was beginning to be fully understood, if not at all times sufficiently recognised.

Towards the end of September, attention shifted again towards Britain's economic circumstances. On the 18 September 1966, Michel Debré wrote an article for the *Sunday Times* in which he outlined France's view on the future of sterling. Commenting on the balance of payments between France and the sterling area since 1963, he was quick to point out that 'during the last three years, we have bought from the United Kingdom $250 million worth of goods more than we sold. I wish that Britain had such a favourable balance with all her trading partners. Year after year, our balance of payments is in deficit with the sterling area.'[64]

'The entry of the Seven into the Common Market is through the stability of the Pound', was the headline of an article by Gilles Gozard of the Gaullist Paper *La Nation* penned on 30 September. The main thrust of the article was to point out the obstacles impeding the entry of the EFTA countries. Readers were left in no doubt as to the largest of these – the present monetary position of the United Kingdom – stating that the countries seeking admission to the EEC must first prove they were in a healthy position. Gozard contended that:

> It would be madness to bring into the Common Market a country whose currency is perpetually in trouble and whose economy seems totally unadapted to modern conditions of production and competition. Unfortunately that seems to be the present situation of Great Britain.[65]

These statements were indicative of the French attitude towards Britain's economic problems, with the French calling for Britain to develop the pound as a fundamental prerequisite for entry into the EEC. What Brown had predicted had begun to materialise: Britain's economic weaknesses were now under the microscope, being directed as yet another reason to block its entry. Furthermore, the article was distinctly critical of both Labour and the Conservatives when it came to the question of Europe. Discussing the British requirements and conditions, it asked:

> Would it not, therefore, be better for London to say honestly and frankly that political leaders, in contra-distinction to the majority of industrialists and no doubt to a great part of the British people, do not wish their country to enter the Common Market, since the conditions which they lay down are incompatible with the structure of the EEC and even more incompatible with the organisation of the Agricultural Common Market?[66]

On 8 October 1966, at the banquet of the National Conference of Editorial Writers held in New York, Brown reiterated the British position:

> I do not believe that the French or General de Gaulle are exercising a veto. It is our business to go on discussing with them and with all the other members of the EEC the possibilities of entering, the complications that it raises for them, and for us, in order to get the earliest arrangement that will protect our essential interests and make it possible for us to join.[67]

Brown's statement emphasises his determination and resolve to find a way to join the Common Market. The question Wilson, Brown and officials in the Foreign Office were desperately trying to answer was how to get into the Common Market. It was widely acknowledged that it would indeed be folly to sit back and lose momentum. Yet, at the same time, it was also recognised that the French obstacle had not disappeared. Their answer was to continue exploring French attitudes, in an attempt to find a way of surmounting the obstacles.

As Con O'Neill advised the private secretary on 26 September 1966: 'the less we ask for – which means the more we are content that our problems should be met by transitional periods – the harder it will be for the French effectively to restrain a British application for membership.'[68]

FIVE

BY LITTLE STEPS TOWARDS THE CONTINENT

—

Europe was increasingly becoming a key issue in British politics and Wilson recognised this. He had taken George Brown's advice and decided to call a meeting at Chequers late in October 1966 to discuss the progress being made in relation to Britain's entry into the EEC. It would be the first meeting of ministers to discuss the topic since the election. On 14 October 1966, the *Financial Times* reported that 'the present view of ministers closely concerned with policy towards the Common Market is that there could be a possibility of formal negotiations starting by 1968'.[1]

Before the meeting took place, an assessment of the mood on the continent was of paramount importance. Officials needed to have a greater understanding of the mood and to examine ways of circumventing a possible French veto. Oliver Wright, who was the British ambassador in Copenhagen, wrote to Michael Palliser that 'one has to wait for the General to be called to his fathers before there is much chance of real progress on the Common Market front. And, of course, that is an event which is bound to happen one day.'[2]

While Brown dismissed the prospect of a veto, Wright maintained it had not yet been lifted – the political and diplomatic classes again adopted different views. Concerned with how the Europeans would view the results of the Chequers meeting, James Marjoribanks wrote to the Foreign Office from Brussels. Commenting on the growing discouragement amongst Britain's allies in Europe owing to its inability to discuss details, Marjoribanks said:

> I fear that if we are not able to enter into more detail after the Chequers meeting and into discussion of solutions to our problems, it will be widely concluded that we are in fact undecided about our readiness to enter the Community, and those who have maintained interest so far will tend increasingly to accept that our membership is a lost cause.[3]

I

Oliver Wright had pointed towards an alternative means to outmanoeuvre de Gaulle. Recognising that recent developments in the financial field had added further weight to the French veto, he maintained that the only thing that would cause the French to think again would concern the political giant at the centre of Europe – Germany and 'a growing belief that France on its own might not be able to contain it'.[4] In contrast to their views on the financial aspects, George Brown and Oliver Wright were in agreement on the need to focus on the German card. Pointing out the fact that 'stagnation is decline', Wright concluded that 'It is the German card that is the most promising one to play if there is to be any hope of causing the necessary shift in French opinion and if we are to maintain any momentum on the Market front.'[5] Palliser was entirely in agreement with Wright's assessment of the prospect of de Gaulle allowing a British entry into the EEC, and contended that 'we probably ought to spend the intervening period in making life thoroughly difficult for the General, by explaining to all and sundry how thoroughly willing we are to go in and thereby forcing de Gaulle to find much more explicit reasons than hitherto for keeping us out'.[6] Frank Roberts sent a telegram from Bonn to the Foreign Office and he maintained: 'As long as de Gaulle is there, the door is almost certainly barred; but most thinking Frenchmen, including Gaullists whether of the Pompidou or Debré variety, want us in as a counterpoise to Germany.'[7] Discussing the German attitude to British entry in more detail, Roberts reported that:

> Despite their polite assurances that they understand our difficulties and their genuine wish not to embarrass us, there is plenty of evidence of increasing doubt among Germans who count about whether we really have 'the political will to join' on the right terms and whether it really is a question of 'when and how' rather than of 'whether'.[8]

Acknowledging that these doubts were of course being fuelled further by the French, Roberts was keen to stress the need for more concrete action. In conclusion he stated:

> I strongly agree with Sir James Marjoribanks' conclusion. The announcement of the Chequers talks has aroused considerable interest in informed circles here, and if we are not thereafter in a position to express willingness to engage in joint study with the Germans and our other European friends of the technical problems involved, it will, I fear, be virtually impossible to sustain German faith in the seriousness of our intentions on this issue.[9]

Speed was now the order of the day. It was not enough to knock politely on de Gaulle's door, rather what was now needed was to persuade those around him to help the British. Nevertheless, a poll conducted simultaneously for a Gallup international enquiry and the *Daily Telegraph* revealed some encouraging signs. According to the leaders of industry, commerce and provisional and administrative affairs in five of the six EEC countries, 'the Germans were the most enthusiastic about British entry into the European Economic Community',[10] with 98 per cent in favour. A nationwide Gallup poll undertaken for the *Daily Telegraph* the previous week had shown that 68 per cent would approve if the government decided to join the European Common Market, leading to the conclusion that 'Both in Britain and on the Continent, every section of influential European opinion is favourably disposed to it'.[11]

II

Two days before this poll was taken, and seven months after the general election, Wilson and his cabinet met at Chequers for their first in-depth discussion on Europe. The morning session was attended by both cabinet ministers and senior civil servants, while the ministers met again in the afternoon in the absence of officials. Much attention was focused on Chequers, as the *Financial Times* reported that 'the meeting could clearly have great significance in shaping future Government policy'.[12] In addition, with Wilson having almost certainly made up his own mind, it was now opportune for the cabinet to make its move. Wilson recognised, however, the need to tread carefully as the cabinet was divided. According to the historian Clive Ponting:

> Nine spoke in favour of EEC entry – Brown, Jenkins, Crosland, Gardiner, Longford, Houghton, Gordon-Walker, Hughes and Benn – while eight expressed opposition – Healey, Peart, Bowden, Marsh, Ross, Castle, Jay and Greenwood. Callaghan was uncommitted and Crossman's attitude was that, although opposed, he would go along with an attempt to enter because 'the General will save us from our own folly'.[13]

This was an attitude echoed by many others who questioned the value of wasting time and energy opposing something that had little chance of materialising in the first place. Denis Healey conveyed this sense of resigned passivity by stating 'We talked absolute tripe about a change in attitude'.[14] There had certainly been no change of attitude on de Gaulle's part. Wary of opposition and scepticism, Wilson was careful not to advocate entry, but instead wanted to encourage further examination of the idea and, if possible, to foster a desire to join. Yet this is where Douglas Jay maintains 'the fatal slide began'.[15] Instead of declaring outright support for an application, Wilson stood back. Michael Palliser claimed that Wilson was 'constantly worried about plots and people undermining his position and was indeed very conspiracy conscious throughout the period I knew him. Wilson was also a Walter Mitty character, and as a result did not know how to handle certain situations'.[16] Yet Robin O'Neill maintains that Wilson's reluctance to declare his intentions was more complex than that and that indeed it was part and parcel of his overall strategy:

> It was typical of Wilsonian policy in general to take time over it, to let others talk themselves into the decision he wanted to adopt. I saw this in the 1970s – with renegotiations. It was clear from the outset that Wilson wanted to stay in the EEC, therefore what he did was let them talk themselves into the ground.[17]

Robin O'Neill added that Wilson:

> presented himself as having a very open mind, in the whole way he handled the issue with the party, the narrowing down of conditions, turning them into things you could achieve. Wilson was a patient man, who absolutely dominated his government. Small creatures (the cabinet) were observed by a stoat (Wilson), apart from Benn that is.[18]

Wilson proposed that he and Brown should embark on a 'tour of the capitals' in order to assess the mood on the continent. The implication was obvious by the end of the meeting at Chequers. While not officially declaring that he wanted to make an application to join the EEC, his colleagues were left in no doubt whatsoever as to where official policy was now moving. Tony Benn, reflecting on the meeting in his diaries, noted:

> We agreed that Harold Wilson and George Brown would visit the six countries of the Common Market to do a 'probe'. Harold was not prepared to let George go alone because he didn't trust George and he thought that George didn't trust him. I came to the conclusion that Britain would be in the Common Market by 1970.[19]

Summarising the outcome of the meeting at Chequers, Burke Trend, the cabinet secretary wrote to the prime minister on 28 October 1966 about the possibility of continuing as they had done in the past (that is, neither trying to approach more nearly to the EEC nor appearing to retreat from it).[20] However, this option was rejected by the majority of those present, for fear of reducing the country 'in political terms, to an international ranking which not many people would willingly accept'.[21] As a result of this, Burke felt that the recent 'probings' in the European capitals had created a general expectation about British intentions which they would either carry forward and develop or allow to fall away once more. It is in this light that a substantial amount of time was dedicated to examining the timescale of the whole exercise and the detail of the difficulties to be overcome, with Trend emphasising that 'There is a great deal here to be thought about'.[22] Yet it was not further thought that was required at that stage, but decisions and actions as had been urged by Marjoribanks and others before the Chequers meeting.

Palliser, reflecting on the meeting, recalled how 'Wilson came down to breakfast with *The Economist* whose main leader was on the technology required for Britain. He then went on to discuss this further and distributed a copy for every Minister at the meeting. Wilson took it as his text, like a preacher for the meeting.'[23] Wilson was now thoroughly convinced of the potential benefits of membership and had begun to link different aspects together in his mind. Michael Palliser remembered how firmly committed Wilson now was to the European option:

> I was waiting outside for coffee, and George Brown told me that Wilson had had an extraordinary idea. Wilson wanted to go to the capitals with George Brown. Until that moment we did not cotton on to Wilson's conviction, his realisation of the importance of Europe. It struck George Brown as unlikely that someone as abstract as Wilson could be a good European.[24]

Palliser regarded this as vital:

> Now Wilson was prepared to identify himself publicly in six countries with Britain's desire to enter the EEC. It was a fairly shrewd move, to visit the capitals, it was entirely Wilson's idea, it was an interesting idea, typical of him – in politics you are active, you do something.[25]

III

After Chequers, the cabinet again discussed Europe on 2 November 1966. A cabinet memorandum issued by Brown on 2 November set out three ideas under discussion in order to accompany the necessary probing. These included:

1. A meeting of EFTA Heads of Government. This was an idea put forward for the first time in cabinet on 1 November
2. Early visits to the capitals of the Six by the prime minister and foreign secretary. This was an idea that was put forward at the Chequers meeting on 22 October.

3. A declaration that Her Majesty's government were prepared to accept the Treaty of Rome, subject to receiving satisfaction on the points on which we saw difficulty.[26]

The following day the cabinet conclusion stressed that, 'with so many uncertainties it was imperative that the Government's freedom of choice must be preserved, both as to whether we were to join the Community, and when we were to do so, until the necessary information was available'.[27] We know that Wilson was decided, but it then became a matter of allowing his troops to follow him voluntarily.

To discuss the visits to be made to the capitals of the EEC by the prime minister and the foreign secretary, a cabinet memorandum by Brown was circulated on 7 November 1966. Seen as a continuation of the probing which had begun in the summer, the memorandum included the hope that the visits:

> Would be seeking on the one hand to explain the principal difficulties we see in accepting Community Policies as they stand and on the other hand to obtain a clear indication of how far each of the Six would be prepared to go in meeting us on those difficulties.[28]

With regard to the political questions it was felt that:

> These are more likely to arise in the discussion with the French Government than in the discussions with the Five. French Ministers (though not General de Gaulle) have said that there is no political veto. Nevertheless General de Gaulle might well raise the question of our close involvement with the United States. If he does, we can only stand firm. Some common ground may be found with him over the question of supranationality.[29]

Writing to President Johnson on 11 November 1966, Wilson was keen to put forward his own view and convey his determination to enter the EEC:

> As you know, I have never been one of the little band of so-called 'Europeans'. I believe that the way our predecessors set about things five years ago was the wrong way, the failure of their attempt was inevitable; and no Government under my leadership is going to get into a similar situation.[30]

Wilson's determination to succeed where his Conservative predecessors failed, while admirable, was to a certain extent flawed from the outset. Wilson recognised that the major obstacle had not been removed or indeed altered; at the same time he exhibited an innate confidence in his own diplomatic ability to change the outcome. This confidence left the Labour administration exposed to the very dangers which had undone Macmillan and his colleagues.

Britain's ties to America, its precarious economic situation, and its agricultural requirements, were just some of the items highlighted by the French in order to show to the British the remaining problems that still obstructed its path into Europe. Wilson was acutely aware of the American dimension, categorising it as the issue:

> Which stuck in de Gaulle's gullet last time. The prophets of doom say that this remains as total an obstacle to our present approach as it proved for our predecessors. We shall see. My own belief is that the General had not changed one iota in his general view of the world or of our own relationship with yourselves.[31]

While Wilson recognised that de Gaulle had not wavered in his general view of the world or in his view of the Anglo-American relationship, he also believed that the world could not remain unchanged, and de Gaulle could not ignore this change. Responding to the prime minister, President Johnson said 'I am immensely heartened by your courageous announcement about joining the EEC. Your entry would certainly help to strengthen and unify the West. If you find on the way there is anything we might do to smooth the path, I hope you will let me know.'[32]

Writing to Patrick Hancock and Norman Statham on 16 November 1966, Con O'Neill was eager to point out the merits of continuing the negotiations begun in 1963, as opposed to launching a new application:

> If and when we decide that we want to negotiate to join the Community, we should do so not by making a fresh application but by asking to continue the negotiations 'interrupted' in 1963. I can see there might be political difficulties for the present government in doing this, but there might be practical and tactical advantages.[33]

This approach was perhaps first mooted publicly in a letter to the *Guardian* on 8 November 1966, which stated that:

> [while] the process of preparing for a formal application for membership seems likely to have started at the Cabinet meeting yesterday such an application is legally unnecessary – that of 1961 has never been withdrawn by Her Majesty's Government.[34]

In Paris, little seemed to have changed. Michel Gabtysiak in the right-wing *L'Aurore* was keen to point out that Brown's reference to 'ties with the United States may have run the risk of a new veto from General de Gaulle for the situation is the same today as after the Rambouillet Conference of 1962, even if France's European partners rally to London's point of view'.[35] *The Times* promptly pointed out the stark truth, that 'no one can accuse the General of being equivocal on this particular subject at this point in time',[36] and went on to portray a sense of 'history repeating itself'. Again, the American card was kept on the table for further scrutiny – 'In the Gaullist book no division of loyalties is tolerable. A country is either pro-American or pro-European.'[37] Vietnam, NATO, the issue of sterling, and Britain's East of Suez policy were all listed as possible contributors to this hypothesis. All of these issues did nothing to dispel the idea in French eyes of Britain as primarily an ally of America at the close of the decade.

On 21 November 1966, the prime minister and the chancellor of the exchequer held a meeting with Eugene Rostow, under-secretary for political affairs (1966–9) and a keen supporter of European integration:

> A strong Anglo-French entente as the nucleus of Europe was the best way forward, according to Mr Rostow. Harold Wilson, reflecting on this, conceded that recently the British had tended to be too anti-French and too pro-Germany. Having said that though, he stressed that this did not necessarily imply an easy route to agreement with the General.[38]

IV

In reply to a question at a debate in Paris concerning the advantages to Europe of British entry, Pompidou acknowledged, 'Great Britain is certainly close to Europe. Whether she is so in every respect is more doubtful', and went on to stress that 'the entry of Britain implies her acceptance of the rules of the Common Market'.[39] Patrick Reilly picked up on this theme, and posed the question as to whether agreeing to the Treaty of Rome and the CAP would make the general's veto all the harder to impose.[40] The need to abandon technical conditions and complicated terms was reiterated by Jean Monnet in a conversation with Reilly.[41] Monnet highlighted the desire, especially amongst younger generations of French people, to see old quarrels set aside and a strong Europe with Britain firmly involved. With regard to de Gaulle, he believed that one of the crucial mistakes made by Heath was to put faith in the leverage of technological agreements. According to Monnet, 'it was impossible to catch the general with any gimmicks, he would always evade it'.[42] Moreover, he firmly believed that de Gaulle did abhor the idea of British entry, but at the same time, if Britain presented their case in a simple straightforward fashion, there was little de Gaulle could do to prevent their accession. This is in contrast to what other officials in the Foreign Office were saying. According to one Foreign Office official, writing to Norman Statham about the French veto:

> The prevailing view of influential French Ministers and officials, and of the General himself, is that our accession now would be inconvenient. French spokesmen talk as if our entry were inevitable in due course. But they would prefer to consolidate the EEC and France's stake in it first.[43]

Yet at the same time:

> The attitude of the Five, and to some extent public feeling in France itself, together with a wish not to appear too obviously vindictive, or reactionary, will make the French hesitant to slam the door in our faces a second time without good and demonstrable reason.[44]

Writing to the permanent under-secretary, Paul Gore-Booth, on 30 November 1966, O'Neill spoke in detail about France, Britain, and the European Community before the foreign secretary was due to hold a meeting on the subject the following day. O'Neill felt that his own views were simple and had been formed in part as a result of living in Brussels. Having outlined the various objections de Gaulle and the French government had voiced ranging from Britain's links with America and the Commonwealth to its economic weakness, Con O'Neill was convinced that one must 'realise that all these reasons advanced by the French to oppose our membership of the Community are no more than pretexts'.[45] In his opinion:

> The real reason for French opposition to our membership of the Community is that they simply do not want a situation which has worked out so much to their advantage to be changed by our getting in to poach in their preserves. The Community has suited them extraordinarily well. Their partners have, so far, been docile.[46]

It was in light of this that Con O'Neill was adamant that the French could easily find further pretexts in the future if need be:

> One important tactical consideration follows from this. We should not be in too much of a hurry to meet the French on the various pretexts they have erected against our membership. If we do, they will erect others. There is much to be said for reserving any major moves we may be able to make (should they be necessary) to meet some of these pretexts for a late stage in any negotiations, when it will be too late for the French to erect other pretexts.[47]

The impression that Christopher Soames, who would replace Patrick Reilly as Britain's ambassador to France in 1968, gained as a result of his talk with Couve on 24 November 1966, was that 'although the French Government does not welcome the British Government's initiative, he feels that it is possible that it may have to succeed'. Likening it to a gamble he asserted, 'All is to play for but the stakes will be high'.[48]

Gladwyn wrote to George Thomson on 2 December 1966, and said 'I personally believe the General will probably go on vetoing till all's blue. He is resolved, I am afraid, to go right ahead on his disastrous course as soon as he has secured his majority in Parliament.'[49] The only way to overcome this gloomy prediction was to make things as difficult as possible for the general: 'The main way and the way the Government has very wisely chosen – is to come out strongly in favour of an extended EEC including Britain.'[50] With regards to gauging the Labour administration's progress with the French and de Gaulle in particular, Soames's main impression was that while there was no greater desire on behalf of the French government to see Britain enter the Common Market, Couve 'was by no means certain that they would be able to succeed in keeping us out'.[51]

On a more negative note, Patrick Reilly, commenting on his meeting with Couve on 14 December, noted that Couve 'clearly could not bring himself to say that the French Government wished to see Britain in the EEC'.[52] Yet this was not the only point on which Reilly pressed him, as Couve 'would not respond to my appeal to say what the political difficulties would be'.[53] Perhaps in the end, an outsider gave the most clear and reliable account – M. P. Harmel, the Belgian foreign minister, recounted that in recent Franco-Belgian talks in Paris 'Pompidou and Couve had shown no ill-will towards the UK but they had equally shown no good-will'.[54]

V

On the same day, George Brown met the foreign minister from the Netherlands, Joseph Luns, at the NATO building in Paris. According to the record of this meeting, Luns urged that Britain should reduce its entry requirements to a minimum: 'The less things that had to be settled before British entry the better. Once she was a member of the EEC, Britain would be in a much better position to make her views prevail.'[55] To which Brown thanked Luns for his interest and advice but mentioned that it was not really feasible to 'sign the contract and only read the fine print later'.[56]

Later in the day, George Brown met Couve de Murville at the Quai d'Orsay to discuss Britain and the EEC. Brown, was in quite a combative mood and was determined to extract some degree of certainty from the French foreign minister. This was the first time that Brown had met Couve since he had become foreign secretary, and he recalled that their last meeting had taken place in London in July. Brown began by emphasising the seriousness of their endeavour, the lengthy discussions that had taken place in the cabinet and the support that the Labour Party had in its objectives. Brown then went on to ask Couve whether the French were approaching the problem in the same manner as the British – as a very serious matter. Couve then replied that the French were indeed taking it very seriously:

> They considered it a very big problem. It was one which would be before them just so long as it remained unsolved. In January 1963 they knew that what had happened was not the end of the story and that the problem would be posed again sooner or later, though they did not know that this would happen less than four years later. The question now was how to solve this very big problem. It was impossible to say what in fact would happen.[57]

Brown urged Couve to approach the problem in a manner similar to the British. He urged them to move beyond outlining the problems towards solving the outstanding issues. Ending on a somewhat stark note, Brown stated:

> If, however, there was another failure, it would be unreasonable to think that there would be yet another chance. Another failure would be a great shock to British opinion, the consequences would be much more serious. It was highly probable that in such circumstances Britain would see other ways of arranging her affairs.[58]

This amounted to little more than a hollow threat. After all EFTA had failed in its aims, the Commonwealth was no longer an alternative source of power and prestige, and 'going it alone' had already been dismissed as a viable option. There was no real alternative and Brown knew this. While the British were demanding to know whether or not the French genuinely wanted them in Europe, the French were equally trying to ascertain the terms of entry Britain was seeking. Respective domestic considerations played a huge part here. Wilson did not wish to tie himself to any stipulations at this stage, and de Gaulle preferred to issue a faint 'perhaps' as opposed to a blunt 'yes' or 'no' before the elections in France. With each side constrained for different reasons, communication across the channel became all the more ambiguous.

On 16 December 1966, Brown met with de Gaulle in the Elysée Palace. Brown began by stressing the sincerity of Britain's desire to enter the EEC and, in particular, his own deep conviction that this should happen. Brown then contended that 'the essential point was that it was not just he himself who was now in favour of a British attempt. The cabinet and the country was behind it. We wanted to come in; did the General want us?'[59] De Gaulle responded by asking: 'under what conditions Her Majesty's Government wished to come in. That was what the French Government did not know.'[60] Discussing Britain's first application, de Gaulle said 'at that time Britain never formulated conditions which would have made its entry possible',[61] and therefore the French reply 'must be that that depended on the conditions for British entry'.[62] De Gaulle went on to add that

> British entry was not an easy matter. Britain was a maritime country . . . Britain had her Commonwealth . . . this was a fact. Britain had the sterling zone, this was also a fact. How could they accept rules which were Continental rules for Continental countries, which had nothing corresponding to the Commonwealth to speak of . . . the French did not know, they did not see, how it could be possible for Britain to come in.[63]

Brown retorted that none of Britain's various links were really an obstacle to entry into the EEC. De Gaulle then asked about British intentions and stressed that 'he was old and had lived a long time and through many different moments. In these he had always seen that Britain would be bound to the United Sates and neither could, nor would, break her links with that country.'[64] While acknowledging that Britain had indeed changed, de Gaulle concluded with a rather dismissive attitude: 'both countries had lived long without the EEC and would continue to do so even if Britain did not enter the EEC'.[65] The man who had lived through numerous changes was now trying to deter the British from embarking on a new direction in foreign policy.

Commenting on Brown's talks with de Gaulle, Patrick Reilly was quite accurate in his estimation that 'the general showed himself not exactly hostile but extremely sceptical about British entry into the EEC'.[66] Having isolated Britain as the problematic country amongst Europeans, de Gaulle made absolutely no attempt to place any faith in their ability to overcome the obstacles. Instead, as one British official put it, 'he laid down a series of road blocks, economic and political and showed little sign of either expecting or hoping that we would circumvent them'.[67] To make matters worse, Reilly maintained that there was an obvious tendency 'to enumerate difficulties at even greater length, as if the old soldier had ordered that new obstacles should be thrown up to slow the British advance'.[68]

The writing was on the wall, with de Gaulle still clearly opposed to Britain joining the EEC, even though he did not put it quite so bluntly. In response, Wilson and Brown decided to pursue their tour of the capitals of Europe, in an attempt to counter much of what de Gaulle had thrown in their way. In discussing tactics for the Wilson/de Gaulle meeting at the end of January 1967, senior officials were keen to emphasise the importance of dispelling the so-called 'de Gaulle myths' (Britain's unsuitability, the problems with sterling, the closeness of ties to the United States, and so on). As Palliser told Wilson: 'Economics are simply the handmaiden of politics, and any economic arguments that he may advance (e.g. about sterling or the CAP) will be adduced for political reasons.'[69] This point was again reiterated by Couve de Murville when answering whether there were political conditions for British entry. He maintained that 'when things are important they are always political even when they are economic'.[70]

In a letter to the prime minister on 6 January 1967, Michael Palliser was keen to emphasise the political basis underlying the whole affair. Ultimately, 'de Gaulle is concerned with power. We have to show that we care too'.[71] It was in this light that Michael Palliser appealed to the prime minister to play on 'de Gaulle's sense of history' and his 'monumental vanity' and present him with a stark choice: either to go down in history as the man who vetoed another British application and succeeded in weakening and dividing Europe, or to be hailed as the figure who made possible the creation of a dynamic European power bloc. Having read this, Harold Wilson penned a few interesting thoughts, especially with regard to America. He considered France and Britain to be more stable than the United States, 'who are more subject to Congressional pressures. The General and I can sign a treaty and carry it. Lyndon Baines Johnson can't be certain (he couldn't pull out of Vietnam if he wanted to).'[72]

Calling on 'the logic of history' Jean Monnet made direct reference to the 'inevitability' of British entry. In his talks with Lord Gladwyn, he put forward two pieces of advice. Firstly, that it was up to Wilson to prevent playing on the obstacles to entry (therefore present the case in simple terms) and secondly he advised against embarking on any secret or clandestine talks with de Gaulle, which would ultimately lead nowhere. If the British followed his advice, he was in no doubt, that at the end of the day, the Germans would rally behind British entry.[73]

There was, however, no guarantee of support from the Germans, because with rekindling of Franco-German relations observers were now talking of Bonn being 'disinclined to embark on a serious dispute with General de Gaulle over Britain should the French leader decide to reject British membership'.[74] Hopes of Britain splitting the delicate Franco-German alliance were dissipating. With individuals such as Walter Hallstein voicing suspicion about 'Britain's readiness to co-operate with the other Common Market nations',[75] it was increasingly obvious that not only did she have to persuade the French of its readiness and suitability to join Europe, but also needed to pay attention to the so-called 'friendly Five'.

Patrick Dean emphasised that 'American support for the idea of an economically and politically unified Europe to include Britain has been repeated so often over the years that it is apt to sound like a conditioned reflex'.[76] Furthermore, Dean recognised that de Gaulle was not immortal and therefore at worst the British would have to play a waiting game; 'If we must wait, we must wait, and in the meantime they hope that we should do whatever possible to keep the option open.'[77]

SIX

GO ON – HAVE A GO!

—

At the beginning of 1967 Britain moved closer to making a formal application to join the EEC. Observing French attitudes on the eve of the visit to Paris in January 1967, Patrick Reilly felt that 'It is for us to persuade the General to change his mind. There is no widespread feeling that public opinion will have much influence on him.' He continued 'Government briefing has been getting progressively more negative. We have been told by French journalists that the Quai d'Orsay spokesman has been raising every sort of difficulty.'[1] The state secretary of Federal Germany, Klaus Schultz, threw further light on de Gaulle's attitude. In talks with George Brown, Schultz recalled a phrase uttered by de Gaulle in reference to British membership: 'the French were more prudent and the Germans more inclined to take chances'.[2]

The 'tour of the capitals' commenced on 15 January 1967, and took Wilson and Brown to Rome, Paris, Brussels, Bonn, The Hague and finally to Luxembourg. Hugo Young maintained that it was:

> In many ways the acme of Wilsonian politics. It applied to Europe several of the defining traits of this remarkable leader. It put on show his fascination with tactics, his professional vanity, his impressionable mind, the grandeur of his self-confidence, his refusal to acknowledge the realities of international power. It was at times comical, at others almost calamitous. But, seen from the distance of history, it did, for all its travails and its ultimate nullity, deposit in the realm of inarguable fact the public commitment of a Labour Cabinet to British entry into the Common Market.[3]

I

It was widely recognised that Paris held the key and should be visited early on in the tour. However, in order not to appear completely at de Gaulle's mercy, they decided to visit another capital first, and Rome was chosen because the founding Treaty of Rome had been signed there ten years previously. The pattern established in Rome was followed in all the other capitals. Wilson would make a general statement and George Brown would follow this with a discussion of more specific problems such as agricultural finance and Commonwealth trade.[4] Wilson's mention of 'a technological community' in Rome was also raised in each of the other capitals, with Wilson keen to emphasise this as one of Britain's key selling points.

The next stage of the journey would be crucial – Paris. Yet before they reached Paris, Wilson's public discourse became even more pro-entry. On 22 January, Wilson delivered a speech to the Assembly of the Council of Europe. He declared:

> We mean business in a political sense because over the next year, the next ten years, the next twenty years, the unity of Europe is going to be forged, and geography and history, and interest and sentiment alike demand that we play our part in forging it and in working it.[5]

Given that this latest declaration of intent was uttered on French soil, the text of the speech had already been delivered to de Gaulle, via Patrick Reilly, as a precaution. However, in his memoirs Wilson recalls that 'on arrival at the Elysée, I found that these fears were ill founded. He began by expressing his deepest appreciation of my action in sending him a copy of the speech I had delivered; it was of the greatest interest. He did not say to what extent he agreed with it'. The talks in Paris, on 24–25 January 1967, were cautious to the point of being painstakingly frustrating for the British. To begin with there were one or two difficulties regarding the procedure. Wilson maintained:

> I had reason to know that the General wanted to meet me alone, before the wider talks. But I discovered that George Brown had sent a telegram – which he had omitted to clear with me – instructing HM Ambassador to insist that all our talks should be together, four or five of us, depending on whether both the French prime minister and the Foreign Minister were going to be present. I decided not to press the matter – but at a crucial point in the talks the General did.[6]

They met at 10.00 a.m. at the Elysée Palace – de Gaulle, Wilson, Couve and Brown with Prince Andronikov and Palliser the respective translators also present.[7] Wilson began by setting out the purposes and intentions of the British initiative. He then acknowledged the importance of bilateral collaboration between the two countries, especially with regard to technology. Wilson discussed the role of France and Britain in Europe, and in particular in building a Europe that could break down the tension between East and West. Finally, the prime minister discussed the task of the European powers:

> Europe had an even wider role to play in the world at large; but she would not be able to play unless she were powerful – and that meant economically powerful.

The task of the great European Powers – of France and of Britain – was not to be mere messenger boys between the two great Powers, They had a bigger role to play – and other nations wished them to play it – than merely waiting in the anterooms while the two great Powers settled everything direct between themselves. That was why France and Britain had to make effective their enormous potential industrial strength by giving that strength a chance to operate on a European and not a national scale, or series of national scales.[8]

In response to the prime minister's statement, General de Gaulle began by stating that he 'was particularly struck by the great difference in what both the foreign secretary in December and the prime minister that day were now saying about Europe in general and the Common Market in particular, compared with the British attitude throughout the years since he had had the honour of directing French affairs'.[9] With regard to east–west relations he agreed that the two countries had very similar approaches and then went on to discuss the independence of Europe. De Gaulle categorically stated that:

Whether or not they achieved economic unity within Western Europe, nothing could be expected to come of this unless they could achieve the complete unity of Europe and the total independence that he sought from the United States. He wished to make it clear that, Europe could only achieve something effective in the world if the European countries were completely independent themselves.[10]

Reflecting on the meeting and, in particular, on de Gaulle's demeanour throughout, Wilson noted:

As ever he (de Gaulle) was relaxed, speaking quickly, fluently, without any notes; yet the whole speech was as logical in its framework and order as if he had written down every word. This he could not have done, as he replied almost point by point to what I had said.[11]

The following morning the French cabinet had its weekly meeting and Pompidou and Couve met with Wilson and Brown in the Hotel Matignon in the afternoon, to discuss agriculture and regional problems. At 4.00 p.m. Pompidou brought the talks to a close as de Gaulle was waiting at the Elysée Palace for their final meeting. Wilson records how Pompidou 'asked me if I would drive by a somewhat less direct route than he was taking, as the President would want him to report on our meeting and then be on the steps when we arrived'.[12] The meeting commenced at 4.15 p.m. that afternoon and amongst those present were Wilson, Brown, Reilly, Trend and Con O'Neill on the British side, and de Gaulle and Hervé Alphand, French ambassador to the USA, on the French delegation. Wilson began by thanking the president for his hospitality and the time that French ministers had devoted to the discussions of the last two days. Wilson then stated that he was:

> sure that the President would have judged for himself that our new approach to the EEC was more in earnest and that, as he himself had said in the House of Commons, we meant business. He agreed that the discussions were not in the nature of negotiations, they were rather an initial approach, designed to show that we were anxious to enter the Community and that we were willing to contemplate those adjustments of policy which membership would undoubtedly entail.[13]

Again, de Gaulle succeeded in giving nothing away, treading a tight balancing act between an encouraging 'yes' and a damning 'no'. He said that he had:

> The impression of an England which now really wished to moor itself alongside the continent and was prepared in principle to pledge itself to rules in the formulation of which it had had no part, and which would involve it in definite links with the system which had grown up on the continent.[14]

At first glance, this can undoubtedly be regarded as a positive sign on behalf of de Gaulle. As Wilson noted in his diaries:

> His reference to 'mooring alongside the Continent' was important, even historic. I had in mind that when the General had abruptly ended the 1961–63 negotiations, he explained his action publicly in terms of the refusal of Britain to moor herself alongside Continental Europe and her insistence on a 'mid-Atlantic' position.[15]

De Gaulle did not intend this as acceptance of the British joining the EEC and quickly moved the goalposts. Towards the latter half of the conversation, de Gaulle raised the question of whether some other form of British participation could be established. The General pointed out that this was the question which constantly played on French minds and he urged the British to examine two alternatives. De Gaulle presented the possibility of 'something entirely new' or 'an agreement for association between Britain and the Community to cover their interests and their exchanges'.[16]

The idea of 'something entirely new' brought further confusion. To start with, Reilly asked Alphand what exactly de Gaulle had meant by this. Alphand replied that his interpretation of what the General meant, was 'an entirely fresh start *ab initio*, which would involve dismantling the European Economic Community, and making a new agreement to include Britain'.[17] It is curious, though, that de Gaulle was not pressed further on this suggestion. According to Wilson's diaries, he himself was 'at pains to make clear that there was no solution in his alternatives, "something entirely new" or "association" presumably under Article 238 of the Rome Treaty'.[18] In Wilson's eyes, 'under such arrangements the British ship would not be moored alongside the Continent, but would come and go. It would be a commuter relationship, at best, an offshore relationship'.[19] Clearly de Gaulle behaved in an obscure manner at the talks. One minute they were becoming closer to 'mooring themselves alongside the Continent', and the next they were being told to look at 'alternatives'.

De Gaulle had earlier commented on the gradual transformation that had occurred in Britain's European policy. Recounting Britain's refusal to join the negotiations at the very start, he then went on to castigate Macmillan and Heath, saying that he:

> Recalled Mr Macmillan speaking about 'economic warfare' and making clear his hope that the Common Market would fail. He also remembered Mr Heath involving the European governments in intermediate negotiations in Brussels which had inevitably produced no result.[20]

With de Gaulle referring to the 1961–3 negotiations as 'interminable', it was as if he could not believe the Britons' blindness to the futility of their actions. On the other hand it was encouraging for Wilson and Brown to hear de Gaulle drawing a firm line between the past and the present when it came to Britain's attitude to Europe.

Palliser, who was present at the meetings, recalled how he 'came away absolutely convinced that there was no question of getting in once the General was there. De Gaulle had been courteous but firm. It was clear to me from the things he said what his intent was.'[21] Yet, at the same time, Michael Palliser remembers Wilson 'professing to me that we had indeed made a dent on the General'.[22] The divergence between the diplomatic and political assessments was obvious. Whereas Palliser was pragmatic, acknowledging not only the likelihood but also the near certainty of a veto, Wilson was content to see the meeting as a success and continued to believe in not only the possibility, but almost the inevitability of persuading the general. Robin O'Neill identified the crux of the problem:

> Yes, there was the funny business of occasional meetings between Wilson and de Gaulle. The ultimate aim at this time was not to give de Gaulle the opportunity to break things off. Yes, Wilson argued his case but he was not unduly assertive. The problem we all felt in the Foreign Office at the time was that all that was possible was to wait until de Gaulle had left the scene.[23]

Finally, the last thing the British could take away from these meetings was the fact that Monnet's advice about de Gaulle not falling for any gimmick certainly rang true. There was no point in the Wilson administration attaching too much weight to the lure of technological co-operation for de Gaulle in return for Britain's entry. As far as de Gaulle was concerned:

> France had no doubt of the great economic and technological capacity of Britain, and it seemed clear that, whether or not Britain joined the Common Market, France and Britain could do much useful work together in a number of fields.[24]

De Gaulle wanted bilateral co-operation within the technological field but Wilson's proposed 'new technological community' was clearly not to mean political and economic integration. In a telegram to the Foreign Office, Reilly raised a valid concern: with regard to the general's suggestion of 'something entirely new', Reilly felt that 'it may represent something which the general would in his heart of hearts like to see; but he must know that at the present time the suggestion has no relation to practical realities'.[25] In giving his initial impression of the talks, Patrick Reilly believed that 'on the political front we have made progress. The General and his ministers will take our approach very seriously. On the economic front, however, the French have kept intact several lines of defence.'[26]

With elections looming on the horizon, de Gaulle was conscious not to appear too hostile or entirely negative towards the British. In private, with other European leaders, de Gaulle was more candid. When playing to his domestic audience he was more circumspect. The attitude of French people to the entry of Great Britain into the Common Market had been closely monitored by the French Institute of Public Opinion. In a poll commissioned by that organisation, between 22 December 1966 and 4 January 1967, the French public when asked 'At the present time, is it in accord with or against the interests of France for Great Britain to enter the Common Market?' the results were quite favourable to Britain. The French indicated 48 per cent in favour and 14 per cent against at the beginning of 1967, an increase from 41 per cent in favour in October 1964 and an even further move away from the low of 35 per cent in January 1963.[27] With the elections due to take place in March and the French public receptive and warming to a British entry, it is not surprising, that de Gaulle was prepared to exercise some caution when it came to portraying his views on this complex subject. One must be careful, however, not to overemphasise this point for Britain's entry into the EEC was never going to be decisive issue in a French election. Richard Crossman, Barbara Castle, who was the minister of transport (1965–8), and even George Brown's memoirs on the subject verify this. Crossman felt that de Gaulle had managed to remove many of his reservations: 'Harold comes back from Paris for the first time determined to enter the Market', and added that 'something seems to have happened during the de Gaulle interview which has made him work unreservedly for entry'.[28] Barbara Castle came to a similar conclusion: 'Harold is straining every nerve to get in'.[29] Even George Brown noted that as the tour progressed 'gradually our line got firmer and firmer, and by the time we had finished we had virtually decided to make our application.[30] Robin O'Neill maintains that by the beginning of 1967 'a bit of the magic was wearing off. My feeling at the time was that the problem was that Wilson was being too deferential. Yet having said that, the aim was not to give de Gaulle the opportunity to break things off.'[31]

II

The conclusions of a cabinet meeting in London on 26 January 1967 raised the issue of association: 'General de Gaulle had also raised at the final meeting the possibility of our being associated with the EEC, though not a member of it, or even of establishing "something new and different", i.e. presumably a wholly different kind of Community.'[32] It was felt that 'Among other things, it might well become purely a device for imposing delay and preventing our entry into the Community.'[33]

> The prime minister said that, while the visit did not in any way appear to have changed the view of General de Gaulle that he would prefer that we should not join the EEC at present, it had clearly made him reconsider a number of aspects and he had said that he now recognised a clear difference between the attitude of the United Kingdom Government on the present occasion and that which the then Administration had demonstrated during the 1961–63 negotiations.[34]

The administration continued to look for positive signs. De Gaulle had stated in a press conference on 14 January 1963 that the Macmillan government had taken 'the first steps down the path which one day, perhaps, will lead it to moor alongside the continent'.[35] The fact that only four years had elapsed made Con O'Neill feel 'that this echo of an almost classical phrase was of real significance, indeed to my mind it was the most significant thing that happened during the Paris visit'.[36] Having read O'Neill's letter, Harold Wilson commented that it was indeed 'a very good point'.[37]

The most accurate gauge of developments came from various foreign observers. American Senator Edward Kennedy discussed British entry into the EEC when he saw the general on 31 January 1967. According to Patrick Reilly:

He had the impression that the General was still against British entry. At his off-the-record briefing he told American journalists that the General wanted to keep the Americans tied up in Vietnam for the same reason he wanted to keep Britain out of Europe. He did not want 'too many frogs in the pond'.[38]

Having spoken to the French at the beginning of February, the opinion of Tyge Dahlgaard, the Danish minister for trade and European integration, was that 'the French had not made up their minds for or against our new approach, although their basic attitude was negative', and they clearly would not make things easy for the British.[39] Furthermore, his final impression was 'that the French were *mal à l'aise* over our approach'.[40]

Ill at ease they certainly were, with Jens Christensen, a Danish Gladwyn-like figure, categorising the French reaction to the British visit as 'nothing more than discouragement shrouded in ambiguity',[41] Christensen also raised a valid point concerning de Gaulle's objections – if he was so concerned about a British entry changing the nature of the EEC irreversibly, then why had he never raised this matter during the 1961–3 negotiations? He also advised against pursuing any 'alternatives': according to most wise opinions this would merely play into de Gaulle's hands, by stirring up opposition amongst the Five. In conclusion, Christensen believed that:

> A consequence of the General's tactics was, however, that because the five wished above all not to prejudice the nature of the community as it now was, we should receive little more than touch-line support from them, the match was really between Britain and France.[42]

The mood in Bonn was no more encouraging. Whereas British officials were trying to point out de Gaulle's transition from categorising Britain as 'an offshore island', to now accepting that perhaps she was indeed ready to moor at the European quay, German politicians such as the Chancellor Dr Kurt Georg Kiesinger (December 1966–October 1969), who had always wanted Britain to 'take the lead' in the post-war era, were more pessimistic about de Gaulle's wishes.

The subject of Britain and the Common Market was discussed in some detail in American political circles. Jeremy Thomson writing to one Foreign Office official stated that 'Both the American and the Germans generally assumed that if we tried to negotiate to join the Common Market this year we should be blocked by General de Gaulle'.[43] Thomson also highlighted the fact that:

> There is an important group in the State Department of convinced Europeans who are so certain of a French rejection that they urged Her Majesty's

> Government not to enter into negotiations at this time. These people, e.g. Messrs Bowie, Owen etc., had changed their tune considerably since last July. Then they were singing of the necessity of a firm British statement and evidence that we meant business. Now that we had more or less done what they wanted they were afraid of the consequence.[44]

In particular it was feared that public opinion in Britain might harden if the French rejected them once more. Other Americans countered this by arguing that if Britain did not decide to negotiate, the Europeans would almost certainly question Britain's sincerity and 'General de Gaulle would have won a victory without fighting a battle'.[45] Thomson maintained that 'if we decide after the present tour of the capitals of the Six not to negotiate our position we will be received with understanding in Washington but we will command more respect if we do negotiate'.[46] In talking to Kiesinger, Frank Roberts concluded that '[Kiesinger] remained gloomy about de Gaulle's real intentions'.[47]

Perhaps the best assessment of the mood in Paris after Wilson and Brown's visit came from Copenhagen. According to Dahlgaard, he had two impressions:

> First, that the French would rather 'see us hanged' than members of the Common Market, but secondly, that they did not wish themselves to be the executioners this time and that the nature of the approach of yourself and the prime minister had got them seriously worried.[48]

The message was reported across all capitals: the British would not get in. Con O'Neill had a visit from the minister for economic affairs at the United States Embassy on 8 February. Reporting to the permanent under-secretary, O'Neill said that Eugene Rostow was under the impression that he had conveyed clearly the United States administration's attitude to the British approach to the Common Market. 'I don't think he ever said so clearly that his Government felt we must accept "everything done under The Treaty of Rom" but on the whole, with rather less precision this was his attitude'.[49] What is perhaps even more noteworthy is Wilson's note in the margins 'on this, let them belt up'.[50]

III

Next up was a visit to Bonn. Emphasising the particular importance of that visit, William Nield wrote from the Foreign Office to the prime minister on 10 February 1967. Nield stressed that:

> The Federal Republic's strength, position in Europe and the Community and her relationship to France, make the importance of this visit parallel to that of the Paris visit. We are dependent upon the Germans to give weight if not leadership to any resistance the Five might offer to French opposition to our candidature. After Bonn, we can pretty well assess the results of the probe, since the reactions of The Hague are the most predictable, and those of Luxembourg the least substantial of the Six. It is, therefore, to the Bonn visit that we must look for whatever elements are still lacking in the results we should like to see from the probing exercise as a whole. The German wicket is probably the most favourable we shall have to play on in Europe – basically easier than the one in Rome.[51]

Wilson and Brown met with Georg Kiesinger, and the foreign minister, Willy Brandt, in the Palais Schaumburg, Bonn, on 15 February 1967. Kiesinger said that he felt obliged to ask 'whether Britain had the same will as the others to advance the European Economic Community to full economic Union and to all that that implied'.[52] Wilson stated the answer was clear. Britain knew it was a developing community:

> The Communities must move forward and Britain would not be amongst those who would be trying to hold them back. Logic and history taught us to recognise that, wherever there had been close economic union, it had led on eventually to political union of one form or another. Just as the speed of a naval convoy was regulated by the slowest ship, so the progress of the European Economic Community would depend on the slowest member. However it was too early to envisage what the situation would be in 10 years time.[53]

Attempting to guess how things would develop over the next year, Patrick Reilly wrote from Paris to the minister of state on 21 February 1967. Reilly outlined two particular problems that the general might be able to exploit. The first referred to Britain's terms and conditions:

> I am afraid that I must repeat what I have said all too often, that from the point of view of French opinion it is of the greatest importance that our terms should be reduced to the absolute minimum and that we should be able to say clearly that we accept the Common Agricultural Policy as well as the Treaty of Rome.[54]

Secondly, Reilly felt that the more time was spent deliberating and waiting before a request was made for formal negotiations, the more time the French had to accumulate:

> Objections designed to stop us before we can even get to a negotiation. The French themselves have shown anxiety about the possibility of an early application

by Her Majesty's Government. This may perhaps indicate that they think that an early move would be more difficult to counter than one made later on.[55]

Discussing the other foreign policies competing with the European policy, Patrick Gore-Booth wrote to the foreign secretary, because he had 'some reason to believe that the prime minister, perhaps without serious practical intent, gave some of his advisers the other day the feeling of a plague on all your houses, can't we do something with the Russians and Eastern Europe instead?'[56] Commenting on relations with the United States, Germany and the Soviet Union, Gore-Booth reiterated that:

> They are claims on our time and not competitors with our European policy. It could of course turn out that the obstacles to entering the EEC are for other reasons too difficult to overcome but this has not yet been proved. The object of these notes is simply to suggest that at the present moment, where the 'antis' have opened up with their broadsides on the home front, we do not need to allow positive, or negative distractions to compel us to wobble about the approach to the Community.[57]

IV

On 23 February 1967, Couve in a French election campaign lunch raised the issue of the change that a British entry would entail for the whole community. The *Financial Times* maintained 'it is the first time any French minister has stated so clearly and in public this latest French objection to the Community's enlargement'.[58] It was this theme that would be later tied with de Gaulle's puzzling suggestion to create 'something entirely new and different'. If the British insisted on knocking at the door, showing no sign of relenting, then a possible solution in de Gaulle's eyes was perhaps to erect a separate edifice suited to British needs, allowing France enjoy the crucial space it had created for itself within the European Community.

Writing on 24 February, Roberts concluded that 'Kiesinger and those around him remain cautious to the point of weakness in their willingness to face strong French opposition'.[59] The main danger 'as seen from Bonn would be in any failure to maintain the momentum of our present approach, since even many of our good friends here are all to inclined to think that the path of wisdom (and clearly the easiest path for the Germans) would be in postponing the crunch for some months or even years'.[60]

It was reported from Paris on 1 March 1967, that French official propaganda was now focusing more on the fact that Britain and other countries would change the very nature of the Community:

The Government have evidently found this theme effective. It appeals to the genuine 'Europeans' who favour our entry so long as we accept the rules and come in alone; and also to French nationalists who want France to stay cock of the European roost and who see the Common Market primarily as a device to further French interests.[61]

It was accepted that this fear of the unknown was genuine and that efforts must be made to dispel such ideas. A paper entitled 'Europe: the next steps' was sent by Con O'Neill to the foreign secretary on 6 March. The first recommendation the paper made was to follow the previous week's advice from *The Economist* which urged:

> '*Go on: Have a Go!*' It was proposed that our best chance of entering the community would be to apply for membership at the beginning of May, at the same time making it clear that the basis on which we will negotiate is acceptance of the Treaty of Rome, acceptance of the Common Agricultural Policy and reliance on transitional periods except insofar as we require a special arrangement for New Zealand.[62]

The argument in favour of '*Go on: Have a Go!*' was to maintain momentum: 'any other course risks losing it', and 'would enable the French to say that we were hesitant or preparing to ask for unacceptable conditions'.[63] O'Neill's advice never wavered as he consistently urged Brown and Wilson to persist. Finally the paper stated:

> It is clear that the French Government have been shaken by our determination to press for membership. If the French had not been shaken, they would have been taking the line that we were asking too much, that we were not in earnest or that we were insufficiently European. Whereas the line which they have in fact been taking is that British membership would alter the character of the Community.[64]

Speaking directly to Pierre Werner at the Ministry of Foreign Affairs in Luxembourg, on 8 March 1967, Brown emphasised the need for more reassurance from the Five, and indeed from France. Brown stated:

> It would not necessarily be easy for Mr Wilson and himself to bring their colleagues in the Cabinet and the Labour Party to the point of taking a definite decision to apply for entry. They would be asked whether the application would simply meet with a second rebuff from General de Gaulle; and as yet they had not been given any clear answer to this question in any of the six capitals which they had now visited. But some answer to this question there must be before the British Government could undertake to make an application. Before we could start on

this road we must have a pretty definite assurance that we should not merely be snubbed again at the end of it.[65]

To which Wilson added 'that "the five" should also remember that a second rebuff would be intolerable for the UK and it would probably mean the end of the road so far as we are concerned. Moreover, it might create such tension within the EEC, as to mean the virtual end of the Community as well.'[66] The conclusion of a cabinet meeting on 9 March stated that 'It was necessary to avoid on the one hand undue haste in coming to a decision and on the other procrastination which (if the decision should be to apply for membership) would dissipate the momentum and interest achieved by the recent series of visits.'[67]

In March 1967, Patrick Reilly met de Gaulle in Paris to discuss the post-visit climate and to reiterate the sincerity of Britain's wishes. The general made it clear that he thought it would be a mistake to attempt to go too fast. he categorised the obstacles that lay in Britain's path as practical and political:

> The practical problem was one not so much of principles but of dimension, the problem of absorbing into the community a country the size of Great Britain. The political problem was that of how Britain could fit into the creation of something which was truly European in the light of her special ties ('liaisons') with the United States.[68]

According to Reilly 'our attitude to the United States was the real criterion, the true touchstone'.[69] Ever the statesmen, de Gaulle constantly thought in terms of power. With his obsession about avoiding succumbing to American influence he remained suspicious of Britain, believing that if Britain were to enter there was no guarantee she would side with the Europeans as opposed to the Americans. Nothing so far had given de Gaulle any assurances to the affirmative.

Patrick Reilly was able to report the following day on worrying developments when it came to the support of the Germans. It was believed that the Germans were becoming more doubtful and were now less likely to conceal their reservations. In fact, one of Reilly's sources was André Fontaine, the diplomatic correspondent of *Le Monde*, who was usually well informed. According to Reilly, Fontaine 'told a member of my staff, yesterday, that officials in the five are speaking much more bluntly among themselves about our chances than they are to us'.[70] In his response, Brown was quick to advise the prime minister against allowing any sign of weakness or vulnerability to emanate from British quarters. He was strongly opposed to the prime minister visiting de Gaulle before the British had made their decision and applied for membership. 'To give any inkling now to the propaganda machine of the

Quai of what you have in mind would be to give altogether too much of a hostage to fortune.'[71]

Brown stated that he did 'not see how a visit before our decision or our application could be interpreted except as a sign of uncertainty or weakness. Whatever passed between you and de Gaulle this is how it would be interpreted by the press and by our friends in Europe – and maybe by some of our colleagues here'.[72] Brown was again adamant that Britain should not be seen to be in a position of weakness and strongly believed that exhibiting such a stance would contribute to a failed venture.

Writing to Fred Mulley, who was the minister of aviation from 1965 to 1967 and the minister for disarmament from 1967 to 1969, Con O'Neill mentioned a Foreign Office paper he was preparing on the political case for going into Europe. O'Neill felt that the overriding political rationale for entering the Community had been forgotten amidst the technical details. In consequence he was drafting a paper on the political rationale: 'The Paper should aim at being a "clincher" in the long argument',[73] and hoped that the foreign secretary would approve of its circulation.' To which Mulley noted:

> I agree that such a paper should be prepared and that the timing of its circulation should be very carefully considered. You may however feel that the form and argument should be revised while bringing out strongly the point that it is easy in the torrent of debate with which the Cabinet is being swamped for the really big issues to get washed away.[74]

The foreign secretary's answer was short and to the point, ordering Mulley to 'Hang on to it. We have enough time to consider'.[75]

V

As summer 1967 approached, momentum gathered. On 18 April, George Brown met with United States Secretary of State Dean Rusk in the State Department. Brown informed the Americans of the timing of the application: 'If the British Application were not put in some time in May there would almost certainly be no action between then and the Autumn, which we would not find tolerable.'[76] In conclusion, Brown 'agreed that it would probably be 'better for them not to play a hand, but said we might later want their help to stiffen the Germans who were clearly very anxious to do nothing to prejudice the recent improvement in Franco-German relations'.[77]

On 24 April 1967, a cabinet memorandum was circulated by the Commonwealth Secretary, George Thomson, which stated that 'there is nothing formally incompatible in Britain's joining EEC and in Britain's continued membership of the Commonwealth'.[78] It also noted:

> The economic value of the Commonwealth to us, and of us to the Commonwealth, is declining. This decline will be markedly accelerated if we join EEC. It is obviously not in our interest that it should decline unless we gain compensating advantages elsewhere.[79]

The same day also saw the circulation of a memorandum by the foreign secretary discussing in detail the approach to Europe. Talking about 'association', George Brown stated that 'when General de Gaulle at the end of our visit to Paris speculated on the subject, I at once rejected his suggestion of associate membership because this would be a kind of second-class citizenship which would impose on us many, perhaps most, of the obligations of membership with few of the rights'.[80] George Brown's consistent advocacy of full membership and nothing less showed that he provided the backbone to this policy. In conclusion it was put forward that:

> The right decision would be to make an early application for entry. In that event, we should make a new application, rather than seek to resume the negotiations initiated by the previous Administration. Clearly we could not contemplate an unconditional application, i.e. one that fails to secure the minimum conditions for entry which our discussions are establishing. On the other hand to demand the prior acceptance of conditions before applying for entry would strengthen opposition to us.[81]

As a result *The Times* the following day declared that 'All the signs last night were that the Government are clearing the way for entry into Europe'.[82]

Frank Roberts, writing from Bonn on 26 April 1967, categorically stated that while the British had the full support of the Federal government:

> Their support would not extend to bringing pressure to bear on the French, still less to contemplating any action which could break up or even temporarily paralyse the Community. Kiesinger had said on several occasions that such pressure would not work, and that his Government neither could nor would attempt to use it. To temper their reluctance to 'make the running for us in Paris', they said 'provided that our arguments and our requirements were demonstrably reasonable in German eyes we should find them ready advocates of our cause'.[83]

With the decision looming to make the formal application in early May, time was of the essence. Assessments such as Patrick Reilly's that 'it is probable that he has not yet made up his mind',[84] whether true or not, were clearly going to spur the British on. With this in mind, Reilly believed that their immediate concern was to prevent a situation whereby de Gaulle could either block or seriously delay the negotiations. Perhaps the best approach would be to allow de Gaulle 'to believe that it is his vision and leadership which had brought Britain into "Europe"' and 'he may in the end yield with a good grace'.[85]

As a word of caution *The Spectator* made an extremely valid point when it condemned 'the facile Foreign Office belief that we only have to trumpet "we're going to get in" loud enough and frequently enough and the walls of Jericho will fall, is a disastrous delusion'.[86] Further ambiguity emanating from the French side of the water only served to make matters worse. Couve's comments to Roberts at the end of April, in which he argued that 'Britain's association with the EEC would be the best solution, implies that Britain's economic interest could be satisfied in this way just as well as by full membership',[87] certainly did nothing to assuage Britain's fears of being fobbed off. In essence Couve was subtly trying to make the British reconsider the idea of joining a political entity and instead presented the case for an economic association. Palliser wrote to the prime minister that 'When one recalls the totally political nature of de Gaulle's veto last time it is indeed ironic to learn of Couve dismissing our political arguments as irrelevant because there is nothing political in the Common Market but this is the kind of thing to be dealt with in your next bilateral with Couve's boss'.[88] However, as the French Finance Minister Wilfrid Baumgartner had pointed out, 'Couve's attitude is well known and any influence he can exert will be in the wrong direction'.[89] he thought that Debré and Pompidou were both in support of British entry, 'but neither Debré nor Pompidou can be relied on to stand up to the general if he barks loud'.[90]

Back in London, Wilson had been adamantly attempting to steer his party towards an application. Up to now it had been an almost exclusively Foreign Office issue. Wilson was now trying to foster more wholehearted involvement, interest, and, it was hoped, support on this issue. James Callaghan recalled how:

> As Chancellor of Exchequer, I was not involved in the day to day discussions of tactics etc., about these matters, and to be truthful, I regarded the management of the domestic economy, and the position of sterling as reserve currency as being of more immediate concern to the Government than the question of the EEC. I did not regard membership as likely at the time, and so it was not my first priority, and I would hazard the view that the attitude of most members of the cabinet who were not passionate advocates of membership, to be that we would believe it when we saw it happen.[91]

Wilson then circulated full details of the meetings that had taken place while on the 'tour of the capitals', so that the cabinet could make a reasoned decision. According to Wilson 'It extended to 140 pages of fairly closely printed foolscap; nothing was omitted. Points and exchanges capable of being interpreted for or against a decision to enter were fully and neutrally reported; nothing was altered or presented anew.'[92] Yet, according to antis such as Douglas Jay, this was not the case,[93] as it was by now widely acknowledged that Wilson was determined to make an application. According to Richard Crossman, 'their idea is to get in by 1969'.[94] Wilson therefore hoped for a decision before the Whitsuntide recess and held a number of cabinet discussions on the subject. The various aspects of membership were discussed in detail from constitutional and legal implications to the CAP. Barbara Castle wrote in her diary on 6 April 1967 that 'I am more than ever convinced that Harold is now a dedicated European and that all this exercise is shadow boxing'.[95] This condition was rooted in the fact that Wilson at every turn minimised the negatives and enhanced the positives. The cabinet was roughly divided into three groups on the subject. Michael Stewart, a moderate pro-European noted the sheer sense of indecision at the time: 'Some, like George Brown, were saying "Yes, certainly", a few, like Douglas Jay, were saying "Not on any account". A good many, like myself, were saying "Yes, if . . ." and who could be described as saying "No, unless . . .".'[96]

On 29 and 30 April 1967, a special two-day ministerial conference was called to come to a decision on whether to apply. The first day of debate would take place at No. 10 and the second would take place at Chequers. At this stage, antis were becoming particularly weary and it was not long before a vote of 13 to 8 in favour of an application was taken.

On 30 April 1967, the cabinet took a vote on whether to apply to the EEC, carried by thirteen votes to eight. On 1 May the cabinet was issued with the prime minister's draft statement to the House of Commons to be delivered the following day. Having discussed the economic aspects, Wilson would shift attention to the political factors:

> Whatever the economic arguments the House will realise that, as I have repeatedly made clear, the Government's purpose derives above all from our recognition that Europe is now faced with the opportunity of a great move forward in political unity and that we can – and indeed must – play our full part in it.[97]

The decision was formally announced in the House of Commons on 2 May 1967. On hearing this de Gaulle wrote to Wilson stating:

> Comme vous le dites, l'adhésion du Royaume-Uni aux traités de Paris et de Rome pose pour vous comme pour nous et pour tous les pays intéressés des problèmes très ardus. Nous avons déjà eu l'occasion entretenir et vous savez que la France ne se le dissimule pas.[98]

With regard to the Paris press comment Reilly classified it as 'reserved but not, in most cases, hostile'.[99] *Le Monde* dedicated two and a half pages to the subject, with the editorial praising the prime minister's turn towards Europe, but at the same time mentioning the difficulties that lay ahead for his country.

Michael Palliser met briefly with Giscard d'Estaing who warned that de Gaulle 'would certainly try to trip us up and to make the negotiations as Byzantine as possible so as to have the maximum good technical excuses for delaying our entry'.[100] With this in mind, he pointed out the need to steer clear of providing the general with another 'Nassau', that is, an excuse for another veto, and added that one needed to be careful so as not to allow the international monetary argument develop into one.

Fred Mulley wrote to Brown on 10 May 1967, and enquired whether he should still speak at the luncheon arranged by the British and French Chambers of Commerce to coincide with the British Day at the Trade Fair (18–19 May). Palliser had expressed concern as to whether it was wise for Mulley to go, given that Britain had made its application and that the general would be giving a press conference on 16 May. Mulley wrote that 'while such a development is pending I do not consider we can afford to leave everything to French initiative and seem to allow our own plans to appear to be subject to French activities and timing'.[101] Brown sanctioned the visit, stating 'you should certainly do the lunch at the British Day. But nothing else please.'[102] At this stage, one must ask whether Wilson had made much progress with de Gaulle. According to Monnet, the prime minister had indeed succeeded in gaining a considerable amount of momentum and in doing so had undoubtedly left the general at times bewildered. In a pragmatic fashion, Monnet recognised that 'We almost certainly could not convince the general of the advantages of British membership. In our tactics therefore, we had to ensure that we gave him no opportunity for diverting our effort into the sand.' [103]

SEVEN

AN APPLICATION AND A VETO

—

Britain officially lodged its bid to join the Common Market on 11 May 1967. James Marjoribanks, Britain's ambassador to the Common Market presented three identical letters from Wilson to Renaat van Elslande, president of the Common Market's Council of Ministers, at 9.00 a.m.

> Mr President,
> I have the Honour, on behalf of Her Majesty's Government in the United Kingdom of Great Britain and Northern Ireland, to inform your Excellency that the United Kingdom hereby applies to become a member of the European Economic Community under the terms of Article 237 of the Treaty, establishing the European Economic Community.
> Please accept, Mr. President, the assurance of my highest consideration,
>
> Harold Wilson.[1]

James Marjoribanks had said on 9 March 1967 in Brussels that 'I profoundly believe that just as there is no future for England in the "Little England" philosophy, there is no future for Europe in the "Little Europe"',[2] and now two months later, in lodging Britain's second application, he stated categorically that he hoped negotiations would begin the next month and that success would be achieved by the end of the year.

I

Reporting on the Paris press reactions to Britain's decision to seek entry into the EEC, Reilly wrote that it was covered 'factually but without much comment. All papers mention the massive vote in the House of Commons in favour of entry, one notes that it was the highest majority for a century, and it is also noted that in contrast with 1961 all three British parties support the move'.[3]

At home in Britain, the *Sun* acknowledged that 'Britain's second bid for membership of the Common Market is being made by a government whose prime minister opposed the first bid. This is a measure of how much the situation has changed in the past four years.'[4] Marjoribanks later reflecting on the historic occasion wrote:

> My last job in the Foreign Service was the six years I spent from 1965 to 1971 as Ambassador to the three European Communities, i.e. Economic Community, Coal and Steel and Atomic Energy. The job required endless patience, owing to General de Gaulle's tiresome habit of slamming the door in our faces every time we tried to apply for entry into the Communities. Harold Wilson said in 1966 that he wouldn't take no for an answer, but that is exactly what he got. On 11 May 1967, I presented the British application to the president of the Community's Council of Ministers, an episode that was widely televised and reported in the press. But it was not until the general had resigned that our application was taken seriously.[5]

'Divert it into the sand' is exactly what de Gaulle tried to do in his surprise Press Conference of the 16 May 1967. At first glimpse, it is ironic that while de Gaulle categorically denied the possibility of a veto, the Press seized upon his statements as being nothing less than a 'velvet veto'. Upon closer inspection, it is not surprising that this was the consensus on the subject. In his press conference, de Gaulle politely told the British that they were clearly not ready to join the EEC. The language employed may have been courteous, but the sentiment was extremely condescending. De Gaulle alluded to his familiar themes: Britain's commitment to Europe; fear of the Trojan horse rearing its head; the position of sterling as a reserve currency; the state of the British economy; and finally, the obvious disruptions that a British accession would create for the rest of the Community.

Yet he was careful to disguise what he was actually saying. De Gaulle stated that:

> For our part there could not be, and moreover, has never been, any question of a veto. It is only a question of knowing whether a successful conclusion is possible in the framework and within the conditions of the Common Market as it is, without introducing destructive difficulties, or alternatively in what other framework and under what other conditions such a conclusion could be reached: unless of course we should decide to preserve what had been established until such time as, if that should come to be, it appears possible to welcome a Britain which had profoundly changed itself and on its own account.[6]

Outlining the only choices available at the moment to be to scrap the EEC in its existing form and create a type of free-trade organisation; to provide some form of association for Britain and other members of EFTA with the EEC;

or to wait until Britain had reached a sufficient stage in its metamorphosis. The official reaction within London circles to the general's press conference was on the whole one of surprise and some could only conclude that 'the president's public bark is worse than his private bite'.[7] The political commentator, Ronald Butt, was quick to point out that:

> It is being said that if the President had been as daunting in private as he now appears to be in public, it would have been a very foolhardy act for the British Government to apply for membership. The intended logic of this appears to be that since the British Government is not foolhardy the French President must have been more amendable in private than in public.[8]

Indeed this 'public bark' did come as somewhat of a shock to the individuals who thought they had succeeded in befriending de Gaulle, and resulted in their humiliation. Reilly had immediately expressed his disgust to the prime minister and accused the French president of exploiting, exaggerating, and even distorting Britain's difficulties. 'The whole statement is so negative that one must ask oneself whether the general's objective has not been while disclaiming any veto, to follow Her Majesty's Government application with a counter attack so powerful as to prevent a negotiation ever starting at all.'[9] Wilson, having read this, was in complete agreement and commented that it was 'a good analysis'.[10]

Elsewhere, the general's statements caused a mixed reaction. In Brussels there was little surprise, with the liberal *Laatste Nieuws* stating that 'If Britain really wants to join', ultimately, 'she will have to be prepared to make concessions',[11] whereas the Dutch reaction was undoubtedly more critical of de Gaulle, with the Catholic Centre paper *Volkskrant* castigating his tone as 'preposterous' and concluding that 'the whole atmosphere reflects the unbending grey, enclosed qualities of an old time, an old man, an old regime'.[12] Even more accusing was the right-wing *Telegraaf* which accused de Gaulle of not stating the main reason behind his attitude: 'his desire for France to be the leader of the Continent'.[13] The cloud of ambiguity that had hovered over the English Channel and that had perplexed British ministers and officials alike was now beginning to disappear. De Gaulle's 'velvet veto' was the first formative step towards putting an end to the Wilson administration's European policy and, moreover, to Britain's chances of securing entry to the EEC for the second time. The reaction of the Irish press was equally pessimistic. Reporting from Dublin to the Commonwealth Office, Andrew Gilchrist noted:

> *The Irish Times* editorial said the only impression could be that the door had been slammed again on Britain and Ireland's applications. While nobody expected de

Gaulle would fail to raise objections their comprehensiveness and pervasive theme of unripeness of timing came as a surprise. Mr Wilson will have other cards to play but it would be inadvisable to rely on any internal rift within the EEC.[14]

What was the Labour government to do now? Changing course was not an option any more than abandoning ship. The only option open to them was to drop anchor and remain patient. As Michael Palliser maintained:

> If we allow the notion to get abroad that we are not prepared to be reasonably patient and that we are adopting a 'take it or leave it' attitude towards negotiation even of the main issues, this will play straight into the General's hands, and enable him to say that it is we who have vetoed ourselves.[15]

Some officials were not able to play a waiting game and were immediately immersed in exploring all possible options. Gladwyn sent Palliser a memorandum detailing a number of possible compromises.[16] Wilson urged a steady hand to be placed on the rudder with no sudden or rash moves to endanger the passengers.

Fred Mulley met Hans Schaffner at the Palais Federal Berne on 7 June. Schaffner asked 'Why should Her Majesty's Government not begin by association only with the community? This might be only a transitional arrangement, but it might avoid a head-on collision between Britain and France.'[17] Mulley was quick to ask 'whether an associate status which would certainly mean effective exclusion from participation in the principal decisions of policy which would nevertheless be binding on associate members, would be acceptable to Switzerland'.[18] This summed up Britain's lack of interest in anything less than full membership.

II

Undeterred, Wilson continued to look forward and decided to meet with de Gaulle in the middle of June. In preparation for these talks, Reilly wrote to the prime minister, outlining a number of crucial points. In particular, he emphasised the recklessness of de Gaulle's arguments and the desire to prevent a British entry as much for his own personal concerns as for any legitimate reasons. O'Neill supported this hypothesis further when he mentioned 'the cosy nest' theory: if Britain, Denmark, Norway and Ireland were to join together, there would 'be an accession of like-minded states',[19] threatening de Gaulle's delicate balance of power. According to Reilly the general 'would have liked to choke us off, but can hardly hope to do so now.

He still wishes to avoid a clear French veto. He will therefore use at every stage every means of delay.'[20] Looking back on recent statements by de Gaulle, Reilly still believed that his underlying fear revolved around British priorities and allegiances:

> A dominant thought in the General's mind is that whatever British feelings may now be, our compulsions (*necessités*) permanent forces – continually push us towards the Americans, our attitude towards whom remains the 'criterion, the touchstone' of our fitness to be accepted.[21]

Preparations for the Grand Trianon Versailles meeting between Harold Wilson and de Gaulle were well under way by the beginning of June. Reilly maintained that 'the primary objective of his visit will be to influence the general in favour of British entry into the European Communities'.[22] The latest opinion poll in France illustrated large support for British entry – with 13 per cent 'in favour' and 47 per cent 'more in favour than not'.[23] Yet this support did not sway the de Gaulle in his convictions. As Reilly assiduously deduced:

> It is probably true that he accepts full British membership as inevitable, one day, but everything suggests that he is deeply reluctant to agree to it now. His use of arguments against it is so reckless that it seems clear that he objects to it for his own sake and primarily for political reasons, although certain economic considerations also weigh much with him.[24]

So while de Gaulle did not wish to invoke a clear veto, he certainly had no intention of opening the gates to Britain. The idea of the meeting had first been raised at Adenauer's funeral in Bonn in April. Wilson recalled how:

> I suggested that perhaps in the forthcoming Whitsun recess, I might come to Paris, Colombey or wherever he liked; as the excuse, I said my wife could do some shopping. '*Paris est à vous*', he replied and it would be good if she were to shop there. Any time. Then remembering he said that it would be better if I came after his mid-May press conference.[25]

On Sunday evening 18 June 1967, Wilson flew to Paris and had a short briefing at the British Embassy. The following morning he went to meet de Gaulle. Wilson reflected on the venue:

> The President's guest house at the Petit Trianon, originally built as a hunting-lodge for the Grand Palace, was much used by Louis XIV and his successors. It had recently been renovated by the French Government – at very great expense,

said General de Gaulle – and this was the first time it had been used for an international rencontre.[26]

A large amount of time was spent discussing the Six Days War in the Middle East and the worsening Vietnam War. Wilson later remembered the mood of the general that day:

> As I walked back on those slippery marble floors to my apartments, M. Burin des Roziers, the President's Chef de Cabinet, said he thought that the President was very depressed. Apocalyptic, I suggested. 'Ah', he said, 'the General is seventy-six and he has little to look forward to' (I was sure he was referring to the General's disappointment following Mr Kosygin's visit). I replied that I was fifty-one and, if I were to take so dejected a view, what purpose was there in remaining in public affairs?[27]

Lunch took place 'en famille' as de Gaulle put it, and Wilson noted how he was lively, without a trace of his morning's depression. Having discussed walking, reading, and the ins and outs of playing patience, the afternoon discussions returned back to the Middle East situation. Later in the afternoon, as Wilson was walking with members of his delegation in the striking Trianon gardens, they were informed that de Gaulle thought it would be fitting to meet outside considering it was such a magnificent day: 'shortly, officers were bringing out the high-backed Second Empire-style chairs, with their deep purple upholstery, which we had admired in one of the ante-rooms, and we sat under the trees'.[28]

Attention turned to the question of Britain's EEC bid. Wilson was keen to emphasise the political nature of the bid from the outset. Following along these lines, Wilson also wanted to prove that Britain was indeed becoming less dependent on the United States. The prime minister mentioned that they had decided not to ask for the Poseidon missile in place of Polaris. 'To that extent I was presenting him not with a new Nassau but a Nassau in reverse. Trianon was the opposite of Rambouillet.'[29] Yet, this was not enough to persuade de Gaulle and he argued that 'the fact remained that British entry would introduce to the Communities an element broadly favourable to the "Atlantic" concept'.[30] De Gaulle made it clear that British entry would make it impossible to avoid such an 'Atlanticist' leaning; 'the purpose of French membership on the other hand was to prevent it'.[31] De Gaulle continued:

> If, during and after the war and even more recently, Britain had seemed to be separate from the United States – and this did not mean opposed to the United States, just as France was not opposed to them – but separate and determined to

make her own way, then France would have been circumspect; and he too, who had observed Britain over the past twenty-seven years, would not be as cautious towards her as he was. But he always observed in war and in peace and whether or not Britain really wanted this, that she was linked to the United States.[32]

Wilson comprehended de Gaulle's innate fear, which was that one day 'Europe would become "Atlantic" and while he had the power, he was not going to speed the process',[33] but whether he recognised the extent to which it permeated de Gaulle's thinking was another question. The meeting was followed by dinner and that was followed by a tour of the Trianon state apartments. De Gaulle then invited Wilson to go for a short drive through the park, to the floodlit Grand Palace. During the drive in a small French car they reflected on the discussion of the afternoon and Wilson was keen to discuss developments over the next ten years. De Gaulle was quick to admit that he would not be there all of ten years. According to Wilson's memoirs:

> It had been a remarkable discussion, friendly above all, with the General fully involved in his exposition. Since our meeting the next morning, 20 June, was very brief, it was my last memory of him. Against the setting of that June Versailles night, it was one I could never forget.[34]

It was becoming increasingly obvious just how de Gaulle viewed the internal balance structure of the EEC. Frank Roberts learned from his conversation with Ludwig Erhard, that this was part of de Gaulle's original blueprint. Erhard recalled a meeting which had taken place between himself and de Gaulle in 1964 in which the general had said 'that if France and Germany agreed on a common policy they had no need to worry about the other countries of Europe – these would be on their knees'.[35] De Gaulle's surprise at Erhard's unwillingness to follow such a ruthless path was evidence of de Gaulle's long-burning desire to create and maintain French hegemony. While on this point, one must also remember that the Anglophile Erhard who was also quite 'Atlanticist' in his leanings had been succeeded by Kiesinger's Grand Coalition in the winter of 1966. This crucial change in personalities, with Kiesinger seriously interested in developing a close Franco-German partnership as well as initiating Ostpolitik was clearly underestimated by the British.

Wilson was frank in his assessment of the talks in a briefing to officials in the United States. Admitting that 'the picture looks pretty sombre for our prospects',[36] and acknowledging that de Gaulle would probably employ all the delaying mechanisms that he could, he still felt optimistic about the eventual outcome. 'If we keep firmly beating at the door and do not falter in our purpose or our resolve I am sure that he no longer has the strength finally to keep us out – a dangerous prophecy as prophecy always is with the General.'[37] Wilson even went so far as to inform the French journalist, Dominique Bromberger, 'that he had been left with the impression de Gaulle would probably support Britain's entry'.[38]

III

The conclusions of a cabinet meeting on 22 June 1967 outlined Britain's position at this time:

> The prime minister, summing up the discussions, said that his conclusion from his talks with the French President, upon whom he had exerted all possible pressure for a quick decision on the question of British entry into the Community, and who was now reviewing his whole position, was that we should continue to press our application for membership of the Community; it might be that by the Autumn we should have further indications of the attitude of the Six and that would be the time to review where we stood.[39]

Commenting on the French position as a result of the recent talks, Reilly felt that the Grand Trianon meeting at Versailles had been significant, but warned of the folly in forcing the French to give a concrete answer. 'I fear that if a decision were forced on him in say, the next six months, it is virtually certain that it would be one to prevent or end the negotiations.'[40] Palliser commented to Harold Wilson that it was 'an admirable letter from Sir Patrick Reilly about the French position in the light of your talks with de Gaulle'.[41] Optimism as opposed to any real sense of pessimism prevailed in official circles in London. Yet nothing de Gaulle had said at Versailles had implied any change in attitude on his part.

How did the British continue to discount any serious discussion of a second veto? The answer, while hard to arrive at, probably lies somewhere between necessity and foreign evaluation. Playing to his party and country, it would have been psychologically damaging for Wilson to return from yet another meeting with the general and concede defeat. Furthermore, the evaluation of the situation presented by various interested foreign parties was not exactly disconcerting. Kiesinger was quick to reassure Wilson that the 'overwhelming tide of European opinion in our favour was a political fact which de Gaulle could not he thought in the long run ignore or override, although he would try to hold back for as long as he could'.[42] Delays Wilson was prepared to consider, but a second veto was not something he could even contemplate at this stage.

The prime minister met with representatives of the CBI at 10 Downing Street on 4 July 1967. According to Wilson 'The Government had concluded that on balance the decision to seek to join Europe was the right course and in reaching this decision, the political considerations had been of greater importance.'[43] The political nature was echoed on the same day by Brown in a speech to the Council of the Western European Union (WEU) at The Hague: 'We in Britain, no less than the present membership of the Community, do not see the issues only in economic terms. Indeed, some of the most decisive considerations for us have been political.'[44]

Writing to the prime minister on 7 July 1967, Michael Palliser declared that 'to say that British foreign policy is in transition is perhaps a platitude; it is certainly a truism. We are in an immensely stimulating but also exceedingly delicate and difficult period in our history.'[45] In discussing this transition he pointed out that the problem was in the process, not to find 'ourselves to have fallen heavily between the two stools of Anglo-American – Commonwealth co-operation and Europe'.[46] The solution in Palliser's opinion would be to mix the old with the new:

> I think it is still true that a successful British foreign policy must depend not simply on avoiding falling between these two stools but on somehow nailing them together to form a single, solid seat for a rather leaner British bottom to sit on. I believe we can do this. But time is becoming an increasingly important factor.[47]

The circles were re-emerging, albeit in a different form.

So with talks under way, a number of strange reports were made, with regard to what the French were saying to those in close quarters. Roberts was quick to report from Bonn that things did not look positive. Citing a recent visit of de Gaulle to Bonn he reported that, 'Dr Arnold summed up his impression of de Gaulle's attitude which presumably coincides with Brandt's, as being that the French position on British entry was now perhaps even more negative than when Kiesinger saw de Gaulle in Paris last January'.[48] This hardening of attitude was bad enough, without the added dimension of the French playing 'the Five' off one another. Alun Chalfont believed that in the current circumstances de Gaulle would have no choice but to 'erode the precious solidarity of the Five'.[49] According to him the French had been explaining to the Germans that, 'one of the main reasons why they are opposed to British entry is that it will prevent Franco-German domination of the community and to their other partners they are saying that if Britain is allowed in, there is bound to be Anglo-German domination!'[50]

Finally, James Marjoribanks was receiving information 'from a highly delicate source, in which he claims to have seen a report from the French

Embassy in Bonn to the effect that in a tête-à-tête with Kiesinger, de Gaulle said that if the United Kingdom joined the Common Market, France would withdraw'.[51] Granted, it is difficult to ascertain whether it was true or not, but given de Gaulle's record of pulling out of organisations if their character became unsuitable to his perception of France's needs or wishes, it would not have been out of character.

Con O'Neill wrote to Norman Statham on 28 July, urging the preparation of a paper outlining the action which the British and indeed the Five should take, in the event that in November or December the French refused to open negotiations with Britain. According to O'Neill:

> My preliminary thought on this is that from our point of view, this will be par excellence the moment for 'not taking no for an answer'. But in addition it is most important that the Five should not themselves be prepared to take this French no for an answer either. What this means in effect is that the Five must *not* acquiesce in the kind of position they adopted in January 1963.[52]

Instead O'Neill advised that if the French did say no, 'the Five must continue loudly and determinedly, in season and out, going on saying no'.[53] Jack Lynch, the Irish taoiseach (1966–1973), conducted an Irish tour of the capitals, and it was reported in the *Irish Times* that 'Ireland's chances of becoming a member of the Common Market by 1970 are much better than 50–50'.[54] Lynch was also quoted as still being mystified as to the possible French action. 'The attitude of France towards the admission of Britain and the other applicants could not be assessed by the five governments I have visited. The French attitude must remain an imponderable.'[55]

It was felt that there was a possibility that the Five would gradually harden against the French. It is in this light that Peter Garran, who was British ambassador at The Hague, sent a translation of an article entitled 'This France is no longer an ally', written by Ernst van der Beugel on France and de Gaulle, to O'Neill on 8 August. The first contention the author made was that it was most likely that in the next few months there would be a second French veto, and furthermore the author pointed out that 'it is becoming increasingly obvious that present French politics – a sometimes brilliant but always objectionable combination of hubris and spite – depend upon one man only'.[56] The point which Peter Garran concentrated on was the suggestion of some sort of working to rule in the EEC: 'Once de Gaulle's motives have been fully understood, this can lead to one conclusion only, – that co-operations with his policies must be reduced to an absolute minimum'.[57]

Thanking Patrick Hancock for the draft paper on action in the event of a French veto, Reilly stated:

I agree of course also that it is now necessary to take seriously the possibility that there may be an early French veto on negotiations. Hitherto I have believed that, while there could be no doubt about the General's deep dislike of the admission of Britain to the EEC, he would go to considerable lengths to avoid a clear political veto.[58]

Reilly then went on to discuss his preference for a longer drawn out refusal as opposed to a quick 'no' if forced to choose between the two:

I have taken the view that, as seen from here, the balance of advantage lies in avoiding a quick break and that we should therefore be ready to play our hand with great patience. I have held this opinion partly because I believe that time is on our side and against the General's, and partly because of the consequence of a quick flat French 'No' are incalculable. Some serious Anglo-French tension would be inevitable and things might be done and said in such a situation which could do real damage and make the initiations of negotiations difficult even after the departure of de Gaulle.[59]

Alun Chalfont met with Franz-Josef Strauss, the German Federal Minister for Finance on 6 September 1967. Strauss pointed out that French resistance could not be overcome quickly, 'The train had started and Herr Strauss hoped it was not going to stop'. In addition to this, 'it was his firm view that the French would abstain from a veto, but that they would make as many difficulties as possible'.[60] 'Bonn sees Britain in Europe's outer circle' was how the *Daily Telegraph* commented on these talks. With a 'two-tiered European Community' it was proposed by the Germans that Britain might 'because of her special American and Commonwealth links prefer to remain in the outer circle'.[61]

O'Neill carried out interviews with some influential officials in Brussels and sent the reports to James Marjoribanks and John Robinson on 11 September. Monsieur Rifflet believed that 'It would be easy enough to get a quick no out of the French, if that were what you wanted'.[62] According to O'Neill:

Rifflet had been much struck by Monnet telling Rey recently (we have also heard this from somewhere) that the best hope of de Gaulle changing his mind is for him to be convinced that he will be damaging his image before history if he keeps us out of the Community, particularly if there were a risk that his action would be reversed by his successor.[63]

'There is a feeling that if negotiations start they will succeed, and therefore that the French will do their utmost to stop them starting.'[64] With hindsight, it is obvious that O'Neill's predictions were closer to the truth then some perhaps at the time wished to recognise.

IV

Two events provided de Gaulle with the necessary ammunition to confront the British. The first of these came in the form of the report released by the Executive Commission of the EEC on 29 September 1967. While acknowledging the advantages of a British entry, the main body of the report was a further blow to the British negotiating position. The report stressed the need for Britain to stabilise its economy, sort out its balance of payments problem and finally re-evaluate the international role of sterling, before joining the Community. It was now obvious to all observers that the very thing Wilson had vowed never to allow had happened – Britain was now negotiating from a position of weakness.

The stark reality of the situation was apparent to the Foreign Office – that the chance of a second 'non' was becoming increasingly possible, if not probable. A paper submitted to the Secretary of State by the Foreign Office official, Roger Jackling, entitled 'EEC: an early French veto', while recognising the need 'to keep at it', was concerned with the need to explore alternative action in the event of a veto in the imminent future. The recommendations in the event of an early veto were to:

> First put pressure on France to reverse her veto; then, if France maintains her position (as must be expected but French responsibility will in that case be even clearer), to profit from the reaction against France throughout Europe which a veto will provoke, to strengthen our position in Europe, and to keep our European options open.[65]

The foreign secretary later saw the paper to which he retorted: 'I am a little surprised and rather sceptical still. But nevertheless the planning is right and the lines proposed seem to be right.'[66] A paper that no one involved in navigating Britain's difficult journey into Europe would have wished to see emerge was now circulating throughout the Foreign Office.

To avoid the development of further problems, the prime minister invited a group of senior French journalists to Downing Street on 10 October 1967. André Fontaine of *Le Monde* and Roger Massip of *Le Figaro* were exposed to the British side of the story, 'to try to ensure that the British view is at least honestly stated in the French Papers'.[67] It is ironic that only a couple of weeks later Wilson himself was to be misrepresented in the British press. The incident took place on 26 October and was widely referred to as the 'Chalfont Affair'. Chalfont briefed journalists on Wilson's so-called retaliatory measures in the event that de Gaulle were to issue a second 'non'. Wilson makes reference to the incident in his memoirs as:

> A storm breaking out over some loose words uttered by Lord Chalfont in Lausanne at what he, at any rate, thought was a non-attributable press discussion. They were sensationalised as implying a direct threat that if General de Gaulle blocked our entry into Europe, we should retaliate by rethinking our entire European policy, including the maintenance of British troops on the Continent.[68]

After some hostile questions in the House of Commons, and much interest in the outburst, the affair subsided. Yet it clearly did nothing to assuage suspicion on the continent that Britain was not truly European.

To gain a clearer picture of the French position, Michael Palliser sent the prime minister a letter he had received from a senior French official whom William Nield had known for years. The senior official believed 'the die is not yet cast' and that the British still had room to manoeuvre:

> The question is to know whether and how you can use this to by-pass the French roadblock. From talks I had a month ago at Strasbourg with Jean Rey and his team, I gained the impression – that only two questions could enable France to continue to block the opening of negotiations: sterling in particular and the problem of agricultural levies.[69]

Pierre Drouin of *Le Monde* had already made this point earlier in the month. Talking in detail about the French attitude, he pointed out that 'the French government is convinced that it is not possible to live both in the European Community and in the sterling area'.[70] According to Drouin, 'France knows that the monetary problem is the most serious that she can place in front of the door of the Common Market in order to block it'.[71]

The second event that applied further brakes to any progress was the devaluation forced on Britain on the 18 November 1967. De Gaulle used the devaluation as the final and damning excuse to put an end to the whole process. The General argued that it merely confirmed what he had been saying all along, that Britain was weak. Wasting no time de Gaulle held a Press Conference on 27 November, indicating that he had indeed made up his mind long ago and was only biding his time until events procured a solution to his dilemma. According to Charles Williams, 'His line was even harder, confirming the opinion of one diplomat that age was hardening his prejudice without blurring his style'.[72] De Gaulle categorised Britain's approach to Europe as a five-act play.

'Act Four came with the beginning of the Wilson Government which was marked by a total lack of interest in the Common Market and by a great emphasis on the maintenance of EFTA and the strengthening of the Commonwealth'. Whereas with Act Five 'came the British candidature supported by every conceivable form of promise and pressure'.[73] Leaving neither political nor economic aspects aside, the general stated that a 'radical transformation must take place if Britain were to join the Continentals'.[74]

Using both the Commission's Report and the recent devaluation, de Gaulle was now able to tie all of his original arguments together under the one umbrella, that Britain was clearly unsuitable to join the EEC. When one looked at both the political and economic obstacles, 'If an attempt were made to force such entry this would lead to a break-up of the Community whose rules could never permit the "monumental exceptions"'.[75] In conclusion, he maintained that 'In order that the British Isles can really make fast to the Continent, there is still a very vast and deep mutation to be effected'.[76] Clearly de Gaulle's second 'non' did not come as such a surprise as his first, and it was less dramatic, but the result was exactly the same. It was even more humiliating for the British – with its weakness magnified for the international community to scrutinise while Britain was told to try again some day.

James Mellon[77] remembers the sense of disappointment at the time and points out that 'we were seen as a great danger to him. Not in terms of logic though. We received a fair amount of stick about it; the blue sea, America, about not being settled down to being Europeans. It was simply a case of stopping us before we got too close.'[78] Michael Palliser remembers Wilson's sense of disappointment at the time: 'It was quite a blow to Wilson. Yet to me it was inevitable. You couldn't have seen it otherwise. It wasn't difficult at all for the general to do it twice. Wilson thought it would be harder to do it twice.'[79]

It was not surprising that British officials were incensed: 'this was the sixteenth press conference which de Gaulle has given as head of the French state, and in substance it was the most outrageous yet'.[80] While finding de Gaulle's statements condescending and at times sarcastic, the British still refused to give up all hope, and immediately turned their attention to cultivating the support of the Five in order to counter such an outcome. However, Wilson's determination would be to no avail, as the Press Conference had effectively put an end to the second British application. James Mellon reflected on the sense of embarrassment but at the same time the inability amongst the other five to do something:

> In the Commission, day in, day out they were very open with us. Although there had been no real sense of progression, there was a great deal of embarrassment when de Gaulle delivered his veto in November. The Germans were clearly embarrassed

but they would not sacrifice Franco-German friendship. The Italians would not go in the trench ahead of us, so as to speak. The Dutch were our only real friends.[81]

Piers Ludlow who has examined Britain's second application from a European perspective verifies the sense of frustration amongst the Five: 'they did not want to accept a French 'no' but did not want to force a 'yes'.[82] Britain would have to wait until the political giant of de Gaulle had left the stage, before she could be admitted into the Common Market.

V

Tactics and the way the British approached the French would present problems again for Edward Heath. Douglas Hurd, who in the run up to the third application was running Edward Heath's office, testifies to the by now age-old problem and indeed the division over the subject:

> With his experience of the first negotiations and the Foreign Office in the late 1960s, Heath was sure that we would only join the EEC by winning round the French, whereas the Foreign Office believed that the Five might force the French along.[83]

Having thoroughly assessed the exchanges between London and Paris for the years 1964 to 1967, one emerges with a number of conclusions. The first of these is that no matter how hard British ministers and officials attempted to draw a line between the past and the present, the past largely dictated the outcome of the second application.

Thomas Barman, commenting on the state of Anglo-French relations in 1967, pointed to another overlooked issue:

> Among the factors that have contributed to the present dangerous state of affairs is the apparent inability of many British politicians – of all political persuasions – to sense what has happened in France, or to perceive that the war and the developments that followed it have left scars on many French minds as deep, perhaps, as the wound left by the loss of Alsace-Lorraine in 1871.[84]

Just as the Second World War sowed the seeds for future British policy for years to come, it also imbued France with a vigorous determination to get back on its feet again and walk as tall as she possibly could, neither aided by nor reliant on anyone else. Anything which threatened to sabotage this goal, ultimately had to be sidelined. In this light it is not surprising that the risk of allowing Britain join the EEC could not be entertained.

What had been achieved in the EEC could clearly not be put at risk by a proposition with neither precedent nor guarantees. Britain at this time did not fully appreciate matters from the French vantage point, and to a certain extent that is understandable. However, this zeal to make France great ('La Gloire') was not the only matter which the British failed to appreciate and would have been against British interests in the first place. Between 1940 and 1967, events had transpired to cause an ironic reversal of fortunes. The balance of power had shifted from one side of the channel to the other. Britain which had proudly stood alone in 1940, was in 1967 standing alone for an entirely different reason. Of the two, Britain had exhibited multiple signs of decline, whereas in contrast, France had not only recovered from its low years earlier, but was surpassing Britain.

British politicians and officials refused to acknowledge their own analysis that they were occupying the weaker bargaining position. The situation could not have been more reversed from those frantic days during the Second World War when de Gaulle was at the mercy of the British. Now, Britain was the one knocking on de Gaulle's door, asking to gain admittance. As Ben Pimlott aptly described the situation at the beginning of 1967, 'The formal meeting with the French President took place at the Elysée Palace on the 24 January. In the official photographs, de Gaulle towered sombrely over the two modestly proportioned British leaders, as if symbolising their difference in world stature.'[85]

Finally, there was de Gaulle: 'It is seldom that one man's psychosis, even when widely shared by colleagues and countrymen, goes far to explain foreign policies or international relations.'[86] A large amount of attention has been devoted to this political giant, for he is the central pivot on which both the first and second applications turned, or failed to turn, as events transpired. Intransigent, opaque, suspicious, stubborn, independent, vain and prudent are just a sample of the adjectives that have been employed to describe the complex character of de Gaulle. Indeed, the majority of these are a succinct depiction of the man who held the keys to Europe in 1967. It is no coincidence that the British application was vetoed twice by the same man. Once Pompidou had assumed the reins of power, Britain was finally allowed to enter the EEC. Memories such as the painful exclusion from the 'Big Three' meetings after the war, Churchill making it perfectly clear that Britain would always 'choose the open seas', Britain's refusal to sign the Treaty of Rome, and the 'Continental Blockade' in 1958 were in time translated into tangible policy, that would result in a loud 'non' not once but twice for Britain. It was as if de Gaulle had etched such grievances against the Anglo-Saxon world in his mind, and was determined at some stage to compensate for France's humiliations.

David Ratford confirms the inevitability of the second veto and the powerlessness of the Wilson administration to alter the outcome:

> There was nothing the Wilson Government could have said or done to circumvent a French veto, because de Gaulle was for his own reasons, connected more with his attitude to the EEC than with his assessment of the UK, determined not to have us in. The important thing for Britain was therefore to ensure, at the very least that nothing was done to harm our long-term position, and if possible that a safe and solid ground was laid for developments after de Gaulle's departure. In that respect, I believe that the Wilson Government's actions were ultimately successful.[87]

Furthermore, speaking quite candidly to Christopher Soames at the beginning of February in 1969, de Gaulle gave a deeper insight into his view of Anglo-French relations.

> Over the centuries, he said it had been the rule and not the exception for relations between our two countries to be bad, a relationship between rivals and not allies. It was only our common fear of Germany which had, exceptionally, brought us together in this century. This fear no longer existed and with it had also disappeared the one spur which had enabled France and Britain to work together.[88]

The United States and the Soviet Union were duly considered ill-matched bedfellows, united only through their fear of Nazism. One cannot consider France and Britain to be cast in the same light. Still, de Gaulle was caught up in his own analysis of the past and to him Britain was undoubtedly more of a rival than an ally. It is only with this in mind that it is not surprising that de Gaulle would see fit to do all in his power to outsmart the British. Not in need of them as an ally, it was much easier to regard them as rivals. Free from the spheres of the superpowers, Paris and Bonn would form the new axis of Europe. The entry of Britain would only dilute this, and as de Gaulle only wanted a 'European Europe', it is not surprising that he regarded the admission of Britain as possibly leading to an 'Atlantic Europe'.

As his biographer Jean Lacouture noted, de Gaulle had said: 'I want her naked! Without her American guardians and her Commonwealth cousins.'[89]

Epilogue

—

When Wilson first met de Gaulle at Churchill's funeral in January 1965, he almost certainly could not have envisaged himself in a similar position to that of Macmillan in January 1963. So why did Wilson make an application in 1967, and why did he fail in his endeavour? Firstly, the Wilson government made an application through a lack of any other viable alternatives. This did not go unnoticed in French quarters. The first Wilson administration was keen to concentrate on other possible options and explore alternatives to a European path. However, as time passed, it became clearly evident that these options were mere fantasies and simply did not exist. There were no 'alternative circles' which Britain could draw, and the 'persistent pressures' of the time left only one option available to Wilson, and that was to make an application to join the EEC. Robin O'Neill illustrated this point:

> The first Wilson administration went through all the alternatives to seeking EEC membership before going for it. The Labour Party had not after all been traditionally a pro-EEC party; and there were many senior figures, like Douglas Jay, who were much opposed to it. So all the alternatives which are examined every time, were raked over again: the Commonwealth; a North American Free Trade Area; widening EFTA; association with the EEC and so on. Again, as always none of them was discovered to be the answer to the problem.[1]

Secondly, while economics clearly affected timing, it was the political element which determined the decision to make an application. The political motives, questions, and gains took precedence over economic ones when it came to Britain's second EEC application.

Thirdly, what was most stark was the apparent inevitability of the second veto. One man's intransigence prevented the British from joining the EEC in 1967. The traditional assessment of the Wilson administration during this period and, in particular, of George Brown's role has always been negative. Criticised at every turn, accused of failure after failure, the handling of the second application could easily be added to that list. Many people assume that if Wilson and his ministers had handled the situation better, developed a personal rapport with de Gaulle, or tweaked the internal dynamics amongst the

Six, then Britain would not have had a second veto in 1967. Whatever other mistakes or misgivings the Wilson administration can be held accountable for, the failure of the second application is not one of them. Responsibility lies solely with one man – de Gaulle. As Oliver Wright maintained, 'the second application, just like the first, was not ever decided on details. There was not a tactical thing you could do to unlock the door that de Gaulle held the keys to'.[2] One of the most Francophile of all participants, the British Ambassador to France, Patrick Reilly reiterated this view: 'From the first, de Gaulle was determined not to let us in, that nothing we could have said or done, would have made any difference. So Christopher Soames came and de Gaulle went, and the tide turned our way.'[3]

In examining Britain's European policy during those critical years, one politician stands out. It is rare to see George Brown cast in the light of anything other than a bumbling buffoon, an alcoholic, incapable of contributing anything other than entertainment to those early Wilson years. Both contentions are not only inaccurate, but also regrettable. While Wilson cannot be blamed for the failure of the second application, it would be an exaggeration to applaud his involvement in the process. That praise should be reserved for George Brown. Exhibiting real vision, consistent in his views, a constant advocate of the European path and dogged in his determination to succeed, Brown played a remarkable, and to date unacknowledged role in shaping Britain's European destiny. It is vital to remember Brown's outspoken declaration: 'we've got to break with America, devalue, and go into Europe'.

De Gaulle's press conference on 27 November 1967 ended British hopes. On 18 and 19 December 1967, the Council of Ministers of the Community met and the French refused to agree to the opening of negotiations with Britain and the other applicants. The following day the president of the Council of Ministers of the Community, Professor Karl Schiller wrote a letter to Wilson noting the deadlock but at the same time reiterating that the application would remain on its agenda. On 20 December, speaking to the House of Commons, Brown stated:

> The Communiqué which was issued after yesterday's meeting of the Community Council of Ministers made clear that our application as well as those of the other countries remain on the agenda of the Council of Ministers. We, in turn, confirm that our application stands. We do not intend to withdraw it.[4]

So the application had been rebuffed by the French but it was not withdrawn by the British. Over the next sixteen months the British government maintained their resolve to 'not take no for an answer' and leave the application 'on the table', refusing any suggestions of compromise, or alternatives short of full membership.

The next major occurance which was to impinge on events took place on 4 February 1969, and is subsequently referred to as the 'Soames Affair'. De Gaulle, having received Christopher Soames, the British Ambassador to France, made proposals to the British in confidence. De Gaulle discussed the possibility of transforming the EEC into a distinctly looser organisation in which Britain could find a place. Discussions of the details could take place amongst all countries concerned at a later date, but could be preceded by secret Anglo-French talks. Reporting back to the Foreign Office, Soames recounted what the general had mentioned: 'he would be quite prepared to discuss with us what should take the place of the Common Market as an enlarged European Economic Association.'[5] Having immediately been informed about the number of telegrams being sent backwards and forwards between Paris and London concerning Soames's audience with de Gaulle, Wilson's initial reaction was interesting:

> Is this connected with Debré's invitation to the Chancellor? or is he trying to put us off taking too hard (i.e. anti-French) a line in Bonn; or is he getting ready to say to President Nixon that he offered us this and that we rejected/dithered? We should follow this up; and we have in mind the possibility that, given encouragement, this could be escalated to higher level meetings – first the Foreign Secretary then possibly myself.[6]

It was indeed discussed in detail and the result was that the British felt compelled to share the details with Kiesinger a week later and it became public knowledge soon thereafter. Michael Palliser had doubts at the time and his gut feeling was to at least inform de Gaulle that they were going to tell the others: 'It was not so much if he should tell him but tell de Gaulle that he was going to tell Kiesinger. I suppose elementary courtesy'.[7]

Yet uppermost in their minds was that the 'Foreign Office saw it as a sinister plot by de Gaulle to trap Britain into the image of a saboteur. If we do not tell the five then de Gaulle will tell the five that it was a British proposal'.[8] Exposing his proposal to the others was therefore their priority for fear of future ramifications – such as being painted in anything but a pro-European light. However, according to Palliser 'de Gaulle was not going to let us in anyway and we had to wait until he disappeared from the scene and Pompidou took over'.[9] This occurred sooner than expected, with de Gaulle's resignation two months later: 'The door was now open. The transformation of our prospects, by this single event, was complete. Everywhere, except at first in France, this was assumed to be the case'.[10] As Robin O'Neill recollects:

I was present at the late night discussions Harold Wilson had with his staff on whether to make public the rash proposition de Gaulle had put to Sir Christopher Soames about a special relationship between France and Britain on European affairs – the 'Soames Affair'. As you know, the worm turned. In a sense it marked part of the decline of de Gaulle, and a turning point between the second and third British applications.[11]

On 15 June, Pompidou succeeded de Gaulle as President. Britain's chances of entry were further enhanced by the departure of Couve de Murville, one of de Gaulle's staunchest allies in keeping Britain out of the EEC. As Michael Butler contends 'As soon as de Gaulle went back to Colombey there was no more veto in principle. Pompidou had not approved of de Gaulle's anti-Britishness – in fact I am pretty sure he didn't.'[12]

Con O'Neill notes that 'the Labour Government immediately recognised that our prospects for membership of the Community had changed from nil to good', and points out that his own experience confirmed that: 'less than four weeks after the General's departure I was approached and invited to the Foreign Office to take charge of the departments concerned with European Integration and to be the official leader of the negotiations now foreseen'.[13]

On 22 July 1969, the Council of Ministers of the Community asked the Commission to provide an updated version of its 1967 'opinion' on Britain's application. The Commission reported back on 1 October, recommending the opening of negotiations 'as soon as possible'. On 1 and 2 December the Six met at The Hague and 'The Communiqué issued after this meeting became on the side of the Community, the charter for the opening of negotiations'.[14]

In June 1970, the Conservatives won the general election and Edward Heath was the man charged with continuing the groundwork laid by the Wilson administration. The official historian of these negotiations, Con O'Neill, adamantly emphasises the continuity between Heath and Wilson's applications and work in the area:

> Looking back, with the benefit of wisdom after the event, my own conclusion is that Monsieur Pompidou and the French Government did in fact effectively take at this Summit meeting the decision which admitted us to the Community. The rest, astonishing though it often was, was no more than the process of negotiation.[15]

Other significant developments had also taken place in the dynamics of the European landscape. As Eric Roll maintained, 'By the time of the third application you also have other changes taking place. For example, the French are beginning to worry that perhaps they are too much in bed with the Germans.'[16]

Oliver Wright maintained this view by pointing out that by the time of the third application 'there was a feeling in France that the Germans were sowing their oats, and were gradually beginning to re-assert themselves'.[17]

On 30 June 1970 the negotiations began, negotiations that were certainly not without problems, obstacles, and delays but negotiations that ultimately succeeded. And so, after the Heath–Pompidou summit in May 1971, Pompidou held a press conference in the same room in the Elysée Palace, Salon des Fêtes as de Gaulle had issued the first veto to Britain in 1963. Yet the outcome would be different this time, for Pompidou effectively declared that Britain would soon be a member of the EEC. Edward Heath, later reflecting on the momentous occasion, stated unequivocally that:

> The French President believed and trusted me. I had known him and his views for many years. I had known his Chief of Staff and there was good rapport between us. Pompidou wanted to settle the whole thing. It went on for two days – these discussions, and everybody obviously assumed it was another failure and that we were trying to cover it up. So we sat down in the gold chairs in the Elysée Palace and declared the outcome. All were flabbergasted that our application had been successful.[18]

After Pompidou's statement, the final negotiations continued and culminated in the Treaty of Accession signed in January 1972, allowing Britain to enter the EEC. So on 1 January 1973 Britain finally became a member of the EEC. Eleven years of tentatively trying, patiently persevering, and endless efforts had paid off.

Notes

INTRODUCTION

1   De Gaulle's press conference, 16 May 1967. A larger extract of his speech can be found in 'Western European Union Assembly, General Affairs Committee 14th ordinary session: the British application for membership of the European Communities 1963–1968'; brief prepared by Mr M. Van der Stoel, Rapporteur (Paris, May 1968), no. 39, pp. 55–8.
2   Winston Churchill, in a speech in Paris, 11 Nov. 1944, quoted in Robert Rhodes James (ed.), *Winston Churchill: His Complete Speeches*, vol. 6 (London, 1974)
3   For further information see Roger Bullen and M. E. Pelly (eds), *Documents on British Policy Overseas*, Series II, vol. 3, no. 114 (London, 1989); Michael Charlton, *The Price of Victory* (London, 1983); Michael Dockrill and John Young, *British Foreign Policy, 1945–1956* (London, 1989).
4   For more information on the above, see John Young, *Britain and European Unity 1945–1999* (London, 1993), pp. 6–52.
5   Sir Oliver Wright joined HM Diplomatic Service in 1945, became assistant private secretary to the secretary of state for foreign affairs in 1960; counsellor and private secretary to the prime minister, 1964–6; ambassador to Denmark, 1966–9.
6   Author's interview with Sir Oliver Wright, 29 May 2001.
7   'What I have called the fraternal association of the English-speaking peoples . . . means a special relationship between the British Commonwealth and Empire and the United States.' Winston Churchill in 1946 Sinews of Peace address to US President Harry S. Truman.
8   TNA, Prem. 11/2985 Harold Macmillan to Selwyn Lloyd, 22 Oct. 1959.
9   Alistair Horne, *Harold Macmillan*, vol. 11 (London, 1989), p. 428.
10 Author's interview with Sir Michael Butler, 22 May 2001.
11 Ibid.
12 Ibid.
13 Ibid.
14 Author's interview with Sir Oliver Wright, 29 May 2001.
15 Harold Macmillan, *At the End of the Day, 1961–1963* (London, 1973), p. 369.
16 Author's correspondence with Sir James Marjoribanks, 16 May 2001.
17 Author's correspondence with Robin O'Neill, 18 Apr. 2001.
18 Harold Macmillan, *Pointing the Way: 1959–1961* (London, 1972), p. 427.
19 Charles de Gaulle 1934 quoted in Dorothy Pickles, *The Uneasy Entente: French Foreign Policy and Franco-British Misunderstandings* (London, 1996), p. 1.
20 'Each time we have to choose between Europe and the open sea, we shall always choose the open sea. Each time I have to choose between you and Roosevelt, I shall always choose

Roosevelt.' De Gaulle, *Mémoires de Guerre: L'Unité, 1942–1944*, vol. II (Paris, 1956), p. 224.
21   Jean Lacouture, *De Gaulle: The Ruler 1945–1970* (London, 1991).
22   Author's correspondence with Robin O'Neill, 18 Apr. 2001.
23   TNA, FO 371/177874, piece no RF 1051/12, Michael Palliser to Jeremy Thomas (Western Dept), 21 Feb. 1964.
24   TNA, FO 371/177874, piece no. 1051/12 FO minute by Crispin Tickell to Michael Palliser, 20 Feb. 1964.
25   Bernard Donoughue, 'Harold Wilson and the renegotiation of the EEC Terms of Membership 1974: a witness account', in Brian Brivati and Harriet Jones (eds), *From Reconstruction to Integration, Britain and Europe Since 1945* (London, 1993), p. 204.
26   Philip Ziegler, *Harold Wilson* (London, 1993), p. 219.
27   Harold Wilson, quoted in *The Times*, 17 Nov. 1964.
28   Cited in Ben Pimlott, *Harold Wilson* (London, 1993), p. 249.
29   www.labour-[arty.org.uk/manifestos/1964/1964-labour

ONE: WAIT AND SEE

1   Ben Pimlott, *Harold Wilson* (London, 1993), p. 319.
2   Robert Stephens in *The Observer*, 7 Feb. 1965.
3   TNA, FO 371/177, piece no. M1093–70, Con O'Neill to R. A. B. Butler, received 25 July 1964.
4   Author's interview with Robin O'Neill, 31 May 2001.
5   Author's interview with Sir Michael Palliser, 5 June 2001.
6   TNA, Prem. 13/317, Record of a conversation between the prime minister and the president of France at the French Embassy, 29 Jan. 1965.
7   TNA, FO 371/182949, piece no. RF1051/6, Pierson Dixon's farewell interview with General de Gaulle, sent to Michael Stewart, 29 Jan. 1965.
8   Ibid.
9   TNA, FO 371/182949, piece no. RF 1051/6, Jeremy Thomas in a FO Brief at the Western Department, 29 Jan. 1965.
10   Press cutting in TNA, FO 371/182949, piece no. RF 1051/12 from H. A. F. Hohler to the Viscount Hood (FO) 5 Feb. 1965.
11   TNA, FO 371/182377, piece no. 10810/11 extract from the transcript of the foreign secretary's interview on BBC Television on 15 Feb.1965 from E. J. W. Barnes.
12   For further detail see ibid.
13   TNA, FO 371/182949, piece no. RF 1051/28, Record of talks between Duncan Sandys and Couve de Murville, 26 Feb. 1965.
14   Ibid.
15   Ibid.
16   TNA, Prem. 13/306, Michael Stewart to Harold Wilson, 3 Mar. 1965.
17   TNA, Prem. 13/324, Patrick Reilly to Harold Caccia (FO) 1 Mar. 1965.
18   TNA, Prem. 13/306, in a letter from Michael Stewart to Harold Wilson, 12 Mar. 1965.
19   Ibid.
20   TNA, Prem. 13/324 Patrick Reilly to Michael Stewart, 18 Mar. 1965.
21   Ibid.

22 Ibid.
23 Ibid.
24 TNA, Prem. 13/324, FO telegram no. 179 of 24 Mar. 1965 from Patrick Reilly.
25 TNA, Prem. 13/324, Patrick Reilly to Harold Caccia, 30 Mar. 1965 .
26 Ibid.
27 TNA, Prem. 13/324, Patrick Reilly to Michael Stewart, 18 Mar. 1965.
28 Harold Wilson, *The Labour Government 1964–1970* (London, 1971), p. 90.
29 Ibid.
30 Ibid.
31 Ibid.
32 TNA, Prem. 13/324, record of a conversation between the prime minister and the president of the French Republic at the Elysée Palace at 3.00 p.m., 2 Apr. 1965.
33 Ibid.
34 TNA, Prem. 13/324, Record of the meeting between the foreign secretary and the French foreign minister at the Quai d'Orsay at 10.00 a.m. on Saturday 3 Apr. 1965.
35 TNA, Prem. 13/324, Harold Wilson to General de Gaulle, 8 Apr. 1965.
36 TNA, FO. 371/182951, piece no. RF 1051/69, telegram no. 138 from Patrick Reilly to FO, 12 July 1965.
37 Ibid.
38 Ibid.
39 TNA, FO 371/182951, piece no. RF 1051/69, Jeremy Thomas, 14 July 1965.
40 Ibid. Jeremy Thomas summarising Alain Peyrefitte's 10 July speech, 14 July 1965.
41 TNA, FO 371/182378, telegram no. 1278 Frank Roberts, (Bonn) to FO, 26 Nov. 1965.
42 TNA, FO 371/182379, piece no M10810/164/9, Rew to MacLehose, 28 Dec. 1965.
43 Ibid.
44 TNA, FO 371/188327, piece no M10810/17(A), address by Con O'Neill to the Committee for Belgian-Netherlands-Luxembourg Co-operation, The Hague, 14 Jan. 1966.
45 Ibid.
46 Ibid.
47 Ibid.
48 Michael Stewart, *The Jekyll and Hyde Years: Politics and Economic Policy since 1974* (London, 1977), p. 25.
49 James Callaghan, *Time and Chance* (London, 1987), p. 148. See also Kenneth Morgan, *Callaghan: A Life* (Oxford, 1997), pp. 226–7.
50 TNA, FO 371/188268, Piece: M1062/6, A speech delivered to the Federal Trust for Education and Research by the Secretary for State, 25 Jan. 1966.
51 Ibid.
52 TNA, FO 371/188268, piece no. M1062/8, A speech by Edward Heath to the Federal Trust, 26 Jan. 1966.
53 TNA, FO 371/188268, piece no. M1062/3, An address by the foreign secretary to the 1966 course at the Imperial Defence College, Jan. 1966.
54 Ibid.
55 TNA, Prem. 13/904, Tommy Balogh to Harold Wilson, 31 Jan. 1966.
56 Lord Gladwyn had been Britain's ambassador to France in the late 1950s, but subsequently devoted himself to advocating British entry into the EEC.

57 TNA, FO 371/188352, piece no. M10811/3, a lecture delivered by Lord Gladwyn in Hamburg, Bonn 2 and 3 Feb. 1966, sent to C. M. MacLehose at the FO, 15 Feb. 1966.
58 Ibid.
59 Ibid.
60 TNA, FO 371/188329, piece no. M10810/44, Robin O'Neill summarising what Spaak had to say, 7 Feb. 1966.
61 TNA, FO 371/188331, piece no. M10810/103 summarised by Patrick Reilly in telegram no. 240 of 17 Mar. 1966.
62 TNA, Prem. 13/904, Harold Wilson's speech at Central Hall, Bristol, 18 Mar. 1966.
63 Ibid.
64 Author's interview with Sir Michael Palliser, 5 June 2001.
65 TNA, FO 371/188332, piece no. M10810/111, telegram no. 56, Frank Roberts (Bonn) to FO, 23 Mar. 1966.
66 Ibid.
67 TNA, FO 371/188331, piece no. M10810/107, press conference by Roy Jenkins, Saturday 19 Mar. 1966.
68 Oliver Kemp, CMG, born 1916, appointed officer in HM Foreign Service 1945. Deputy Head of the United Kingdom Delegation to the European Commission, Luxembourg, 1965–7.
69 Edmond Wellenstein, formerly a senior official in the European Commission and ECSC High Authority Secretary.
70 TNA, FO 371/188332, piece no. M10810/116, letter from Oliver Kemp to Sir James Marjoribanks, 21 Mar. 1966.
71 The leading Italian daily independent newspaper which leans to the right and represents the views of the Milanese business community.
72 TNA, FO 371/188333, piece no. M10810/ M10810/135, Alfredo Pieroni in *Corriere Della Serra*, 30 Mar. 1966.
73 Ibid.
74 Author's interview with Robin O'Neill, 31 May 2001.

TWO: HAROLD, GEORGE AND PERSISTENT PRESSURES

1 Harold Wilson, Hansard, Apr. 1965, col. 623.
2 Harold Wilson, Hansard, 10 Nov. 1966, col. 1540.
3 Harold Wilson at the Lord Mayor's banquet, Guildhall, 14 Nov. 1966, in Frances Nicholson and Roger East, *From the Six to the Twelve: The Enlargement of the European Communities* (Harlow, 1987).
4 Author's interview with Sir Oliver Wright, 29 May 2001.
5 Ronald Butt, 'The Common Market and Conservative party politics 1961–62', *Government and Opposition* 2 (1967), p. 373.
6 Author's interview with Robin O'Neill, 31 May 2001.
7 George Brown, *In My Way* (London, 1970), p. 14.
8 Ibid.
9 Hugh Gaitskell had succeeded Attlee as leader of the Labour Party in Dec. 1955, and after suffering a rare disease died in January 1963.

10 Author's correspondence with Robin O'Neill, 18 Apr. 2001.
11 Ben Pimlott, *Harold Wilson* (London, 1993), pp. 329–31.
12 Author's correspondence with Sir Jeremy Thomas, 16 Apr. 2001.
13 Lord Jenkins of Hillhead, speaking on *The Last Europeans*, Channel Four TV, 26 Nov. 1995.
14 George Brown (interviewed by Kenneth Harris) 'Why I am what I am', *Observer*, 14 Aug. 1966.
15 Ibid.
16 Brown, *In my Way*, p. 140.
17 Ibid., p. 129.
18 Author's interview with Lord Roll, 29 May 2001.
19 Author's interview with Sir Oliver Wright, 29 May 2001.
20 Brown, *In my Way*, p. 208.
21 Harold Wilson, *The Labour Government 1964–1970* (London, 1971), p. 272.
22 Brown, *In My Way*, p. 205.
23 Douglas Jay, *Change and Fortune: A Political Record* (London, 1980), p. 363.
24 Uwe Kitzinger, *The Second Try: Labour and the EEC* (London, 1968), p. 13.
25 Sir Nicholas (Maxted) Fenn, GCMG, Born in 1936, assistant private secretary to the secretary of state for foreign and commonwealth affairs, 1963–7.
26 Sir Derek (Malcolm) Day, KCMG, born 1927. Entered HM foreign service in 1951. Second, then first secretary in the Foreign Office 1959–62; first secretary in the British Embassy, Washington 1962– 66; first secretary in the Foreign Office 1966–7; assistant private secretary to the secretary of state for foreign affairs.
27 Author's correspondence with Sir Nicholas Fenn, 1 Aug. 2001.
28 Author's correspondence with Sir Derek Day, 16 Apr. 2001.
29 TNA, Prem. 13/1476, Harold Wilson at a meeting with President de Gaulle in the Elysée Palace, 24 Jan. 1967.
30 Brown, *In my Way*, p. 140.
31 TNA, FO 371/188343, piece no. M10810/393(G), George Brown to Harold Wilson, 1 Aug. 1966.
32 Author's correspondence with Sir David Ratford, 19 Apr. 2001.
33 Author's correspondence with Lord Callaghan, 1 May 2001.
34 Anthony Sampson in *Le Monde*, 20 Oct. 1967.
35 Leonard Beaton, *Guardian*, 15 June 1966.
36 Richard Crossman, *The Diaries of a Cabinet Minister, vol 1, Minister of Housing 1964–66* (London, 1975), p. 472. Tony was Anthony Crosland, George Brown's deputy in 1964, who went on to become secretary of state for education in 1965 and president of the Board of Trade in 1967.
37 Author's interview with Robin O'Neill, 31 May 2001.
38 John Robinson in an interview with Hugo Young, 20 Aug. 1993; Hugo Young, *This Blessed Plot: Britain and Europe from Churchill to Blair* (London, 1999), p. 180.
39 Author's correspondence with Robin O'Neill, 18 Apr. 2001.
40 Author's interview with Sir Oliver Wright, 29 May 2001.
41 Author's interview with Robin O'Neill, 31 May 2001.
42 TNA, Prem. 13/904, Thomas Balogh to Harold Wilson, 31 Jan. 1966.

43 TNA, Prem. 13/907, Thomas Balogh to Burke Trend and David Mitchell, 1 July 1966.
44 Ibid.
45 TNA, Prem. 13/907, Thomas Balogh to Harold Wilson, 4 July 1966.
46 Author's correspondence with Robin O'Neill, 18 Apr. 2001.
47 Ibid.
48 TNA, FO 371/188340, piece no. M10810/317/9, Con O'Neill to David Mitchell (DEA) 1 June 1966.
49 TNA, FO 371/188343, piece no. M10810/388, Con O'Neill to the permanent under-secretary, 13 July 1966.
50 TNA, FO 371/188346, piece no. M10810/458, Con O'Neill to Wilson's private secretary, 18 Aug. 1966.
51 Ibid.
52 TNA, Prem. 13/908, additional notes made by Harold Wilson to Balogh's letter to him, 20 Oct. 1966.
53 TNA, FO 371/188347, piece no. M10810/475/G, Con O'Neill to the private secretary, 21 Oct. 1966.
54 Ibid.
55 *Sunday Times*, 2 Jan. 1966.
56 *Financial Times*, 13 Oct. 1966.
57 TNA, FO 371/188347, piece no. M10810/478, John Robinson to Norman Statham, 31 Oct. 1966.
58 TNA, Prem. 13/1473, John Davies speaking at a meeting between the prime minister and representatives of the CBI at 10 Downing Street, 4 July 1967.
59 See TNA, Prem. 13/312, UK Delegation, Brussels, 18 May 1965.
60 Ibid.
61 *Daily Telegraph*, 24 Oct. 1966.
62 Ibid.
63 TNA, Prem. 13/909, Burke Trend to Harold Wilson, 28 Oct. 1966.
64 Both men had only recently been involved in a bid for leadership of the Labour Party.
65 Author's interview with Lord Roll, 29 May 2001.
66 Ibid.
67 Ben Pimlott, *Harold Wilson* (London, 1993), p. 364.
68 Author's correspondence with Lord Callaghan, 1 May 2001.
69 Ibid.
70 George Brown, cited in Barbara Castle, *The Castle Diaries 1964–1970* (London, 1984), p. 148.
71 D. Gowland and A. Turner, *Reluctant Europeans: Britain and European Integration 1945–1998* (London, 2000), p. 159.
72 Author's correspondence with Robin O'Neill, 18 Apr. 2001.
73 Author's correspondence with Sir Jeremy Thomas, 16 Apr. 2001.
74 Tony Benn, *The Benn Diaries* (London, 1996), 30 Apr. 1967, p. 171.
75 TNA, FO 371/188352, piece no. M10811/3, Gladwyn's speech 'The changing British attitude towards Europe' sent to C. M. Maclehose, 15 Feb. 1966.
76 Author's interview with Sir Michael Palliser, 5 June 2001.

THREE: NO ALTERNATIVE CIRCLE

1 John Darwin, 'British decolonisation since 1945: a pattern or a puzzle?' *Journal of Imperial and Commonwealth History* XII: 1 (1983), p. 206.
2 TNA, FCO 30/224, piece no. MEK 4/1/1/. Transcript of interview with Chalfont on *Independent Television News*, 9 Oct. 1967.
3 In 1960, Macmillan gave a speech in Cape Town, South Africa and discussed the process of imperial disintegration. For further detail see Dennis Judd, *Empire: The British Imperial Experience from 1765 to the Present* (London, 1996), pp. 367–71.
4 Harold Macmillan, *Hansard*, vol. 645, 55, col. 1480, 2 Aug. 1961.
5 Author's correspondence with Sir Jeremy Thomas, 16 Apr. 2001.
6 Miriam Camps, *Britain and the European Community, 1955–63* (London, 1964), p. 538.
7 Roy Jenkins, *A Life at the Centre* (London, 1991), p. 143.
8 Hansard, 3 Aug. 1961 vol. 645 cols 1651–70.
9 TNA, Prem. 13/306, Harold Wilson to Michael Stewart, 5 Mar. 1965.
10 TNA, Prem. 13/306, Michael Stewart to Harold Wilson, 12 Mar. 1965.
11 See Robert J. Lieber, *British Politics and European Unity* (Berkeley, 1970), pp. 261–2.
12 TNA, CAB 128/42, CC (67) 26 Conclusions, 20 Apr. 1967.
13 Michael Stewart, *The Jekyll and Hyde Years: Politics and Economic Policy since 1974* (London, 1977), p. 77.
14 Michael Wheaton, 'The Labour Party and Europe 1950–71', in Ghita Ionescu (ed.), *The New Politics of European Integration* (Basingstoke, 1972), p. 95.
15 Author's interview with Sir Oliver Wright, 29 May 2001.
16 General Smuts, 25 Nov. 1943, cited in A. P. Thornton, *For the File on Empire: Essays and Reviews* (London, 1968), p. 372.
17 Dennis Judd, *Empire: The British Imperial Experience from 1765 to the Present* (London, 1966), p. 371.
18 Robert Holland, *The Pursuit of Greatness: Britain and the World Role 1900–1970* (London, 1991), pp. 329–30.
19 Ibid., p. 330.
20 Hugo Young, *This Blessed Plot: Britain and Europe from Churchill to Blair* (London, 1999), p. 188.
21 TNA, Prem. 11/4811, Pierson Dixon to R. A. B. Butler; 'Europe and Atlantic relations'; 16 July 1964.
22 TNA, Prem. 11/4811, Oliver Wright's covering note on Pierson Dixon's despatch on 'European and Atlantic relations', 16 July 1964.
23 TNA, Prem. 13/103, Paymaster General to Harold Wilson, 20 Oct. 1964.
24 Author's interview with Robin O'Neill, 31 May 2001.
25 Ibid.
26 TNA, Prem. 13/910, Harold Wilson to President Lyndon Johnson, 11 Nov. 1966.
27 Author's correspondence with Lord Callaghan, 1 May 2001.
28 TNA, FCO 30/224, piece no MEK 4/1/1, Harold Wilson in a speech to the National Press Club in Washington, 1 Apr. 1963.
29 Author's interview with Sir Michael Palliser, 5 June 2001.
30 TNA, FCO 30/224, piece no. MEK 4/1/1, interview on Independent Television, 'Anglo-American relations and Europe', 9 Oct. 1967.

31 A. M. Rendel for *The Times*, 10 Oct. 1967.
32 Department of State to the president, 14 July 1966, LBJ National Security files, cited in Christopher Lord, *British Entry to the European Community under the Heath Government of 1970–4* (Aldershot, 1993), p.16.
33 Author's interview with Robin O'Neill, 31 May 2001.
34 TNA, Prem. 13/1475, Patrick Dean to the foreign secretary 12 Jan. 1967.
35 TNA, Prem. 13/1477, Michael Palliser, 25 Feb. 1967.
36 TNA, FCO 30/226, piece no. MEK 4/1/1, telegram no. 1246 Patrick Dean (Washington) to the FO 18 Apr. 1967.
37 George Ball in *Sunday Telegraph*, 7 May 1967.
38 Author's interview with Robin O'Neill, 31 May 2001.
39 TNA, FCO 30/223, piece no. MEK 4/1/1, Patrick Dean to Con O'Neill, 13 Jan. 1967.
40 Author's interview with Sir Michael Palliser, 5 June 2001.
41 Ibid.
42 TNA, Prem. 13/906 telegram no 5288, President Johnson to Harold Wilson, 23 May 1966.
43 TNA, FO 371/188346, piece no. M10810/459, FO minute by Patrick Hancock, 1 Sept. 1966.
44 TNA, Prem. 13/909, telegram no 217, Patrick Dean to FO, 2 Nov. 1966.
45 TNA, FO 371/188343; piece no. M10810/387, J. A. Thomson to Mr Greenhill, 26 July 1966. Report on George Ball's speech at Chatham House the previous day.
46 Interview with Sir Michael Palliser, 5 June 2001.
47 Ibid.
48 TNA, FO 371/188362, record of conversation at lunch in the State Department, 16 May 1966.
49 TNA, FO 30/223, piece no. MEK 4/1/1, Patrick Dean to Con O'Neill, 13 Jan. 1967.
50 TNA, Prem. 13/1475; Patrick Dean to the foreign secretary 12 Jan. 1967.

FOUR: HOW TO GET INTO THE COMMON MARKET

1 TNA, FO 371/188335, piece no. M10810/188 foreign secretary's speech in Stockholm, 5 May 1966.
2 Ibid.
3 Ibid.
4 Ibid.
5 TNA, FO 371/188335, piece no. M10810/188 first secretary's speech in Stockholm, 5 May 1966.
6 Author's interview with Sir Michael Palliser, 5 June 2001.
7 Ibid.
8 TNA, FO 3271/188336, piece no. M10810/220, FO minute by Norman Statham, 6 May 1966.
9 Ibid.
10 Ibid.
11 TNA, FO 371/188344 , piece no. M10810/421/G Norman Statham to Con O'Neill, 11 May 1966.
12 TNA, Prem. 13/906, Eric Roll's opinion according to Thomas Balogh, 16 May 1966.
13 TNA, Prem. 13/906, Thomas Balogh in a letter to Harold Wilson, 16 May 1966.
14 TNA, Prem. 13/906, George Brown to Harold Wilson, 16 May 1966.
15 Ibid.
16 TNA, Prem. 13/906, Wilson's personal minute, 19 May 1966.
17 TNA, FO 371/188337, piece no. M10810/223, J. E. Galsworthy to J. A. Snellgrove 23 May 1966.

18 Ibid.
19 TNA, FO 371/188337, piece no. M10810/227, telegram no. 423, from Patrick Reilly, 25 May 1966.
20 Ronald Koven in *The Herald Tribune*, 25 May 1966.
21 TNA, Prem. 13/906, Michael Palliser to Harold Wilson, 31 May 1966.
22 Ibid.
23 TNA, Prem. 13/906, George Brown to Harold Wilson, 23 June 1966.
24 Ibid.
25 Ibid.
26 Ibid.
27 TNA, FO 371/188340, piece no. M10810/309, transcript of the programme *Britain in Search of a Continent*, 9 June 1966.
28 Ibid.
29 Ibid.
30 Ibid.
31 Michel Gabrysiak in the *Sunday Times*, 26 June 1966.
32 TNA, Prem. 13/907, George Brown to Harold Wilson, 29 June 1966.
33 TNA, Prem. 13/509, telegram no. 512, Patrick Reilly to the FO, 25 June 1966.
34 TNA, FO 371/188344, piece no. M10810/325, Oliver Kemp to James Marjoribanks, 4 July 1966.
35 TNA, FO 371/189122, piece no. RF 1051/31, FO Guidance telegram no. 202, 4 July 1966.
36 TNA, Prem. 13/1509, Conversations with Couve de Murville and Georges Pompidou, Terence Prictie reporting, 4 July 1966.
37 Ibid.
38 Author's interview with Lord Roll, 29 May 2001.
39 TNA, Prem. 13/1509, Record of a Conversation during the french prime minister's luncheon for the prime minister at the French Embassy on Friday, 8 July 1966.
40 TNA, FO 371/188359, piece no. M10823/9, Douglas Hurd to John Snellgrove, 1 Aug. 1966.
41 Ibid.
42 Ibid.
43 Ibid.
44 Ibid.
45 Author's interview with Sir Michael Palliser, 5 June 2001.
46 Ibid.
47 Ibid.
48 Ibid.
49 Author's interview with Lord Roll, 29 May 2001.
50 TNA, FO 371/188359, piece no M10823/9, Douglas Hurd to Anthony Snellgrove, 1 Aug. 1966.
51 TNA, FO 371/188346, piece no. M10810/458, FO paper 'How to get into the Common Market', sent by Con O'Neill to the private secretary 18 Aug. 1966.
52 Ibid.
53 TNA, FO 371/188346, piece no. M10810/458, notes on the FO paper 'How to get into the Common Market'.
54 TNA, FO 371/188346, piece no. M10810/458(A), Nicholas Fenn to Con O'Neill, 23 Aug. 1966.
55 Author's interview with Lord Roll, 29 May 2001.
56 Author's correspondence with Sir Jeremy Thomas, 16 Apr. 2001.

57 TNA, FO 371/188346, piece no. M10810/459, FO minute by Patrick Hancock, 1 Sept. 1966.
58 TNA, Prem. 13/908, Thomas Balogh to Harold Wilson, 6 Sept. 1966.
59 Ibid.
60 TNA, FO 371/188346, piece no. M10810/459, Patrick Hancock's FO Paper, 'The American attitude to British membership', 1 Sept. 1966.
61 *Financial Times*, 12 Sept. 1966.
62 TNA, Prem. 13/908, telegram no. 682, Patrick Reilly to FO, 13 Sept. 1966.
63 TNA, Prem. 13/908, Harold Wilson's covering note on telegram no. 682, 13 Sept. 1966.
64 Michel Debré in the *Sunday Times*, 18 Sept. 1966.
65 TNA, FO 371/188365 piece no. M10829/11, telegram no. 720 from Patrick Reilly to the FO, 30 Sept. 1966.
66 Ibid.
67 TNA, FO 371/188345, piece no. M10810/443, Lord Carodan (New York) to the FO, 10 Oct. 1966.
68 TNA, FO 371/188346, piece no. M10810/464/9, Con O'Neill to the private secretary 26 Sept. 1966.

FIVE: BY LITTLE STEPS TOWARDS THE CONTINENT

1 *Financial Times*, 14 Oct. 1966.
2 TNA, Prem. 13/897, Oliver Wright to Michael Palliser, 18 Oct. 1966.
3 TNA, FO 371/188346, telegram no. 104, James Marjoribanks to the FO, 19 Oct. 1966.
4 TNA, Prem. 13/897, Oliver Wright to Michael Palliser, 18 Oct. 1966.
5 TNA, Prem. 13/897, Oliver Wright to Michael Palliser, 21 Oct. 1966.
6 Ibid.
7 TNA, FO 371/188346, piece no. M10810/451/(B), telegram no. 1480, Frank Roberts (Bonn) to FO 20 Oct. 1966.
8 Ibid.
9 *Daily Telegraph*, 24 Oct. 1966.
10 Ibid.
11 TNA, Prem. 13/909, Burke Trend to Harold Wilson, 28 Oct. 1966.
12 *Financial Times*, 14 Oct. 1966.
13 Clive Ponting, *Breach of Promise: Labour in Power, 1964–70* (London, 1989), p. 207.
14 Denis Healey cited in ibid., p. 207.
15 Douglas Jay cited in Hugo Young, *This Blessed Plot: Britain and Europe from Churchill to Blair* (London, 1999), p. 191.
16 Author's interview with Sir Michael Palliser, 5 June 2001.
17 Author's interview with Robin O'Neill, 31 May 2001.
18 Ibid.
19 Tony Benn, *The Benn Diaries* (London, 1995), 22 Oct. 1966, p. 165.
20 TNA, Prem. 13/909, Burke Trend to Harold Wilson, 28 Oct. 1966.
21 Ibid.
22 Ibid.
23 Author's interview with Sir Michael Palliser, 5 June 2001.

24 Ibid.
25 Ibid.
26 TNA, CAB 129/127 C (66) 146, 2 Nov. 1966.
27 TNA, CAB 128/41, CC 54 (66) 3 Nov. 1966.
28 TNA, CAB 129/127, C (66) 149, 7 Nov. 1966.
29 Ibid.
30 TNA, Prem. 13/910, telegram no; 10190 (Personal) Harold Wilson to President Johnson, 11 Nov. 1966.
31 Ibid.
32 TNA, Prem. 16/910, telegram no. 10293 (Personal) President Johnson to Harold Wilson, 15 Nov. 1966.
33 TNA, FO 371/188351, piece no. M10810/59, Con O'Neill to Patrick Hancock and Norman Statham, 16 Nov. 1966.
34 *Guardian*, 8 Nov. 1966.
35 TNA, FO 371/188365, telegram no. 868, Paris to FO, 17 Nov. 1966.
36 *The Times*, 18 Nov. 1966.
37 Ibid.
38 TNA, Prem. 13/910, Extract from a meeting between the prime minister, the chancellor of the exchequer and Eugene Rostow at no. 10 Downing Street, 21 Nov. 1966.
39 TNA, Prem. 13/910, telegram no. 897 of 25 Nov. 1966; text of a reply by Pompidou at a dinner debate organised by *Les Echoes* (daily economic paper).
40 TNA, Prem. 13/910, telegram no. 898, Patrick Reilly to FO, 25 Nov. 1966.
41 Jean Monnet (1888–1979), architect of European unity, never elected to public office but worked behind the scenes with European and American governments.
42 TNA, Prem. 13/910, telegram no. 931, Patrick Reilly to FO, 1 Dec. 1966.
43 TNA, FO 371/188366, piece no. M10829/65, A. H. Campbell to Norman Statham, 28 Nov. 1966.
44 Ibid.
45 TNA, FO 371/188366, piece no. M10829/51 (G), Con O'Neill to the permanent under-secretary 30 Nov. 1966.
46 Ibid.
47 Ibid.
48 TNA, Prem. 13/922, summary of a record by Christopher Soames of his conversation with Couve de Murville, 1 Dec. 1966.
49 TNA, FO 371/188306, piece no. M10829/49a, Lord Gladwyn to George Thomson, 2 Dec. 1966.
50 Ibid.
51 TNA, Prem. 13/922, Christopher Soames to Harold Wilson, 14 Dec. 1966.
52 TNA, FO 371/188366, piece no. M10829/60. telegram no. 996, Patrick Reilly to FO, 15 Dec. 1966.
53 Ibid.
54 TNA, Prem. 13/1475, record of a meeting between the foreign secretary and the Belgian foreign minister at NATO Building, Paris, 14 Dec. 1966.
55 TNA, Prem. 13/1475, record of a meeting between the foreign secretary and the Netherlands foreign minister, 14 Dec. 1966.
56 Ibid.

57 TNA, Prem. 13/1475, record of a meeting between the foreign secretary and the French minister for foreign affairs at the Quai d'Orsay on Wed. 14 Dec. 1966.
58 Ibid.
59 TNA, Prem. 13/1475, Record of a Conversation between the foreign secretary and President de Gaulle at the Elysée Palace on 16 Dec. 1966.
60 Ibid.
61 Ibid.
62 Ibid.
63 Ibid.
64 Ibid.
65 TNA, Prem. 13/1475, Record of meeting between the foreign secretary and President de Gaulle, Elysée Palace, 16 Dec. 1966.
66 TNA, Prem. 13/1475, Patrick Reilly to George Brown after Brown's talks with de Gaulle, 4 Jan. 1967.
67 Ibid.
68 Ibid.
69 TNA, Prem. 13/1475, Michael Palliser to Harold Wilson, 6 Jan. 1967.
70 TNA, Prem. 13/1475, telegram no 23, Paris to FO, 9 Jan. 1967, reporting on an interview by André Fontaine of *Le Monde* and Maurice Delarve of *France Soir* on French Radio, Saturday 7 Jan. 'Prospects for '67'.
71 TNA, Prem. 13/1475, Michael Palliser to Harold Wilson, 6 Jan. 1967.
72 TNA, Prem. 13/1475, Harold Wilson's notes on a letter from Michael Palliser, 6 Jan. 1967.
73 TNA, Prem. 13/1514, Lord Gladwyn to Michael Palliser, 12 Jan. 1967.
74 *New York Times*, 16 Jan. 1967.
75 *New York Times*, 10 Jan. 1967.
76 TNA, Prem. 13/1475, Patrick Dean to foreign secretary, 12 Jan. 1967.
77 Ibid.

SIX: 'GO ON – HAVE A GO!'

1 TNA, FCO 30/66, piece no. Mek 1/2/3, telegram no. 64, Patrick Reilly to FO, 18 Jan. 1967.
2 TNA, Prem. 13/1475, Record of talks between the secretary of state and the state secretary of Federal Germany, Ministry of Foreign Affairs at the FO, 23 Jan. 1967.
3 Hugo Young, *The Blessed Plot: Britain and Europe from Churchill to Blair* (London, 1999), pp. 191–2.
4 For more detail on the content of the discussions see Harold Wilson, *The Labour Government 1964–1970: A Personal Record* (London, 1971), pp. 326–33.
5 Harold Wilson at Strasbourg, 22 Jan. 1967, cited in Uwe Kitzinger, *The Second Try: Labour and the EEC* (London, 1968), p. 1.
6 Harold Wilson, *The Labour Government 1964–1970: A Personal Record* (London, 1971), Jan.–Feb. 1967, p. 334.
7 Wilson notes in his memoirs that 'both on this occasion and on my next visit in June 1967 [de Gaulle] courteously went out of his way to pay tribute to Michael Palliser's command of the language and his power as an "interpreter"'. Ibid., p. 335.

8   TNA, Prem. 13/1476, record of a conversation between the prime minister, the foreign secretary, the president of France and the French foreign minister at the Elysée Palace, 24 Jan. 1967.
9   Ibid.
10 Ibid.
11 Wilson, *Labour Government*, p. 336.
12 Ibid.
13 TNA, Prem. 13/1476, record of a meeting held at the Elysée Palace on Wednesday 25 Jan. 1967.
14 Ibid.
15 Wilson, *Labour Government*, p. 340.
16 TNA, Prem. 13/1476, record of conversation between the prime minister, foreign secretary and the president of France and the French foreign minister, 24 Jan. 1967.
17 TNA, Prem. 13/1476, record of a meeting held at the Elysée Palace on Wednesday 25 Jan. 1967.
18 Wilson, *Labour Government*, p. 437.
19 Ibid.
20 TNA, Prem. 13/1476, Record of a conversation between the prime minister, foreign secretary and the president of France and the French foreign minister at the Elysée Palace, 24 Jan. 1967.
21 Author's interview with Sir Michael Palliser 5 June 2001.
22 Ibid.
23 Author's interview with Robin O'Neill, 31 May 2001.
24 TNA, Prem. 13/1476, Record of a conversation between the prime minister, foreign secretary and the president of France and the French foreign minister at the Elysée Palace, 24 Jan. 1967.
25 TNA, Prem. 13/1476, telegram no. 107, Patrick Reilly to FO, 26 Jan. 1967.
26 Ibid.
27 See ibid.
28 Richard Crossman, *The Diaries of a Cabinet Minister*, vol. II (London, 1981), 26 Jan. 1967, p. 212.
29 Cited in Ben Pimlott, *Harold Wilson* (London, 1993) p.440.
30 George Brown, *My Way* (London, 1970), p. 206.
31 Author's interview with Robin O'Neill, 31 May 2001.
32 TNA, CAB 128/42, CC 3(67), 26 Jan. 1967.
33 Ibid.
34 Ibid.
35 TNA, Prem. 13/1477, Con O'Neill's letter to John Pilcher, 3 Feb. 1967.
36 Ibid.
37 TNA, Prem. 13/1477, Michael Palliser to Nicholas Fenn, 13 Feb. 1967.
38 TNA, FCO 30/223, piece no. MEK 4/1/1, telegram no. 135, Patrick Reilly to FO, 2 Feb. 1967.
39 TNA, Prem. 13/1476, E. Melville to Con O'Neill, 6 Feb. 1967.
40 Ibid.
41 TNA, Prem. 13/1476, telegram no. 29 Copenhagen to FO, Oliver Wright, 6 Feb. 1967.
42 Ibid.
43 TNA, FCO 30/223, piece no. MEK 4/1/1, J. A. Thomson to J. Rennie, 7 Feb. 1967.
44 Ibid.
45 Ibid.
46 Ibid.
47 TNA, Prem. 13/2089, telegram no. 268, Bonn to FO, Frank Roberts, 9 Feb. 1967.

48 TNA, Prem. 13/1477, telegram no. 34 Copenhagen to FO, 9 Feb. 1967.
49 TNA, Prem. 13/1477, Con O'Neill to the permanent under-secretary, 9 Feb. 1967.
50 TNA, Prem. 13/1477, Harold Wilson's covering note.
51 TNA, Prem, 13/1477, W. A. Nield to the prime minister, 10 Feb. 1967.
52 TNA, Prem. 13/1477, record of a meeting between the British prime minister and foreign secretary and the Federal German chancellor and foreign minister, Palais Schaumburg, Bonn 15 Feb. 1967.
53 Ibid.
54 TNA, FCO 30/82, piece no. MEK 1/4/1, Patrick Reilly to the foreign secretary, 21 Feb. 1967.
55 Ibid.
56 Ibid.
57 TNA, FCO 30/82, piece no. MEK 1/4/1, Paul Gore-Booth to the Secretary of State, 23 Feb. 1967.
58 Paul Lewis in *Financial Times*, 24 Feb. 1967.
59 TNA, FCO 30/88, piece no. MEK 1/6, telegram no. 351, Frank Roberts (Bonn) to FO, 24 Feb. 1967.
60 Ibid.
61 TNA, Prem. 13/1478, telegram no. 46, Paris to FO 1 Mar. 1967.
62 TNA, FCO 30/82, piece no. MEK 1/4/1, 'Europe: the next steps', sent by Con O'Neill to the Private Secretary, 6 Mar. 1967.
63 Ibid.
64 Ibid.
65 TNA, Prem. 13/1478, Record of a conversation between Harold Wilson, George Brown, Pierre Werner and Gregoire at the Ministry of Foreign Affairs, Luxembourg, 8 Mar. 1967.
66 Ibid.
67 TNA, CAB 128/42, CC 11 (67) 9 Mar. 1967.
68 TNA, Prem. 13/1478, telegram no. 255, Patrick Reilly, 20 Mar. 1967.
69 Ibid.
70 TNA, Prem. 13/1478, telegram no. 259, Patrick Reilly to FO, 21 Mar. 1967.
71 TNA, FCO 30/83 piece no. MEK 1/4/1, George Brown to the prime minister, 9 Apr. 1967.
72 Ibid.
73 TNA, FCO 30/154, piece no. MEK 2/6, Con O'Neill to Fred Mulley, 11 Apr. 1967.
74 TNA, FCO 30/154, piece no. MEK 2/6, Fred Mulley's note to George Brown, 11 Apr. 1967.
75 TNA, FCO 30/154 piece no. MEK 2/6, George Brown's response to Fred Mulley, 11 Apr. 1967.
76 TNA, FCO 30/226, piece no. MEK 4/1/4, telegram no 1246, Washington to FO 18 Apr. 1967.
77 Ibid.
78 TNA, CAB 129/129, C (67)59, 24 Apr. 1967.
79 Ibid.
80 Ibid.
81 TNA, CAB 129/129, C (67) 60, 24 Apr. 1967.
82 *The Times*, 25 Apr. 1967.
83 TNA, Prem. 13/1473, telegram no. 667, Frank Roberts (Bonn) to FO, 26 Apr. 1967.
84 Ibid.
85 TNA, Prem. 13/1473, telegram no. 363, Patrick Reilly to FO, 26 Apr. 1967.
86 *The Spectator*, Fri. 28 Apr. 1967.

87 TNA, Prem. 13/1480, telegram no. 692 Bonn to FO, Frank Roberts, 29 Apr. 1967.
88 TNA, Prem. 13/1480, Michael Palliser to Harold Wilson, 29 Apr. 1967.
89 TNA, Prem. 13/1496, Letter from Lord Cobbold to the prime minister summarising Baumgartner's opinion, 5 May 1967.
90 Ibid.
91 Author's correspondence with Lord Callaghan, 1 May 2001.
92 Wilson, *Labour Government*, p. 373.
93 See Douglas Jay, *Change and Fortune* (London, 1980), pp. 381–4.
94 Pimlott, *Harold Wilson*, p. 440.
95 Barbara Castle, *The Castle Diaries: 1964–1970* (London , 1984), 6 Apr. 1967, p. 239.
96 Cited in Pimlott, *Harold Wilson*, p. 440.
97 TNA, CAB 129/129 C(67) 72, 1 May 1967.
98 TNA, Prem. 13/1481, de Gaulle to Wilson, 2 May 1967 .
99 TNA, Prem. 13/1481, telegram no. 392, Patrick Reilly to FO, 3 May 1967.
100 TNA, Prem. 13/1481, Michael Palliser to Harold Wilson, 4 May 1967.
101 TNA, FCO, 30/91, piece no. MEK 1/7/1, Fred Mulley to George Brown, 10 May 1967.
102 TNA, FCO, 30/91, piece no. MEK 1/7/1, George Brown's response, 10 May 1967.
103 TNA, Prem. 13/1482 – Michael Palliser to Harold Wilson, 11 May 1967.

SEVEN: AN APPLICATION AND A VETO

1 TNA, Prem. 13/1482, 11 May 1967.
2 Contained in Author's correspondence with Sir James Marjoribanks on 16 May 2001.
3 TNA, FCO 30/91, piece no. MEK, telegram no. 426, Patrick Reilly to FO 12 May 1967.
4 *The Sun*, 12 May 1967.
5 Author's correspondence with Sir James Marjoribanks, 16 May 2001.
6 TNA, Prem. 13/1482, General de Gaulle's press conference on 16 May 1967.
7 *Financial Times*, 18 May 1967.
8 Ibid.
9 TNA, Prem. 13/2646, telegram no. 443, Patrick Reilly, 17 May 1967.
10 TNA, Prem. 13/2646, covering note by Harold Wilson to telegram no. 443 of 17 May 1967.
11 TNA, Prem. 13/2646 telegram no. 256 Brussels to FO, J. Wright, 17 May 1967.
12 TNA, Prem. 13/2646, telegram no. 186, The Hague to FO from Peter Garran, 17 May 1967.
13 Ibid.
14 TNA, FCO 30/230, piece no. MEK 4/1/4, telegram no. 38, Andrew Gilchrist (Dublin) to the Commonwealth Office, 17 May 1967.
15 TNA, Prem. 13/1482, Michael Palliser to Harold Wilson, 18 May 1967.
16 See TNA, Prem. 13/1482, Lord Gladwyn's paper 'Britain and Europe'.
17 TNA, FCO 30/37, piece no. MEF 3/7/4, record of a conversation between Fred Mulley and Hans Schaffner at the Palais Federal Berne, 7 June 1967.
18 Ibid.
19 TNA, Prem. 13/1521, Con O'Neill to Harold Wilson, 8 June 1967.
20 TNA, Prem. 13/1521, Patrick Reilly to Harold Wilson, 7 June 1967.

21　Ibid.
22　Ibid.
23　Ibid.
24　Ibid.
25　Harold Wilson, *The Labour Government, 1964–1970: A Personal Record* (London, 1971), May–June 1967, p. 402.
26　Ibid.
27　Ibid.
28　Ibid.
29　Ibid., p. 408.
30　TNA, Prem. 13/1483, Record of a conversation between the prime minister and the president of France at the Grand Trianon, Versailles, Monday 19 June 1967.
31　Ibid.
32　Ibid.
33　Harold Wilson, *Labour Government*, p. 529.
34　Ibid., p. 413.
35　TNA, Prem. 13/1483, Frank Roberts to Con O'Neill, 17 June 1967.
36　TNA, Prem. 13/1521, Harold Wilson to the UK Mission in New York, 21 June 1967.
37　Philip Ziegler, *Harold Wilson* (London, 1993), pp. 335–6.
38　Ibid.
39　TNA, CAB 128/42, CC 41(67) 22 June 1967.
40　TNA, Prem. 13/1483, Patrick Reilly to Paul Gore-Booth at the FO, 28 June 1967.
41　TNA, Prem. 13/1483, Michael Palliser to Harold Wilson 29 June 1967.
42　TNA, Prem. 13/1483, telegram no. 987, Bonn to FO, 30 June 1967.
43　TNA, Prem. 13/1473, notes of a meeting between the prime minister and representatives of the Confederation of British Industry (CBI) at 10 Downing Street, 4 July 1967.
44　TNA, Prem. 13/1473, A statement on behalf of Her Majesty's Government, made by George Brown to the Meeting of the Council of WEU at The Hague 4 July 1967.
45　TNA, Prem. 13/2636, Michael Palliser to Harold Wilson, 7 July 1967.
46　Ibid.
47　Ibid.
48　TNA, Prem. 13/1490, telegram no. 1056. Bonn to FO, Frank Roberts, 15 July 1967.
49　TNA, Prem. 13/1484, Lord Chalfont to the foreign secretary, 19 July 1967.
50　TNA, Prem. 13/1489, Michael Palliser to Harold Wilson, 15 July 1967.
51　TNA, Prem. 13/1484, telegram no. 204, Brussels to FO, James Marjoribanks, 19 July 1967.
52　TNA, FCO 30/107, piece no. MEK 1/7/12, Con O'Neill to Norman Statham, 28 July 1967.
53　Ibid.
54　*Irish Times*, 29 July 1967.
55　Jack Lynch quoted in *Irish Times*, 29 July 1967.
56　TNA, FCO 30/107, piece no. MEK 1/7/12, Peter Garran to Con O'Neill, 8 Aug. 1967.
57　Ibid.
58　TNA, FCO 30/107, piece no. MEK 1/7/12, Patrick Reilly to Patrick Hancock, 29 Aug. 1967.
59　Ibid.
60　TNA, Prem. 13/1484, Record of a conversation between Chalfont and the German Federal Minister for Finance (Herr Strauss) at the Bundeshaus, Bonn, 6 Sept. 1967.

61 *Daily Telegraph*, 7 Sept. 1967.
62 TNA, FCO 30/109, piece NO: MEK 1/7/13, Con O'Neill to James Marjoribanks, 11 Sept. 1967.
63 Ibid.
64 TNA, FCO 30/109, piece no. MEK 1/7/13, Con O'Neill to the private secretary, 18 Sept. 1967.
65 TNA, FCO 30/107, piece no. MEK 1/7/12, Roger Jackling's paper 'EEC: an early French veto', submitted to the permanent under-secretary, 1 Oct. 1967.
66 TNA, FCO 30/107, piece no. MEK 1/7/12, P. M. Kelly for the Secretary of State to Roger Jackling, 2 Oct. 1967.
67 TNA, Prem. 13/1503, Notes by Norman Statham of a meeting between the prime minister and a group of senior French journalists at 10 Downing Street, 10 Oct. 1967.
68 Wilson, *Labour Government*, p. 445.
69 TNA, Prem. 13/1513, A senior French official's view reported by Michael Palliser to the prime minister, 31 Oct. 1967.
70 Pierre Drouin in *Le Monde*, 17 Oct. 1967.
71 Ibid. and see TNA, Prem. 13/1485, telegram no. 1023, 17 Oct. 1967.
72 Charles Williams, *The Last Great Frenchman* (London, 1995), p. 456.
73 TNA, Prem. 13/2646, General de Gaulle's Press Conference, Monday 27 Nov. 1967.
74 Ibid.
75 Ibid.
76 Ibid.
77 Sir James Mellon, KCMG, born 1929, Foreign Office 1963–64, UK Delegation to European Commission 1967–72.
78 Author's interview with Sir James Mellon, 23 July 2001.
79 Author's interview with Sir Michael Palliser, 5 June 2001.
80 TNA, Prem. 13/2646, telegram no. 1191, Patrick Reilly to FO, 27 Nov. 1967.
81 Author's correspondence with Sir James Mellon, 23 July 2001.
82 Piers Ludlow in a paper 'The second British application: the E.C. reaction' delivered to a conference held at the Institute of Contemporary British History on The Second Try: Wilson and Europe, 1964–7', 13 Jan. 2000.
83 Author's correspondence with Lord Hurd, 27 Apr. 2001.
84 Thomas Barman, 'Britain and France: 1967', *International Affairs* 43 (1967), p. 29.
85 Ben Pimlott, *Harold Wilson* (London, 1993), p. 439.
86 David Thomson, 'President de Gaulle and the Mésentente Cordiale', *International Journal* 23 (1968), p. 217.
87 Author's correspondence with Sir David Ratford, 14 Oct. 2001.
88 TNA, FCO 30/414, piece no. MWK 4/12, telegram no. 124, Christopher Soames to FO, 5 Feb. 1969.
89 Jean Lacouture, *De Gaulle: The Ruler 1945–1970* (London, 1991), p. 360.

EPILOGUE

1 Author's correspondence with Robin O'Neill, 18 Apr. 2001.
2 Author's interview with Sir Oliver Wright, 29 May 2001.
3 Patrick Reilly, contained in author's correspondence with Jane Reilly, 1 Apr. 2001.

4 TNA, FCO 75/1, Con O'Neill's Report on the Negotiations for Entry into the European Community, June 1970–Jan. 1972.
5 TNA, FCO 30/414, piece no. MWK 4/12, telegram no, 124, Christopher Soames to the FO, 5 Feb. 1969.
6 TNA, FCO 30/414, piece no. MWK 4/12, Harold Wilson's personal minutes on the telegrams 121, 123, 124, 125 of 4 and 5 Feb. 1969.
7 Author's interview with Sir Michael Palliser, 5 June 2001.
8 Ibid.
9 Ibid.
10 O'Neill's Report.
11 Author's correspondence with Robin O'Neill, 18 Apr. 2001.
12 Author's interview with Sir Michael Butler, 22 May 2001.
13 O'Neill's Report.
14 Ibid.
15 Ibid.
16 Author's interview with Lord Roll, 29 May 2001.
17 Author's interview with Sir Oliver Wright, 29 May 2001.
18 Author's correspondence with Sir Edward Heath, 4 June 2001.

Bibliography

PRIMARY SOURCES

State papers are available at the National Archives, Kew (TNA).

Papers consulted include minutes and papers of the Cabinet and its committees (CAB); the Foreign Office (FO) and the Foreign and Commonwealth Office (FCO); the office of Harold Wilson, as Prime Minister (PREM); and the Treasury (T).

CORRESPONDENCE

Lord Armstrong of Ilminster (Sir Robert Armstrong), 12 May 2001
Sir Christopher Audland, 14 April and 10 May 2001
Lord Callaghan of Cardiff (James Callaghan), 1 May 2001
Sir Derek Day, 16 April 2001
Sir Nicholas Fenn, 1 August 2001
Francis G. K. Gallagher, 19 May 2001
Sir Edward Heath, 4 June 2001
Lord Hurd of Westwell (Douglas Hurd), 27 April 2001
Sir James Marjoribanks, 17 April and 16 May 2001
Sir James Mellon, August 2001
David Morphet, 9 November 2001
Robin O'Neill, 18 April and 7 July 2001
Sir David Ratford, 19 April and 14 October 2001
Jane Reilly (daughter of the late Sir Patrick Reilly), 18 April 2001
Neil Smith, 10 May 2001
Sir Norman Statham, 7 May 2001
Sir Jeremy Thomas, 16 April 2001

INTERVIEWS

Sir Michael Butler, 22 May 2001
Robin O'Neill, 31 May 2001
Sir Michael Palliser, 5 June 2001
Lord Roll of Ipsden (Eric Roll), 29 May 2001
Dr Kenneth Whitaker, 19 February 2001
Sir Oliver Wright, 29 May 2001

PUBLISHED COLLECTIONS OF DOCUMENTS

Bullen, Roger and M. E. Pelly (eds), *Documents on British Policy Overseas*, series II, vol. 3 (London, 1989).

DIARIES, MEMOIRS, AUTOBIOGRAPHIES

Benn, Tony, *The Benn Diaries* (London, 1996).
Boothby, Robert, *Recollections of a Rebel* (London, 1978).
Brown, George, *In My Way* (London, 1970).
Callaghan, James, *Time and Chance* (London, 1987).
Castle, Barbara, *The Castle Diaries: 1964–1970* (London, 1984).
Couve de Murville, Maurice, *Une Politique Etrangère 1958–1969* (Paris, 1974).
Crossman, Richard, *The Diaries of a Cabinet Minister: vol 1, Minister of Housing 1964–66* (London, 1975).
Crossman, Richard, *The Backbench Diaries of Richard Crossman* (London, 1981).
Dalton, Hugh, *High Tide and After: Memoirs 1945–1960* (London, 1962).
Eden, Anthony, *Memoirs: Full Circle* (London, 1960).
de Gaulle, Charles, *Mémoires de Guerre: L'Unité, 1942–1944* (Paris, 1956).
de Gaulle, Charles, *Memoirs of Hope: Two Volumes*, trans. by Terence Kilmartin (London, 1971).
Gladwyn, Lord, *The European Idea* (London, 1961).
Gore-Booth, Paul *With Great Truth and Respect* (London, 1974).
Heath, Edward *The Course of My Life* (London, 1998).
Healey, Denis, *The Time of My Life* (London, 1990).
Jay, Douglas, *Change and Fortune: A Political Record* (London, 1980).
Jenkins, Roy, *A Life at the Centre* (London, 1991).
Macmillan, Harold,, *Tides of Fortune: 1945–1955* (London, 1969).
Macmillan, Harold, *Riding The Storm 1956–1959* (London, 1971).
Macmillan, Harold, *Pointing The Way 1959–1961* (London, 1972).
Macmillan, Harold, *At the End of the Day 1961–1963* (London, 1973).
Marjolin, Robert, *Architect of European Unity: Memoirs 1911–1986* (London, 1989).
Maudling, Reginald, *Memoirs* (London, 1978).
Monnet, Jean, *Memoirs* (London, 1978).
Stewart, Michael, *The Jekyll and Hyde Years: Politics and Economic Policy since 1974* (London, 1977).
Wilson, Harold, *The Labour Government 1964–1970: A Personal Record* (London, 1971).

THE PRESS

France Soir
Le Monde
Daily Telegraph
Daily Express
The Economist
Evening Standard
Financial Times
Guardian
Herald Tribune
Irish Times
New York Times
The Observer
The Spectator
The Sun
Sunday Telegraph
Sunday Times
The Times

SECONDARY SOURCES

Barman, T., 'Britain and France: 1967', *International Affairs* 43 (1967), pp. 29–38.
Brivati, B. and H. Jones, *From Reconstruction to Integration, Britain and Europe Since 1945* (London, 1993).
Butt, R., 'The Common Market and Conservative party politics 1961–62', *Government and Opposition* 2 (1967), pp. 372–86.
Camps, M., *Britain and the European Community, 1955–63* (London, 1964).
Charlton, M., *The Price of Victory* (London, 1983).
Darwin, J., 'British decolonisation since 1945: a pattern or a puzzle?' *Journal of Imperial and Commonwealth History* XII: 1 (1983), pp.187–209.
Dockrill, M. and J. Young, *British Foreign Policy, 1945–1956* (London, 1989).
Gowland, D. and A. Turner, *Reluctant Europeans: Britain and European Integration 1945–1998* (London, 2000).
Holland, R., *The Pursuit of Greatness: Britain and the World Role 1900–1970* (London, 1991).
Horne, A., *Macmillan, vol. II: 1956–1986* (London, 1989).
Judd, D., *Empire: The British Imperial Experience from 1765 to the Present* (London, 1996).
Kitzinger, U., *The Second Try: Labour and the EEC* (London, 1968).
Lacouture, J., *De Gaulle: The Ruler 1945–1970* (London, 1991).
Lieber, R. J., *British Politics and European Unity* (Berkeley, 1970).
Lord, Christopher, *British entry to the European Community under the Heath Government of 1970–4* (Aldershot, 1993).
Morgan, K., *Callaghan: A Life* (Oxford, 1997).
Nicholson, F., and R. East, *From the Six to the Twelve: The Enlargement of the European Communities* (Harlow, 1987).
Pickles, D., *The Uneasy Entente: French Foreign Policy and Franco-British Misunderstandings* (London, 1996).
Pimlott, B., *Harold Wilson* (London, 1993).
Ponting, C., *Breach of Promise: Labour in Power, 1964–70* (London, 1989).
Rhodes James, R. (ed.), *Winston S. Churchill: His Complete Speeches, Vol.6* (London, 1974).
Thomson, D., 'President de Gaulle and the Mésentente Cordiale', *International Journal* 23 (1968), pp 211–20.
Thornton, A. P., *For the File on Empire: Essays and Reviews* (London, 1968).
Wheaton, M., 'The Labour Party and Europe 1950–71' in G. Ionescu (ed.), *The New Politics of European Integration* (Basingstoke, 1972).
Williams, C., *The Last Great Frenchman* (London, 1995).
Young, H., *This Blessed Plot: Britain and Europe From Churchill to Blair* (London, 1999).
Young, J., *British Foreign Policy, 1945–1956* (London, 1989).
Young, J., *Britain and European Unity, 1945–1999* (London, 1993).
Ziegler, P., *Harold Wilson* (London, 1993).

Index

Acheson, Dean, 29
Adenauer, Konrad, 2, 43
   funeral of, 104
Alphand, Hervé, 84–5
Andronikov, Prince, 15–16, 83
Arnold, 108
L'Aurore, 23–4

balance of payments, 37, 59, 111
Ball, George, 52, 54–5
Balogh, Thomas, 22, 30, 35–6, 57, 65
Barman, Thomas, 114
Baumgartner, Wilfrid, 97
Beaton, Leonard, 33
Benn, Tony, 43, 70–1
Beugel, Ernst van der, 109
Brandt, Willy, 91
Britain/British
   agricultural issues, 74
   application to join EEC, first, 3, 38, 86
   application to join EEC, second, 100:
      conditions of, 59, 111; decision, 98; failure of, 117; German views of, 94, 96; Italian views of, 64; reasons for, 21, 43–4, 60, 117–18; timing of, 41, 95–6; US views of, 18, 52, 65–6, 88–90
   becomes member of EEC, 121
   –Commonwealth relations, 46, 76, 108
   economy, 33, 52, 59, 66–7, 74, 76, 111
   European policy, 1, 10, 86, 108
   foreign policy: 2, 8, 49, 79, 108; East of Suez, 48, 75
   –French relations, 2, 4, 13, 16, 114–15; rebuilding, 18

   –German relations, 15, 60, 62
   international co-operation, 12
   role of, international, 46
   terms of entry to EEC, 77–9, 91
   –US relations: 2–3, 6–7, 14, 20, 46, 50–1, 59, 65, 73–4, 76, 79–80, 108; weakening of, 105
Bromberger, Dominique, 107
Brown, A. J. Stephen, 38
Brown, George, *see also under* Wilson, Harold, 9, 20, 40, 59–60, 62, 64–5, 77–8, 83–4, 87–8, 93–5, 98
   assessments of, 117–18
   attempts to resign, 42
   attitude to Europe, 29, 32, 78–9
   becomes foreign secretary, 29–30
   determination of, 96
   influence on Harold Wilson, 31–2
   popularity of, 29
   speeches by: The Hague 1967, 108; New York 1966, 67; Stockholm 1966, 56–8
   views of: on Treaty of Rome, 58; on the US, 54
   vision of Europe, 30–1
Brussels Negotiations, 5
Brussels Treaty (1948), 2
Butler, Michael, 3–4, 13, 120
Butt, Ronald, 102

cabinet
   European conference, April 1967, 98
   European views of, 70, 97
Caccia, Harold, 13–14
Calais Fair (1965), 17

Callaghan, James, 21, 33, 40–2, 48, 50, 97
Camps, Miriam, 46
Castle, Barbara, 87–8, 98
CBI, 108
   pro-European stance of, 38–9
Chalfont, Alun, 45, 51, 110, 112
'Chalfont affair', 112
Channel Tunnel, 11, 17
Christensen, Jens, 89
Churchill, Winston, 2, 6
   funeral of, 11
Common Agricultural Policy, 47, 59, 75, 80, 91, 93, 112
Common Market, *see* EEC
Commonwealth, 21–2, 46–8, 79, 96, 113, 117
   political importance of, 47
   trade, 44, 47
Concorde, 11
Conseil National du Patronat Français, 38
Conservative Party, 24
'Continental Blockade', 115
Corriere della Sera, 25
Couve de Murville, Maurice, 12–13, 16, 61, 77–8, 80, 83–4, 92, 97, 120
Crosland, Anthony, 34
Crossman, Richard, 34, 87–8, 98

Dahlgaard, Tyge, 89–90
Daily Mirror, 25, 39
Daily Telegraph, 40, 110
Darwin, John, 45
Davies, John, 39
Day, Derek, 31–2
Dean, Patrick, 52–5, 81
Debré, Michel, 58, 66, 69, 97, 119
de Broglie, 57
defence cuts, 48
de Gaulle, Charles, *see also under* Wilson, Harold
   boycotts EEC institutions, 23
   character of, 4, 80, 115
   criticism of, 15
   disputes with NATO, 25
   foreign policy of, 4

   hostility to Britain joining EEC, 58–9, 63, 79, 82, 91, 94, 103–6; suggests alternative, 85–6, 88, 92, 96, 101; reaction to, 102
   intransigence of, 118
   resignation of, 101, 119
   threatens to leave EEC, 109
   vetoes Britain's applications: first, 4, 97; second, 1, 101, 112–16 (reactions to, 113–14), 118
   views about: of George Brown, 29; of Foreign Office, 5; of Macmillan, 6
   views of: on Anglo-American relations, 50; on Anglo-French relations, 116; on the EEC, 11, 106; on Europe, 3–6, 19; on France, 5–6; on the US, 7, 11, 19, 61, 74, 106
d'Estaing, Giscard, 16, 99
devaluation, 33, 41–3, 46, 112
Dixon, Pierson, 11, 49
Donoughue, Bernard, 8
Drouin, Pierre, 112

Economist, The, 72, 93
EEC, 3
   Executive Commission, report on British application, 111, 113
   implications of Britain joining, 98
EFTA, 44, 66, 72, 78, 101, 113, 117
elections, general
   British: October 1964, 10, 47; 1966, 56
   French: December 1965, 18; March 1967, 87, 92
Elslande, Renaat van, 100
'empty chair' crisis, 23
Erhard, Ludwig, 58, 106
Europe, role of, 83–4
Europe, Council of, 2
European Economic Organisations Department, 18, 58

Fenn, Nicholas, 31, 64–5
Figaro, 111
Financial Times, 38, 66, 68, 92

Fisher, H. A. L., 56
'Five', the, 73, 76, 81, 89, 91, 93, 113–14, 119
    relations among, 4
Fontaine, André, 94, 111
France Soir, 23
French–German relations, 69, 80, 95, 106, 114

Gabrysiak, Michel, 60, 74
Gaitskell, Hugh, 8–9, 29
Galsworthy, John, 58
Garran, Peter, 109
Gilchrist, Andrew, 102–3
Gladwyn, Lord, 22–3, 43, 77, 80, 103
global change, 45
Gore-Booth, Paul, 34, 76, 92
Gozard, Gilles, 66–7
Guardian, 33, 74
Guerin, André, 24

Hallstein, Walter, 39, 80
Hancock, Patrick, 53–4
Harmel, M. P., 77
Healey, Denis, 48
Heath, Edward, 21, 49, 60, 75, 86, 114, 120
Herald Tribune, 58
Hurd, Douglas, 63–4, 114

Indo-Pakistan war, 47
Irish Times, 109

Jackling, Roger, 111
Jay, Douglas, 31, 71, 98, 117
Jebb, Gladwyn, *see* Gladwyn, Lord
Jenkins, Roy, 9, 25, 34, 46
Johnson, Lyndon, 50, 53, 74, 80
Judd, Dennis, 48

Kemp, Oliver, 25, 61
Kennedy, Edward, 88–9
Kiesinger, Kurt Georg, 89–92, 106, 119
King, Cecil, 39
Koven, Ronald, 58
Kreisky, Bruno, 14

Labour Party
    anti-Europeans in, 8–9, 28, 117
    manifesto, 9
    pro-Europeans in, 28
Lacouture, Jean, 116
Lloyd Hughes, Trevor, 28
Luns, Joseph, 77
Lynch, Jack, 109

Macmillan, Harold, 1, 3–5, 28, 38, 54, 86
    foreign policy, 49
    'Grand Design' of, 46
Marjoribanks, James, 5, 68–9, 100–1, 110
Marshall Plan, 2
Massip, Roger, 111
media
    British, 38–9
    French, 23–4, 100
    Irish, 102–3
Mellon, James, 113–14
Messina Conference (1955), 2
Middleton, Drew, 11–12
ministers' meeting, Chequers (October 1966), 68, 70–2
Le Monde, 23, 33, 94, 99, 111–12
Monnet, Jean, 75–6, 80, 87, 99, 110
Mulley, Fred, 95, 99, 103

Nassau Agreement, 11, 63
Nasser, Gamal Abdel, 2
La Nation, 66
National Plan 1965, 20–1, 33–4, 40–1
NATO, 2, 23, 49, 62, 65, 75
New York Times, 11–12
Nield, William, 90–1
Nixon, Richard, 119
Norman, Gerry, 38
nuclear energy, 65

Observer, 10
O'Neill, Con, 10, 19–20, 34–8, 64–5, 67, 74, 76, 84, 88, 90, 93, 95, 103, 109–11, 120
O'Neill, Robin, 5–7, 10, 26, 28–9, 34, 36, 43, 50, 52, 86, 117, 119–20
Ostpolitik, 106

Palewski, Jean-Paul, 66
Palliser, Michael, 7, 11, 34, 44, 50, 52–4, 57, 59, 62–3, 68, 71–2, 80, 83, 97, 99, 103, 107–8, 113
party politics, 33–4
Peyrefitte, Alain, 17–18
Pimlott, Ben, 10, 115
Pompidou, Georges, *see also under* Wilson, Harold, 16, 60–1, 69, 75, 77, 84, 97, 115, 119
　becomes president, 120
Ponting, Clive, 70
Prittie, Terence, 61
public opinion
　British, on Europe, 39–40, 57, 70
　French, on Britain, 87, 104

Rambouillet meeting, 4, 63, 75, 105
Ratford, David, 32–3, 116
Reilly, Patrick, 13–15, 58–9, 61–2, 66, 75, 77, 82, 84–5, 87–9, 91–2, 94, 96, 99, 100, 102–3, 107, 109–10, 118
Rey, Jean, 110, 112
Rhodesia crisis, 47–8
Rifflet, 110
Roberts, Frank, 18, 24–5, 69, 90, 92, 96, 106, 108
Robinson, John, 34–6, 38–9, 110
Roll, Eric, 30, 41, 57, 61, 64, 120
Rostow, Eugene, 75, 90
Rusk, Dean, 52, 95

Schaffner, Hans, 103
Schiller, Karl, 118
Schultz, Klaus, 82
Schuman Plan (1950), 2
seamen's strike (1966), 41
'Six', the, 3, 12, 73, 107
　dynamics of, 61
　growth in, 44
Six Days War, 105
Smith, Ian, 48
Smuts, General Jan, 48
Soames, Christopher, 77, 116, 118
'Soames Affair', 119–10

Spaak, Paul-Henri, 23, 39
'special relationship', *see* Britain/British–US relations
Spectator, The, 97
Statham, Norman, 38, 57
sterling, 58, 66, 75, 79–80, 97, 111
Stewart, Michael, 12–16, 20–2, 31, 34, 47, 59, 62, 98
Strauss, Franz-Josef, 110
Suez crisis, 2–3, 34, 45–6
Sun, the, 100–1
Sunday Times, 38, 60, 66

'technological community', 83
Thomas, Jeremy, 7, 11, 18, 43, 65
Thomson, George, 54, 62, 95–6
'three circles' concept, 2, 18, 45, 49
Tickell, Crispin, 7–8
Times, The, 75, 96
Treaty of Rome, 4, 12, 57–9, 73, 75, 82, 90–1, 93
　Article 237, 100
　Article 238, 86
Trend, Burke, 40, 71, 84

unemployment, 42

Vietnam War, 50, 65, 75, 80, 105
'velvet veto', 1, 101–2

Wellenstein, Edmond, 25
Die Welt, 18
Werner, Pierre, 93
Wheaton, Michael, 47
Williams, Charles, 112
Wilson, Harold
　becomes prime minister, 8
　character of, 82
　criticism of, 64–5
　decides to make EEC application, 98
　determination of, 73–4
　European policy, 20, 24
　foreign policy, 49
　influences on, regarding Europe, 33–4, 37

meetings with de Gaulle: April 1965, 15–17 (preparations for, 13–15); January 1967, 83–8; June 1967 (Trianon), 103–7
meeting with Pompidou (July 1966), 62–4
misrepresenation of, in the press, 111–12
paranoia of, 71
pragmatism of, 50–1
reaction to de Gaulle's veto, 113
relationship with Pompidou, 63–4
speeches by: Bristol (1966), 24, 56; to Assembly of Council of Europe (1967), 83
tactical skill of, 28–9, 71
views of: on the Commonwealth, 8–9, 47; on Europe, 8, 27–8, 33, 47, 57; on France, 80; on the US, 54, 80
visits: to European capitals (with George Brown), 27, 71–3, 79–80, 82, 90–2, 98; to Washington, 49–50

Wright, Oliver, 2, 4, 16, 28, 30, 35, 48–9, 57, 68–9, 121

Young, Hugo, 82

Ziegler, Philip, 8